THE ACTUALITY OF WALTER BENJAMIN

THE ACTUALITY OF WALTER BENJAMIN

Edited by
Laura Marcus
Lynda Nead

AAKAR

THE ACTUALITY OF WALTER BENJAMIN
Edited by Laura Marcus and Lynda Nead

First Published in India 2015

ISBN 978-93-5002-317-4

Published in agreement with Lawrence and Wishart Limited, London for publication and sale only in the Indian Subcontinent (India, Pakistan, Bangladesh, Nepal, Maldives, Bhutan and Sri Lanka)

Published by
AAKAR BOOKS
28 E Pocket IV, Mayur Vihar Phase I, Delhi 110 091
Phone : 011 2279 5505 Telefax : 011 2279 5641
aakarbooks@gmail.com; www.aakarbooks.com

Printed at
Saurabh printers Pvt. Ltd., Noida

Contents

NOTES ON CONTRIBUTORS

Zygmunt Bauman is Professor Emeritus of Sociology at the University of Leeds. His most recent books include *Globalization: The Human Consequences* (1998) and *Work Ethic, Consumerism and the New Poor* (1998).

Andrew Benjamin is Professor of Philosophy at the University of Warwick. His publications include *The Plural Event: Descartes, Hegel, Heidegger* (1993) and *Present Hope: Philosophy, Architecture, Judaism* (1997).

Victor Burgin is Professor in the History of Consciousness Department at the University of California, Santa Cruz. His books include *In/Different Spaces: Place and Memory in the Visual Culture* (1996) and *Some Cities* (1996).

Iain Chambers teaches history of English cultures at the Instituto Universitario Orientale, Naples. He is author of *Migrancy, Culture, Identity* (1994) and co-editor, with Lidia Curti, of *The Post-Colonial Question. Common Skies, Divided Horizons* (1996).

Martin Jay is Sidney Hellman Ehrman Professor of History at the University of California, Berkeley. He is the author of *Cultural Semantics* (1998).

Axel Honneth is a professor at the Institute for Philosophy at the Gaethe-University in Frankfurt/Main. He is the author of *The Struggle for Recognition* (1995) and *Critique of Power* (1992).

Laura Marcus has taught at Birkbeck College and, from 1999, is Reader in English at the University of Sussex. Her publications include *Auto/biographical Discourses* (1994) and, as co-editor, *Culture, Modernity and 'the Jew'* (1998).

Lynda Nead is Reader in the History of Art at Birkbeck College. Her publications include *The Female Nude: Art, Obscenity and Sexuality* (1992) and co-editor of *Law and the Image: The Authority of Art and the Aesthetics of Law*, forthcoming.

Julian Roberts is Professor of Philosophy at the University of Munich. His next publication is *The Philosophy of Law: An Introduction*.

Gillian Rose was Professor of Social and Political Thought at the University of Warwick. Her publications include *The Broken Middle* (1992); *Judaism and Modernity* (1993) and *Love's Work* (1995).

Sigrid Weigel is Professor of German Literature at the University of Zurich. She is author of *Body and Image – Space: Re-reading Walter Benjamin* (1996).

Irving Wolfarth is Professor of German at the University of Reims. He has written important articles on Benjamin's work in *New German Critique*, No 70, and contributed to *Walter Benjamin and the Demands of History* (1996).

Janet Wolff is Professor of Art History and Director of the Program in Visual and Cultural Studies at the University of Rochester. Her most recent publication is *Resident Alien: Feminist Cultural Criticism* (1995).

Editorial

The centenary in 1992 of Walter Benjamin's birth provided the context for a critical reappraisal of his work and its implications for a cultural politics of the 1990s. Centenaries are usually the occasions to celebrate a knowable body of work; a canon which is somehow already in place, set for commemoration. Although it is true that Benjamin's place in the canon of twentieth-century critical theorists is now established, the boundaries of his work still resist classification and demarcation. His writings are not easily summarized or assimilated; they remain an uneasy but thrilling combination of the actual and the mystical, of Marxism and messianic utopianism.

So if we are to search for the actuality of Walter Benjamin, perhaps it is to be found in his quietly determined failure to belong – to a speciality, to an institution, to an easily specifiable tradition of thought. It is this indeterminacy and refusal to remain within boundaries which signifies Benjamin's contemporaneity, his rich place within a cultural epoch in which belonging and abiding have come to seem so philosophically troubling.

Benjamin's intellectual career prior to 1955, when Theodor Adorno produced a two-volume German edition of his work, had been one of startling obscurity. Since then, however, Benjamin seems to have been made and remade as the necessary ancestor of the varieties of the left that grew through the 1960s and beyond. The appearance in German of his *Collected Writings* (1972-1989), including the notes for his great unfinished project, the *Passagenwerk* (Arcades Project), prepared the ground for a mass of secondary literature which took on the vexed task of interpreting Benjamin's relevance for a contemporary political and intellectual history.

Devastated by the rejection of his doctoral dissertation on the 'Origin of German Tragic Drama' by the University of Frankfurt in 1925, Benjamin turned away from a career as an academic literary critic and made himself, almost single-handedly, into the kind of cultural theorist who, in later decades, would be both celebrated and emulated. From the mid-1920s to 1933, Benjamin scraped a living through journalism and the writing of articles commissioned by the Frankfurt Institute for Social Research. Much of his work for the Institute was related to his projected history of nineteenth-century French ideologies and included the now well-known 'The Work of Art in the Age of Mechanical Reproduction'. The positions embodied in his work during this period are not easily assimilated with those represented in his writings from earlier years and in his final piece, 'Theses on the Philosophy of History'. Written after the Nazi-Soviet pact of 1939, the 'Theses' envisage intellectual activity as a form of magical remembrance and revolution as a utopian ending of time and the beginning of a new temporal order.

The diversity of Benjamin's work and themes is reflected in the diversity of the contributions to this collection. Yet the themes of temporality and memory emerge as one of the most powerful common strands. In a century in which memory has been more than ever before under threat, Benjamin offers us a body of work in which the demands of modernity are investigated alongside the ethical demands of memory. To speak, write and think in memory of Walter Benjamin, to commemorate his centenary, is to be in memory of a writer for whom the requirements of memory were pressing and ineluctable – it is to be in memory of the fragile value of memory itself.

The relationships between memory and history, mourning and melancholy, are explored by a number of contributors to this volume. In her analysis of Benjamin's complex and difficult relation to Judaism, Gillian Rose shows how Benjamin, 'the taxonomist of sadness', negotiates, or fails to negotiate, the passage between mournfulness and melancholy, *aberrated mourning* and *inaugurated mourning*; 'in his work', Rose writes, 'the hard heart of judgement does not melt into grief, into forgiveness, or into atonement'. Axel Honneth, pursuing the theme of atonement, links Benjamin's anthropologically fashioned concept of experience and his philosophy of history, and argues that Benjamin's emphasis on the recovery of lost modes of experience has as its corollary a symbolic restitution to a past in need of redemption, a moral debt paid to preceding generations. Honneth expresses doubts about the viability of a project of reparation conceived in these terms, while emphasizing the continuing need for the task of historical remembering.

Zygmunt Bauman, in his discussion of Benjamin the intellectual, takes up the theme of redemption, but argues that, in Benjamin's version of revolutionary action, historical narrative becomes an act of construction rather than restitution. Rebelling against the concept of 'historical necessity', Benjamin's idiosyncratic version of historical materialism entails a replacement of 'the false certainty of progress with the unprocessed, untamed, un-domesticated hope of free creation'. Disruptions of time, history and knowledge are also the focus of Iain Chambers' analysis of the Baroque, the aesthetic which Benjamin explored in *The Origin of German Tragic Drama*. The Baroque, Chambers argues, in its allegorical, ironic crossings of the borders of different worlds, of life and death, creates 'a rent in the fabric of our knowledge'. Its critique of permanency and essentialism returns to haunt western modernism, calling out 'for an ethical reply to the needs of another scene, another story, another possibility, reminding us that historical reason is itself to be judged'.

Martin Jay, like Axel Honneth, takes Benjamin's concept of 'experience' as his starting-point. He argues that Benjamin could have found a form of 'absolute experience' – one which transcended the subject-object dichotomy without the need to invoke magic or metaphysics – in the language of the novel. Jay links the 'indirect free style' characteristic of the modern novel not only with Benjamin's own styles of intransitive writing (his suppression of expressive subjectivity), but also with recent historiographical debates about the representation of the 'unrepresentable' (in particular, the Holocaust), and the politics of the 'middle voice', seen either as the proper mode of articulation for unspeakable sentences/histories or as an evasion of political agency. Andrew Benjamin also engages with the consequences of representation understood as a mode of thinking, and with the temporalities of memory, in his analysis of the enduring problem, for philosophy as well as for history, of thinking the Holocaust as event and occurrence. Like Bauman, Andrew Benjamin argues for a fuller analysis of the meanings and the temporalities of 'hope'.

Janet Wolff's essay offers a cultural analysis of Benjamin's work and of the 'legendary' status that certain aspects of his life and writing have acquired. She argues for a new willingness on the part of critics 'to explore the origins and connotations of the images which figure in their analysis'. Where Martin Jay points to an evacuation of authorial subjectivity in Benjamin's writing, Wolff sees Benjamin – author of numerous 'autobiographical' sketches – as a significant forerunner of the move in feminist theory and cultural studies towards the inclusion of the 'personal moment', an acknowledgement of the subjectivity of the theorist and of the nature of his/her commitment to the theoretical object. Sigrid Weigel's essay provides a response to Wolff's call for a deconstruction of the fascinating image and for an interrogation of the concept of the 'dialectical image'. She explores the function of the whore/prostitute – and the feminine generally – as image and sign in Benjamin's work, and the representation of the whore as an allegory of modernism. The 'dialectical image' is profoundly and problematically gendered in Benjamin's work, Weigel argues, and she shows how concepts of time and space become linked to representations of the female/feminine in Benjamin's mappings of the city. Building on historically fashioned links between 'body' and 'city', Victor Burgin pursues the metaphor of porosity and a competing dialectic of interior and exterior in Benjamin's writings on the city. Burgin argues that the ambivalence between these two metaphoric structures 'marks the representational space of modernism in general', but that such spatial representations need to be understood in psychic/psychoanalytic as well as cultural/historical terms. Subjectivity is also intensely spatialized: 'today, the autistic response of total withdrawal, and the schizophrenic anxiety of the body in pieces, belong to our psycho-corporeal forms of identification with the tele-topological puzzle of the city in pieces'.

Julian Roberts draws out a radical 'aesthetics of conflict' from Benjamin's writings. The theme of conflict guides Benjamin's work on Baudelaire in which, Roberts argues, Benjamin reveals the failure of modern writers and intellectuals to achieve collective solidarity and to resist the demands of the market or the state. The theme of conflict is also central to Benjamin's aesthetic system itself, for he points up the need to relinquish the utopian or nostalgic aesthetic of the symbol, to celebrate 'melancholy' as one of a number of attitudes to beauty, and to valorize a principle of construction – 'that form of art which thematizes its own instability'. In contrast to a number of critics, Roberts argues that Benjamin's aesthetics, and more broadly, his sense of history, are both secular and systematic.

Irving Wohlfarth's essay provides the title of this collection – *The Actuality of Walter Benjamin*. Like Bauman, Wohlfarth takes up the vexed questions of historical understanding versus historicism, of the 'actuality' of Benjamin's 'now', and of the (im)possibility of transposing Benjamin's 'actuality' into our own time. Interrogating the desire to 'celebrate' and commemorate, Wohlfarth gives us our keynote in Benjamin's words:

> 'Celebration' or apologetics aims to smooth over the revolutionary moments of the historical process. Its concern is to construct a continuity . . . what it misses are the jagged edges which offer a foothold to someone who wants to get beyond that work.

The essays which follow, we believe, both point to the steps beyond and show us how extraordinarily substantial were the footholds which Walter Benjamin supplied.

Most of the material included in this collection was delivered at the centenary conference, *Walter Benjamin 1892-1940*, which was held at Birkbeck College, London on 16th-18th July 1992. The conference was made possible by support from the British Academy, the Lipman Trust, the Goethe Institute in London and the German Academic Exchange Service. Thanks are also due to all those who participated in the conference both as speakers and as audience. We are grateful to Elmar Brandt, William Outhwaite, Steve Connor, John Kraniauskas, Richard Salmon and James Donald for their help.

This book is dedicated to the memory of Philip Brady.

Laura Marcus
Lynda Nead

THE MEASURE OF THE POSSIBLE, THE WEIGHT OF THE REAL AND THE HEAT OF THE MOMENT: BENJAMIN'S ACTUALITY TODAY*

Irving Wohlfarth

For Christa Wolf

I PRO DOMO

Let me begin by citing a number of scattered passages from Benjamin's writings which cast an unflattering light on the event we are celebrating – or should I say perpetrating? – today. 'There is no document of culture', said Benjamin, 'which is not at the same time a document of barbarism'.[1] He was not thereby *reducing* culture to barbarism, merely – merely! – claiming that culture is implicated in a web of inescapable guilt (*Schuldzusammenhang*). There is no way round this implication. Will there ever be a way through it?

> 1. [Brecht] was the first to pose to intellectuals the far-reaching requirement that they should not supply the apparatus of production without also transforming it, as far as possible [*nach Massgabe des Möglichen*], in the socialist interest [. . .]. To supply the apparatus of production without also *transforming* it, as far as possible, [is] a highly suspect procedure even if the materials supplied appear to be of a revolutionary character. We have, in effect, to face the fact that the bourgeois apparatus of production and publication can assimilate and even propagate astonishing quantities of revolutionary themes without thereby seriously putting in question its own existence and that of the class which owns it. This remains the case at least as long as it is routinely supplied by hacks (*Routiniers*), even revolutionary ones.[2]

'What remains' – in Christa Wolf's phrase – of the revolutionary hopes which sustained these sentences is a question which may provisionally be left open. If Benjamin's generation was forced to recognize that 'capitalism will not die a natural death',[3] ours has had to learn the further lesson that capitalism is not, for the foreseeable future, going to die at all. Benjamin's distinction between supplying and transforming a cultural apparatus nevertheless remains as pertinent now as then, if in reduced measure. And this distinction directly concerns us here, inasmuch as conferences too are part and parcel – above all, parcel – of the bourgeois cultural apparatus[es]. How, then, can we, the assembled suppliers, avoid serving up a culinary Benjamin to the jaws of the culture industry? How can we avoid the fate of the revolutionary hack?

The fact that Benjamin had an extremely measured conception of revolutionary change corners us that much more effectively. It does not allow us to claim (as Adorno, among others, was wont to do) that the – *the* – revolutionary chance has, regrettably, been missed. Every historical moment, according to Benjamin, has its *own* revolutionary chance[4] – including, therefore, those moments whose possibilities are severely reduced. This notion of a perpetually renewed – and perpetually missed – opportunity is Benjamin's version of Trotsky's demand for 'permanent revolution'. Actuality, thus conceived, is a matter of actualizing the specific potential of this particular now. To do so is to act 'within the measure of the possible' – no more and no less. This measured phrase keeps cropping up in Benjamin's writings. *Nach Massgabe des Möglichen*: the possible is both a 'measure' (*Mass*) and a 'gift' (*Gabe*).

To stand 'entirely to the left of the possible' – this, by contrast, is in Benjamin's eyes the empty, ultra-radical gesture of the revolutionary hack who prefers 'left melancholy'[5] to actual action. It is necessary, in other words, to stand to the left *within* the possible in order to measure the gift.

'Men make history', wrote Marx, 'but not in conditions of their own choosing'. As a historical materialist, Benjamin recognised that the 'melting-process' through which social and cultural relations were to be 'recast' depended on the 'temperature'[6] of the class struggle. We know today, and therein lies the pitfall of a new left melancholy, how low that temperature has meanwhile dropped. What, then, are we to make of our revolutionary chance – that of a geopolitical conjuncture which allows for no more revolutionary transformations, except possibly those that are confined to catching up with the bourgeois revolutions of yesteryear?[7] The more pointed question which confronts us here is whether we – but who are we? – can extract from this conference the modest opportunity it affords.

> 2. But from what can something from the past be saved? Not so much from the contempt and disregard into which it has fallen as from the

> particular way in which it has been handed down. The way in which it is celebrated (*gewürdigt*) as our 'heritage' is more ominous than any oblivion.[8]
>
> 'Celebration' or apologetics aims to smooth over the revolutionary moments of the historical process. Its concern is to construct a continuity. It accentuates only those elements of a work which have already entered posterity. What it misses are the jagged edges which offer a foothold to someone who wants to get beyond that work.[9]

In Central Park, Benjamin writes:

> The souvenir (*Andenken*) is the secularized relic. [. . .]. The souvenir is the counterpart of so-called 'experience' (*Erlebnis*). It marks the increased estrangement that consists in drawing up an inventory of one's inanimate possessions . . .[10]

The reified souvenir (*Andenken*) is, according to Benjamin, as irreconcilably opposed to true remembrance (*Eingedenken*) as are pseudo-experience (*Erlebnis*) to true experience (*Erfahrung*), and 'celebrating' (*würdigen*) the past to 'saving' (*retten*) it. Saving the past involves the 'firm, apparently brutal grasp'[11] which may help us 'get beyond' it. Benjamin is, in other words, implicitly asking posterity to find ways of commemorating his work that are also so many footholds to places beyond it. But one can only leave behind what one has worked through. 'To annihilate something', Benjamin once wrote, 'one must not only know it. To do the job completely, one must also have felt it.'[12] Flowers and plaques will not, therefore, do the job. The birthday cake we need to eat is Benjamin's own corpus. What is called for is the combined work and wake of mourning, remembrance and critique which might begin to save us from Benjamin, and Benjamin from himself. It might even begin to save us – in Nietzsche's phrase, but not the way he meant it – from salvation itself.

> 3. Mistrust in the fate of literature, mistrust in the fate of freedom, mistrust in the fate of European humanity, but three times mistrust in all reconciliation: between classes, between nations, between individuals. And unlimited trust only in I.G. Farben and the peaceful perfection of the air force. But what now, what next?[13]

These sentences were written at the end of the 1920s – the good old days when Brecht could still oppose those 'in the dark' to those 'in the light'. In an age when some 'give' work (*Arbeitgeber*) and others 'take' it

(*Arbeitnehmer*), the fronts have, of course, hardly disappeared. They have shifted, ramified and been smoothed over, notably by talk of the 'end of class conflict', the 'end of ideology', the 'end of socialism' and, last not least, the 'end of history'.

The trust that the above lines placed in the future manufacturer of Zyklon B was to prove more than justified. But with the alleged collapse of socialism – the real, existing collapse, that is, of 'real, existing socialism' – Benjamin's Marxist agenda has yielded to a seemingly irrevocable disenchantment with Marxism itself. *Die Weltgeschichte ist das Weltgericht*. The Left has internalized the images that the right (and its own former zealot) have created of it, and now pleads guilty as charged ('the god that failed', 'the opium of the intellectuals' etc.). As a result, an all too limited 'measure of the possible' is now deemed possible. What is surely required in this situation is more, and more accurate, mistrust, not a generalized disenchantment. Mistrust, certainly, of ourselves as well as of 'them' – unlimited confidence that the worst is still possible – trust, too, that *le pire n'est pas sûr*. The 'disenchantment of the world' is, certainly, a world-historical force to be reckoned with. But why add insult to injury?

Can one imagine an international Benjamin conference which, instead of fostering harmless, disenchanted understanding, made a little difference?

II WEIGHTS AND MEASURES

> There may be timeless images, but there are certainly no timeless theories.[14]
>
> As Rabbi Hillel [used to say], standing on one leg . . .[15]

The Actuality of Walter Benjamin was the title of a remarkable volume of essays which appeared in 1972 to mark his eightieth anniversary.[16] There are at least two good reasons for renewing this question twenty years later. Firstly, actuality is always the order of the day – especially in relation to a thinker who saw in the fulfilment of its claims both the categorical imperative and the pleasure principle. Actuality is, *pace* Nietzsche, the eternal return of what is not the same. And to *this* eternal return, says Benjamin, we cannot but say yes. The author of the *Trauerspiel* book would hardly have denied Baudelaire's claim that 'we are all celebrating some funeral'. But he would have added that we are all constantly celebrating particular, unrepeatable birthdays. That melancholy and that joy each give the other its specific weight.

This already indicates the second reason why the question of Benjamin's actuality should pre-empt today's agenda. 'Benjamin's actuality' can *also* be taken to mean his own particular *notion* of actuality. How to come to terms with this idiosyncratic, remote, yet immensely seductive conception of 'the now' is the second, related task that he leaves us. I will approach this 'now' by first assembling an anthology of relevant passages from his work.

First, in 1921, there is the 'announcement' (*Ankündigung*) – or should one say 'annunciation' or even 'a-now-ncement'? – of a journal, *Angelus Novus*, which was never to see the light of day:

> The true vocation of a journal is to announce the spirit of its epoch. Such actuality means even more to it than its own unity or clarity. A journal would, like a newspaper, be condemned to insignificance if there did not take shape within it a life which was powerful enough to redeem even what is questionable by the act of affirming it.[17]

Benjamin here locates 'true' actuality between two fronts, and describes its medium, the journal, as the utopian mean between journalism and philosophy. The philosopher's spurious claim 'to master, from some lofty vantage-point, the intellectual horizon of the times'[18] does no more justice to true actuality, in Benjamin's view, than does the journalist's unconditional surrender to passing fashion. Standing both in and against its time, the journal that Benjamin envisages is, in a Nietzschean sense, 'untimely'. Focusing on 'the genuinely actual which takes shape under the unfruitful surface of the new, whose exploitation it leaves to the newspapers', it is to 'woo' actuality, instead of 'ogling' the public.[19]

Benjamin's announcement of his prospective journal closes with the following explanation of its name. It

> refers to the ephemeral nature of the journal [. . .]. This is the just price demanded by its wooing of true actuality. For, according to Talmudic legend, angels are created anew every moment in innumerable throngs to sing their hymn before God and then disappear into nothingness. May the name of this journal mean that such actuality, the only true kind, has fallen to it.[20]

It is no accident that these lines monotheistically invoke the true actuality. An analogous phrase in the *Theses on the Philosophy of History* describes the ephemeral nature of 'the true picture of the past'.[21] In Benjamin's writings 'truth' and 'actuality' almost invariably appear in the singular, usually accompanied by the definite article. Countless angels appear and vanish each moment, but the short-lived journal that is destined to capture their fleeting passage bears the singular name: *Angelus Novus*.

The notion of actuality conjured up by this name turns out, on closer inspection, to be the 'temporal core' (*Zeitkern*)[22] of a Messianic theology of history. 'To the spiritual *restitutio in integrum* which leads to immortality corresponds', according to the *Theologico-Political Fragment*,

> a worldly restitution which leads to the eternity of decline; and the rhythm of this eternally transient worldly existence [. . .] is happiness. For nature is Messianic by virtue of its eternal and total passing away[23]

What the *Theologico-Political Fragment* says of the death and rebirth of nature as an eternal form of transience the announcement of the Angelus Novus says of the Messianic rhythm of history. The Messianic 'now' resides in the fragile intimations of the 'genuinely actual' that announce their virtual existence under the unfruitful surface of the merely new.[24] In an early essay Benjamin had called these intimations the 'elements of the end-state' which are 'deeply embedded in every present as its most endangered, disreputable and ridiculed creations and thoughts'.[25] Thus, the truly actual, which lodges 'in the oddest and most crabbed of phenomena',[26] points from the heart of the present beyond itself. In this sense, the hymnic happiness of the Messianic present is also the Messianic promise of a happiness yet to come. A coming fulfilment is being symbolically anticipated in the performative act of promising it. Benjamin's announcement thus prefigures a Messiah who constantly defers his arrival: it announces the projected journal *Angelus Novus*, who – had he ever arrived on the doorstep – would in turn have announced the Messiah. Such deferral is not, however, a series of empty postponements. If the 'true price' of genuine actuality is its transience, its reward is a fulfilled intimation of immortality.[27]

To weigh Benjamin's actuality is also, I am arguing, to ponder his *concept* of actuality, and, to do so, inevitably, from the standpoint of our own now. But it is also, from his perspective, to consider our (concept of) actuality from the standpoint of his.

For critique, as Benjamin understands it, is a matter of the critical conjuncture between the present and the past. 'For it is not a question', he writes,

> of presenting written works in the context of their time, but of articulating the time which grasps them – namely ours – in the time in which they originated.[28]

In defining the present as the medium of the past and vice versa, Benjamin is implicitly prescribing how his own writings are to be read. Our actuality is to be read through his, and his through ours, each being the condition of the other. If we then ask what Benjamin actually means by actuality, we soon find ourselves amidst the world of Jewish Messianism.[29] Theology may, as Benjamin's first *Thesis* claims, no longer dare to show its face in public. It is, however, very much in evidence in Benjamin's notion of actuality. His 'now time' comes with strings attached, and these strings are pulled by a not-so-invisible dwarf.

We secular readers thereby find ourselves confronted with the following problem. We may be entirely willing to follow Benjamin's lead in giving first priority to the urgencies of the present. We may also be inclined to include among these needs the less tangible 'claims' which, Benjamin insists, the past makes on the present.[30] We may, however, balk at buying into the Jewish Messianism to which Benjamin owes his own peculiar conception of actuality. We may, in particular, feel uncomfortable with Benjamin's monotheistic affirmation of a single – *the* single – true actuality. Does not our actuality demand that we eye such Messianic claims with the same 'cautious detachment' that 'the historical materialist' of the seventh *Thesis* bring to the 'cultural treasures' of the past? That we 'dissociate' ourselves from them 'as far as possible?'[31] *Nach Massgabe des Möglichen*. But just how possible is that?

'We have become poor', Benjamin writes in 1931 . . .

> We have given up one piece after another of mankind's inheritance, often pawning it for a hundredth of its value in exchange for a meagre advance in the small change of the 'actual'[32]

Benjamin's work meanwhile constitutes our postwar inheritance, and it is safe to assume that parts of it now need in turn to be exchanged for our currency. The metaphor of the pawnshop is, moreover, still all too theological: there is, in effect, no guarantee that the family heirlooms we leave behind will ever be 'redeemed'.

According to the *Theses on the Philosophy of History*, a 'particular life' has to be 'blasted out' of the 'epoch', 'a particular work' out of the 'life-work' – and so on (we may interpolate) in ever greater detail.[33] Such cultural sabotage aims to expose the jagged edges by which we may clamber beyond the slippery blocks of a monumentalized past. 'Some hand things down to posterity by making them untouchable and thus conserving them', Benjamin writes in *The Destructive Character*; 'others hand on situations by making them practicable and thus liquidating them.'[34] In this sense, but perhaps no longer quite in this sense, the task facing today's students of Benjamin is to find ways through his work; to renew his efforts to 'blot out'[35] the theology in which it was steeped; in short, to avoid canonizing a work which leaves instructions for the dismantling of cultural monuments.[36] Benjamin, for his part, admitted his inability to achieve a 'complete transformation'[37] of his thinking and had, here too, to work within 'the measure of the possible'. This is not the place to speculate whether the persistent presence of Jewish theology in Benjamin's thinking – a backlog emblematized by the hunchback of the first *Thesis* – had to do, as he himself might have argued, with the 'temperature of the class struggle' or, more or less synonymously, with the massive world-historical fact that the Enlightenment has remained, in Habermas's phrase, an 'unfinished project'; nor to speculate whether that project should and must remain incomplete. I simply want for now to raise the following questions. What concept of actuality remains if we attempt to blot out the Messianic dimension of Benjamin's thinking? Has it meanwhile become more possible to extricate actuality from theology? Do we not still need a 'weak Messianic'[38] concept of actuality?

These questions will perhaps prompt the following objection. Is not any attempt to get beyond Benjamin by playing him against himself necessarily circular? But what if there is no way round this circle? No other way out than through? As far, that is, as possible?

Leaving these questions in suspense, I return to Benjamin's image of actuality, the *Angelus Novus*, in order to recall the 'devastating events'[39] to which he is already exposed in Benjamin's own subsequent writings. 'The Kabbala recounts', he writes in 1933 in his autobiographical piece *Agesilaus Santander*.

> that God creates at every instant a throng of new angels who are all destined for the space of a moment to sing his praise before his throne before passing away into nothingness. Mine was interrupted . . .[40]

This motif of the arrested halleluja is echoed seven years later in the ninth *Thesis* where another *Angelus Novus* is inexorably propelled into the future by the 'storm we call progress'. A hymnic actuality is here supplanted by an infernal one. The good news announced by the angels of yesteryear is drowned out by news that is hardly deserving of the name – the age-old news of a Fall from the name. This nameless catastrophe is mutely named by the speechless expression on the angel's face. It is the wide-eyed, wide-angled, apotropaic gaze of the Medusa as camera(wo)man. Before being carried off into a now non-theological void from which no newer angel can ever hope to be born, this last *Angelus Novus* momentarily contemplates a – 'the'-

'dialectical image' of world history and thereby symbolically arrests it in its tracks.

What we in turn should keep firmly in view is the implicit lesson contained in this image. Only an angel *in extremis* can still see the world as it actually is. One might speak here of a theological alienation-effect. History has been wreaking havoc with theology, yet history can itself be 'sighted', in Benjamin's phrase, only from a vanishing theological vantage-point. The relation between the sacred and the profane is thus one of mutual, though unequal, dependence. The angel's hymn of praise is interrupted by the whirlwind we call history; but history is in turn frozen for an instant by the angel's petrified look of horror. The 'last snapshot of the European intelligentsia'[41] is thus the superimposition of two opposing actualities – historical and theological – on one another. Salvation may be the straw at which the drowning man grasps, but without a modicum of theology the actual present cannot be grasped. If history finally succeeds in relegating theology to oblivion, it will presumably have become oblivious to itself. This, at least, would seem to be the moral of Benjamin's ninth *Thesis*.

It would not, on the other hand, be difficult to show that Benjamin's *Theses* attempts to secularize a Messianic conception of actuality and thereby to reactualize it.[42] This transition is nicely summed up in the following statement, made in 1928, which contains in a nutshell the 'temporal kernel' of Benjamin's subsequent theory of materialist historiography:

> The innermost structures of the past are illuminated for each present only in the light which emanates from the incandescence (*Weissglut*) of their actualities.[43]

Far from representing a linear series of discrete moments, as an over-literal reading of the Talmudic legend would suggest, actuality is conceived here as the molten fusion of two actualities. The metaphor of white-hot 'incandescence', which recalls those of the 'melting-process' and the 'temperature' of the class struggle, leaves the present-day reader with the following questions. To what extent can such a 'fusion of horizons' – to cite Gadamer's term – still take place in a colder climate? To the extent, no doubt, of the possible. But how do we measure it? We all still live, said Nietzsche, from the 'old fire'. But can we still actually warm ourselves around that metaphysical hearth? What, alternatively, would be the specific revolutionary chance sparked off by the dying fire? Or are even the sparks going out nowadays?

In the *Theses on the Philosophy of History* Benjamin develops the notion of an interplay of actualities into a far-reaching theory of historical constellations. This time the heat of the critical moment is no longer that of a revolutionary melting-process; it is that of acute 'danger'.[44]

> The materialist historian grasps the constellation which his own era has formed with a definite earlier one. He thus establishes a concept of the present as the 'time of the now' (*Jetztzeit*) which is shot through with chips of Messianic time.[45]

The opportunity granted to each historical moment lies, according to this theory, in its 'secret agreement'[46] with a corresponding moment of the past. Benjamin thereby replaces the phantasmagoria of an eternal return of the same with a 'rational astrology' whose object is the permanently changing conjunction of life- and world-historical planets. This theory has, certainly, far more in common with Proustian *mémoire involontaire* and Baudelairian *correspondances* than with the usual methods of professional historians. The scene recalls that of Baudelaire's sonnet *À une passante*. Like the poet and his passing muse, two 'very specific' moments look one another in the eye for the duration of a transient, immortal, melting moment. Benjamin thereby transposes a theory of aura and 'magical observation'[47] borrowed from early German Romanticism, on which he superimposes the mystical notion of the 'now' (*Nu, Jetztzeit*), onto the relation between world-historical epochs. From this he extract a theory of historical knowledge which renews the old philosophical topos of a homology between individual and collective experience.

The 'now' of this 'twinkling of an eye' (*Augenblick*), in which two corresponding moments exchange a lightning glance, is in an equally literal sense a main-tenant. The materialist historian is defined by his ability to hold fast the *nunc stans* of an unrepeatable constellation that is about to slip through his fingers.[48] It is all a matter of seizing the day. This today may be meagre (*dürftig*), Benjamin observes,

> But however it may be, one must grasp it firmly by the horns if one is to question the past. It is the bull whose blood must fill the pit if the spirits of the departed are to appear around its edge.[49]

Only if the bull is grasped by the horns can the dilemma be resolved. The primacy that Benjamin accords to politics over history[50] is, as this image makes clear, not to be confused with spuriously radical calls for 'relevance', which amount merely to judging the past by the standards of the present. Such calls are, as Nietzsche already knew, merely the obverse side of the historicist *refusal* of the present. 'Actuality', as Benjamin understands it, assumes only the primacy, not the superiority, of present-day concerns over the past. The historian can see the past only from his present viewpoint – but this 'viewpoint' is not the elevated vantage-point of a historicist God who reviews history like a general reviewing his troops. The image of the bull whose blood has to be sacrificed if the spirits of the dead are to be conjured up suggests a quite different relation between past and present. Not that the self-sacrifice of the present is a distinterested act; it is rather, in Benjamin's eyes, the condition of its self-discovery. Such sacrifice thus has nothing in common with the self-effacing posture of the historicist, who fondly imagines that he can abstract from the conditions of his existence and who himself, as a result, turns into a bloodless shade. For Benjamin as for Nietzsche, such selfless objectivity is in fact 'empathy' with the 'victor'[51]. Historicism is thus far from disinterested; but the interests it represents are far from its own. The 'methodological' bracketing-out of the present, coupled with the contrary enthronement of the present as the sole presiding, sole surviving judge of the past – this constitutes the basic contradiction of historicism. The primacy of politics over history defines not merely the task of the historical materialist but also actual historicist practice. In the latter case, however, present interests go largely unadmitted and unchecked. Hölderlin's lament over a 'meagre' age is matched by Brecht's maxim: 'Don't seize upon the good old things, but upon the bad new ones'.[52] However impoverished the present may be, it is all that we have at our disposal. Benjamin is here inverting the historicist claim that the historian who wants to know the past 'as it actually was'[53] must 'rid his head'[54] of everything that happened meanwhile. To this he opposes the following thesis:

> The Copernican turn in historiography is this: one used to take the 'past' as the fixed point and to see the present as groping its way towards this firm basis of knowledge. Henceforth this relation is to be inverted, with the past acquiring its dialectical fixity from the synthesis which waking achieves with the various contradictory dream images. Politics acquires primacy over history.[55]

In the second preface to the *Critique of Pure Reason*, Kant claimed to have introduced a Copernican revolution into epistemology by having the object revolve henceforth around the subject. Benjamin's theory of historical constellations marks a parallel inversion. The experience of the present is no longer to be considered a *quantité négligeable* which the historian is at liberty to ignore. It is, on the contrary, the medium of all historical knowledge. Certainty now lies not in the 'eternal image'[56] of a past that allegedly 'will not run away from us',[57] but in a present which is constantly escaping us. This fleeting, fleeing moment is, according to Benjamin, the 'vanishing point'[58] of every historical construction. Historicism thus rests on an optical illusion. It is mediated through and through by the present to which it fondly believes it has turned its back.[59] How seriously Benjamin took his claim that the materialist historian writes history 'for his own person'[60] can be gauged from his observation that 'everything one is thinking at any given moment must at all costs be incorporated into the work in which one is currently involved'.[61]

It is time to break off this extrapolation of Benjamin's theory of historiography from his concept of actuality. Such philological exercises, while necessary, can only serve as a preliminary to the actual business at hand – that of inquiring into the topicality of a bygone topos – the actuality of Benjamin's 'now'. A final quotation will serve to bring the problem into clearer focus.

'All historical knowledge' Benjamin writes in his notes to the *Arcades Project*,

> can be represented in the image of a weighing scale. One pan is weighed down by the past, the other by knowledge of the present. The facts assembled in the former can never be too numerous or too insignificant. The latter may, however, contain only a few heavy, massive weights.[62]

This, then, is Benjamin's image of materialist historiography. *The Theses on the Philosophy of History* will define such historiography in contradistinction to bourgeois historicism. In one of the most incisive articles to have appeared on Benjamin in the past decade, Hans-Dieter Kittsteiner has challenged this opposition and presented Benjamin as a 'materialist historicist'.[63] But does not the above-quoted passage perhaps indicate that the opposition between the two is not always as exclusive as a casual reading of the *Theses* might suggest? One would, at the very least, have to discriminate between historicisms. Does not the image of the scale in fact suggest a possible balance between the 'religious' devotion to petty detail characteristic of a certain antiquarian historicism and the 'economic(al)' definition of present priorities which remains a primary task of the materialist historian? The scales of justice are not, however, intended to represent some middling compromise but rather a dynamic equipoise calculated to do justice to both sides – historical justice to the past, political justice to the present, and never the one without the other.[64] In this sense, historical materialism must take into its service not only theology, as the first *Thesis* claims, but also a certain form of historicism. Then every moment can justly be 'that of a judgment over certain moments which preceded it'[65] – a Messianic moment in which the scales of historical justice, indeed time itself, momentarily stand still.[66]

By way of this necessarily historicist reconstruction of Benjamin's mystico-materialist notion of 'now time', I now return to the critical issue of our own actuality. Can the theory of unrepeatable constellations outlined above still serve as a model for the possible interplay between Benjamin's now and today's? Does some 'secret agreement' somehow exist between the present conjuncture and particular moments of Benjamin's work? What other aspects have meanwhile forfeited their actuality? Which ones have become more 'legible' (in Benjamin's, or some other, sense of the term) through the critical passage of time? Does not Benjamin's theory demand to be applied to itself? And what, above all, are the few, well-chosen weights which must today be placed on one – let's say the left – side of the scale?

Benjamin's own answer to this last question can be elicited from the following sentences which he copied in 1935 from an article by Louis Aragon:

> If I insist on the mechanism of contradiction in the biography of a writer, it is because the development of his thought cannot neglect facts which have a different logic from that of his thought when considered on its own. No idea that he holds really holds up . . . when confronted by certain basic and very simple facts: the fact that the workers face a police force armed with cannons, the fact that war looms and that fascism is already in power . . . It is a matter of human dignity to subject one's ideas to these facts and not to insinuate them by some sleight-of-hand into one's own ideas, however ingenious these may be.[67]

'The construction of life', Benjamin had written in 1927,

> is at present in the power of facts far more than of convictions, and of such facts as have scarcely ever become the basis of convictions.[68]

Benjamin, who elsewhere reflects on the 'shock' which gave rise to Baudelaire's *Loss of a Halo*, is here recording an equivalent shock – the intellectuals' encounter with facts whose impact they can no longer absorb into their systems. Whereas the image of the scale describes a possible equilibrium between the many small facts of the past and the few massive ones of the present, the above-quoted passage from Aragon accentuates the massive disproportion between the objective facts and the subjective convictions of the bourgeois intellectual.

However unmasterable this opposition may be, the facts themselves are all too clear; naked class struggle, rising fascism, approaching war. What, then, are today's equivalent weights? Instead of attempting to narrow down the present conjuncture to a comparable list,[69] I shall confine myself for now to raising a few further questions. Who would seriously claim, more than fifty years later, that Benjamin's account of his present can be simply transposed to our own? At the opposite extreme, who (apart from Francis Fukuyama) would risk the contrary proposition that the old conflicts can, at least in principle, be overcome by the new world order? But could it perhaps be that the urgencies of our present cannot be handily reduced to a handful of weights, and that it is correspondingly more difficult for us to get a handle on them? Have, then, the dangers become more diffuse, the fronts more ambiguous, and the 'facts', while no less stark, that much more complex? How actual(izable) – how present, how commensurable – is our actuality? Could it be an essential structural feature of the current period that it should, precisely, elude a 'firm, apparently brutal grasp'? What opportunities would such an ungraspable dilemma still afford? Do – or can – such questions serve to obscure the view from below? Are today's Western intellectuals simply that much more insulated against the life-threatening pressures that would cause the present constellation to 'crystallize' into its own essential truth? 'Where thinking suddenly stops in a configuration pregnant with tensions', writes Benjamin in the *Theses*, 'it gives that configuration a shock, by which it crystallizes into a monad.'[70] Is the 'conviction' that underlies such a metaphor – part metaphysics, part alchemy, part astrology – still a match for the 'facts' of today? What if advanced capitalism can no longer be grasped by such 'illegitimately poetic'[71] means? Do not Benjamin's images, metaphors and correspondances effectively short-circuit the 'system'[72] But how effectively? Is not his 'anthropological materialism' all too romantic a venture? Does not the brave experiment he undertook in the Arcades Project – to defy his own theory of the decay of experience – obstruct a more sober conceptual analysis of the deep structures of the modern world?[73]

How else to explain the embarrassing difficulty one has in taking the bull by the horns, in short-listing the 'simple and fundamental facts' of the present? Instead of trying to tackle this massive question head-on, we are perhaps better advised to approach it more obliquely by way of specific, limited, substantive analyses. But the pressure which that overarching question ought to exert on such detailed research will have to be no less palpable than the 'claim' which, according to Benjamin, specific moments of the past have on the present.

This much, at least, seems clear. It is scarcely conceivable that a socio-political diagnosis in the manner of Benjamin's *Theses on the Philosophy of*

History could be envisaged today. If we could measure more precisely the distance which separates us from that diagnosis, we would already have made a beginning.

To this end, let me briefly recall how, under the immediate impact of the Hitler-Stalin pact, Benjamin himself chose to weight the scales. 'In more than one sense', he wrote of the *Theses*, 'the text is . . . reduced.'[74]. If we compress it still further, the following schematic analysis emerges. Under the pressure of the Hitler-Stalin pact, the present political conjuncture has polarized into two opposed fronts. On the one hand, 'the enemy' who has 'not ceased to be victorious';[75] on the other, an alliance between theology and historical materialism – two 'foreign friends' who are to abandon their hostilities and make common cause against their common enemy. But the 'strategic value' (*Kampfwert*)[76] of the *Theses* lies above all in their resistance to another, more insidious enemy – one who dangerously confuses the fronts and saps the home team from within. This internal enemy is the bourgeois belief in 'progress'. For when the smoke has cleared, progress turns out, as Marx showed, to be that of the bourgeoisie. It is, in other words, the hegemonic ideology with which the victors colonize the minds of the defeated. Would-be progressives abet fascism, Benjamin argues, by reducing it to a relapse into barbarism, instead of recognizing it as a product of the barbarism which lurks within so-called progress itself. The belief in progress amounts, in short, to a new opium of the people, a false, secular religion which can only be counteracted, according to Benjamin's first *Thesis*, by the introduction of actual theology into the apparatus of historical materialism.

What the tradition of the oppressed actually teaches us, according to the eighth *Thesis*,

> is that the 'state of emergency' in which we are living is not the exception but the rule. We must attain to a conception of history that is in keeping with this insight. Then we shall clearly recognize that it is our task to bring about a real state of emergency, and this will improve our position in the struggle against Fascism. One reason why Fascism has a chance is that in the name of progress its opponents treat it as a historical norm.[77]

Seen from below, the *so-called* 'state of emergency' brought about by Fascism is, in Benjamin's eyes, merely the exacerbation of a *permanent* state of emergency, which could in turn only be ended by a revolutionary state of emergency. But the only forces which could bring about this unprecedented exception to the rule of myth are, according to the above analysis, themselves being increasingly weakened by the new fetishistic myth of progress.

Progress progresses the way capital capitalizes itself – as a kind of automat or automobile, a self-moving mover which will, like a train, deposit mankind at its final destination. This myth already lurked, Benjamin suspects, within Marxism itself, with its strangely fetishistic notion of 'the' dialectic. But the myth acquired hegemonic proportions, according to Benjamin, only with the political emasculation of historical materialism. In persuading the working class to abandon its 'hatred' and 'spirit of sacrifice', social democracy cut 'the sinews of its greatest strength'.[78]

Tertium non datur. Behind Benjamin's indictment of this fatal betrayal stand the classic alternatives between revolution and evolution, Marxism and reformism, radicalism and revisionism. It should, however, be added that Benjamin increasingly came to conceive revolution as a purely preventive measure intended to avert the worst. This is what, by the late thirties, the 'measure of the possible' had come to.

The above-cited *Thesis* does, however, contain one phrase which offsets what might otherwise amount to a doctrinaire alternative. Benjamin speaks of 'improving' the position of those who are struggling against Fascism. Such a touchingly meliorist notion of improvement might appear to be strangely inappropriate to a situation which seems to allow no middle ground between two irreconcilable states of emergency. Such measured formulations are, however, as much a feature of Benjamin's thinking as its immoderate faith in extremes. It is this steady insistence on 'the measure of the possible' that distinguishes Benjamin's political Messianism from other forms of political Romanticism . . .

In an extreme situation, indeed *in extremis*, Benjamin nevertheless saw no alternative but to distribute the political weights between two extremes. 'The enemy' looms at the other side of the chess-board. Even and especially in the darkest hour, the fronts are as clear as day.

What is, however, equally clear is that the weights are not today what they were then, and that the rules of the chess-game have changed. There are a number of simply inescapable facts which no 'actual' reading of Benjamin's *Theses* can today afford to ignore. Did they not, after all, make a point of denouncing as 'historicism' all attempts to relive the past by screening out what happened meanwhile? And did not Aragon warn against forcing massive new facts into the mould of pre-existing convictions?

Three such facts, which cannot but weigh heavily on any present-day reading of Benjamin's *Theses*, should be mentioned here. Firstly, it was not the theologico-political strategy proposed in the first *Thesis* that won the war against Fascism; the 'allied victory' was a quite different, much messier, more mixed affair. Secondly, we now know that the attempt to bring about a revolutionary state of emergency under post-revolutionary conditions led, when literally acted out, to the dead end of urban terrorism. Thirdly, the political system that has, mercifully, outlasted Fascist and Communist totalitarianisms is also the one which, even and especially in its most benign, enlightened form, represents the opposite, indeed the betrayal, of everything that Benjamin stood for. The future lies for the time being with social democracy, and revolution, like the little hunchback of Benjamin's first *Thesis*, is today obliged to keep out of sight. It has at best returned to its former existence as 'spectre' and 'mole'. Did not Benjamin himself finally visualize historical materialism as a puppet smoking a hookah? As much as to say that *le grand soir* had become a pipe-dream already by then? Another of the 'phantasmagorias' from which we were to awaken? What we were, however, to awaken to was itself a specific revolutionary opportunity – even if it was that of a meagre, a brave new, bad new day.

So the weights have shifted, and the *Theses on the Philosophy of History* need to be read in the historical context of their times. But does not the tired acknowledgement that the times have changed carry with it the stale smell of historicism? True, Benjamin's rejection of historicism is inseparable from his condemnation of social democracy, and needs to be subjected to a similarly agonizing reappraisal. This does not yet mean, however, that his indictment of them has lost all its teeth.

'Where a chain of events appears before us', writes Benjamin in the ninth *Thesis*, the angel of history sees 'one single catastrophe'.[79] If *he* is identifiable as the guardian angel of historical materialism, then we stand indicted as mere historicists. And it is he alone who fulfils the historicist claim to see history 'as it actually was' (*wie es eigentlich gewesen*). But who, we might retort, who but an expiring angel could ever afford so undifferentiated a perspective on history? Yet who would dare rush in to place the angel's optic 'in historical perspective'? Who would presume to blink at the staring angel with the eyes of Nietzsche's 'last men' and reduce his absolute horror to relative terms? Does so-called progress not advance apace today? Hasn't the mounting rubble now reached the ozone layer? Perhaps, then, we have to live, or balance, between two barely compatible truths. Firstly, the present undeniably perpetuates a permanent state of emergency. Secondly, and no less undeniably, Benjamin's *Theses on the Philosophy of History* have to be understood in terms of a then prevailing state of emergency with which ours cannot remotely be compared. The relation between Benjamin's now and ours is one of intense closeness and distance – not the empathic closeness or the safe distance which form the two sides of the historicist coin.

In his materialist phase Benjamin was willing to renounce those convictions which no longer withstand the 'facts'. In defiance of all empirical verification, he had issued some of his own earliest convictions in the form of oracular *faits accomplis*. Scholem wrote of the young Benjamin as an esoteric 'producer of [. . .] quotable and interpretable sentences' which characteristically began with the authoritarian formula 'It is a metaphysical truth that. . .'.[80] 'Underneath the pavement', so ran one of the surrealist mottoes of the student movement, 'is the sand'. Below the 'unfruitful surface' of the facts, Benjamin likewise claimed to see a quite different order of reality. There were moments when Benjamin, like Zarathustra, thought he had penetrated to the heart of the world 'For at bottom', he once claimed, 'at their most hidden, things do not really go on this way, but from one extreme to another'.[81] Such (un)dialectical leaps have a tangential[82] relation – no more and no less – to Hegelian and Marxian dialectics. They are elsewhere described as the 'paradoxical reversal' that occurs whenever one proceeds 'ruthlessly (*rücksichtslos*) and radically' enough.[83] Radicalism is here implicitly defined against the politics of the *juste-milieu* as well as all other forms of 'bourgeois compromise.[84]

What the last two quotations also suggest is that Benjamin's political radicalism is, in the last instance, grounded not merely in a dialectic but in an *ontology* of extremes.[85] It is sustained by a serene theologico-political faith in a divine immediacy – in the unerring, unmediated, unfallen power of extremes to subvert fallen norms and lead us back home. *Wirf weg*, Adorno liked to say, *damit du gewinnst*: 'Throw away that you may win'. It is enough, Benjamin likewise implies, to proceed 'regardless' (*rücksichtslos*) – regardless of any mediation, any considerations, any considerateness (*Rücksichten*) – in order to 'awaken in God's world' and discover oneself *dans le vrai*. The truth, for Benjamin, is one, the truth is radical, and the royal road that rejoins it is not the highway of progress but an eccentric zigzag path full of detours, leaps and about-turns.

Benjamin's faith in the redeeming (un)dialectical 'leap'[86] was itself no doubt a redemptive leap of faith. Was it, then, a 'conviction' that flouted 'the facts'? But does not today's realism tend in turn to deny any reality that is not grey, inert and middling? The question remains whether Benjamin's motto 'always radical, never consistent'[87] is equal to the all-too-consistent logic of today's facts, and whether the subterranean energies to which it implicitly appeals have effectively survived the 'disenchantment of the world'.

To this question Benjamin gave various answers, all of which intimate that the old forces are, in one reduced form or another, weathering the storm.[88] His last word on the subject was the parable of the hunchback dwarf. But we today have to wonder about the fate of another dwarf, who has meanwhile replaced Benjamin's hunchback. 'Marxian theory', wrote Hans-Dieter Kittsteiner several years ago,

> is now in the enviable position which Benjamin reserved in the First *Thesis* for theology: it is small and ugly and cannot allow itself to be seen. It is out of fashion, and it may now be time to reflect on the energies that are contained in obsolete things from which the vogue has withdrawn.[89]

The question of 'what remains' today concerns not merely the Messianic idea but its secular heir. With the majestic collapse of 'effectively existing socialism', the ghost of a revolution that never materialized has been driven back underground. But it continues to haunt Europe with the desperate question that the young Lukács asked on the eve of the Russian Revolution: 'Who will save us from Western civilisation?'

The most viable answer to the radical opposition between revolution and reformism on which the *Theses on the Philosophy of History* could still take their stand is perhaps to be found today in the critical revision of the Marxian canon which Jurgen Habermas has undertaken in the name of a 'radical revisionism'.[90] The basis for an independent dialogue with Benjamin has thereby been established, and it is in this force-field, perhaps, that our own peculiar (post-)revolutionary opportunity lies.[91]

Habermas's intellectual stamina and unresigned commitment to social democracy also set his position apart from the disenchantment prevalent among those who identified with Benjamin in '68 and are now busy foreswearing the sympathies and empathies of their revolutionary past. One can, of course, hardly reconcile the confidence of a Habermas in the 'uncompleted project of modernity' with the young Lukács' vote of no-confidence in Western civilization. The contradiction is, however, truer than its parts. It was Benjamin who taught us that we do not always have to choose between seemingly ineluctable alternatives. His 'freedom to put together things and thoughts which are considered incompatible'[92] rested, however, on a quasi-religious confidence in the capacity of extremes to generate a 'force-field of tensions' from which the right decisions were to 'crystallize'as if of their own accord. And it is this confidence that one can no longer *entirely* share today.

Perhaps, then, everything depends today on the quality of our disenchantment. Benjamin's notion of sobriety lay somewhere between the far-flung poles of Brecht's 'crude thinking' and Hölderlin's 'holy soberness'. We in turn will have to navigate between Weber's stoical acceptance of the late-capitalist reality-principle, and Benjamin's Messianic expectation of a grand fairytale awakening from the spell of myth. One can hardly imagine a new *Angelus Novus* singing an ecstatic hymn to the welfare state. Two cheers for democracy were all that E. M. Forster could muster. For the moment, a moderately inspired spirit of sobriety is perhaps the most we can hope for.

Let me, in conclusion, take up an observation of Brecht's which Benjamin entered without comment into his diary in 1938. It might just 'offer a foothold to those who want to get beyond [Benjamin]'.

> 'It is good to be caught up by a reactionary epoch in an extreme position. That way one ends up in a middle position.' This is, [Brecht] says, what happened to him; he has become mild.[93]

The point of this remark lies in the fact that Brecht's justification of an undialectical 'middle position' is itself placed within a historico-dialectical perspective. 'All roads lead to Rome', remarked Schonberg, 'except the middle one'. '*All* roads?', the worker in Brecht's poem *Fragen eines lesenden Arbeiters* might innocently have enquired. Does rejection of the middle way preclude all recourse to common sense? Is there really no difference between a speculative and a materialist dialectics? Or, at least, between idealist and materialist speculation? As Benjamin himself put it to his Hegelian-Marxist interlocutor Adorno, the 'necessarily daring flight' of speculation is doomed to failure if it entrusts itself to 'the waxen wings of the esoteric'.[94]

Benjamin once observed that in the economy of his thinking a certain limited number of relations enabled him to 'maintain a counter-pole to that of [his] original being'.[95] These relations (*einige wenige gezählte Beziehungen*) were as limited in number as the counterweights (*enige wenige schwere massive Gewichte*) that, in the metaphor of the scale, stand for the knowledge of the present. This is because they were, precisely, intended to set limits on – and to oppose a counterweight to – his 'original being'. His relation with Brecht was a case in point. It was an 'extreme' that was calculated to counteract his own theological bent. This particular extreme, however, vindicated 'middle positions' and thereby implicitly put into question the model into which Benjamin inserted it – that of a providential 'force-field' of 'radical' tensions and polar 'extremes' which, if left to themselves, would produce the truth. Where Benjamin was tempted to reject the middle way in the name of a theologico-political dialectic of extremes, Brecht rejected radicalism in favour of the actual dialectics of the real. This was a resistance that Benjamin knew he needed. In a reactionary period, extremism needed to be exchanged for – or at least channelled into – something messier, less heady, more viable. The 'weak Messianic power'[96] of each passing moment had, more than ever, to reckon with the gravity and inertia that weighed down the real.[97]

Today we again find ourselves overtaken by a political shift to the right. If we do not want to remain to the left of what is currently possible, we need, as Brecht suggested, to give ground. Benjamin's extreme mistrust of compromise[98] will have to be counterbalanced by negotiated compromises with some of the middle positions we used to abhor. If, as Kittsteiner has suggested, historical materialism has today inherited the role of the theological dwarf, the moral of the first *Thesis* should perhaps be amended to read as follows. The middle ground to which the left is currently obliged to retreat will only be distinguishable from social democracy as long as the invisible hand of a materialist dwarf still guides the moves.

Benjamin speaks of the 'now' as the 'strait gate' through which the Messiah may enter at any moment.[99] This Biblical image recalls another – that of the rich man who can no more enter the gates of heaven than a camel can pass through the eye of a needle. It is in the same spirit that Benjamin speaks of narrowing down our knowledge of the present to a few well-chosen weights. Under straightened circumstances there is, Benjamin argued against Bloch, no point in displaying one's cultural riches: the only thing to do with Oriental carpets at the scene of an earthquake is to cut them into blankets.[100] The corresponding question now facing Benjamin's readers is how much of his wealth we can still afford without living beyond our political and existential means. As indispensable as his faith in extremes is to the life of the mind, it is one of those 'convictions' which will have to pass the means test of today's actuality. True, Benjamin's portrait of 'the destructive character' can be read as an attempt to find a way between Jewish Messianism and Brechtian pragmatism. The question is to what extent the latter is thereby incorporated into a dialectic of extremes which it should counteract. What if, 'at bottom', things *do* 'go on this way', and not 'from extreme to extreme'- if indeed there is any 'bottom' at all?

Benjamin learned from Brecht that dialectics consists of 'thinking inside' – not above or beyond – 'other peoples' heads'. And he sought to implement Brecht's idea of exchanging the Good Old for the Bad New. But what if *his* Bad New has meanwhile become *our* Good Old, so that the operation now needs to be repeated?

This much, at least, is clear. Since the 'small change of the actual' continues to be the only currency that has any purchase in the world we actually live in, the going rate of exchange, however bad it may be, is the only possible – and hence the best possible – alternative. No conception of actuality, however straightened, can entirely do without some such residual faith.

It was 'good', Brecht observed, that political conditions should have forced him into the middle. What he had lost in radicalism, he had gained in mildness. *À quelque chose malheur est bon*, says the poet in Baudelaire's prose poem *Perte d'Auréole* after losing his halo. Can the loss of revolutionary paraphernalia likewise represent a new opportunity for the Left? Not that the massive collapse of so many socialist hopes is not a *malheur*.

Whatever hymns our actuality can still muster will be tinged by the sadness of so many defeats. But the weight of Benjaminian 'remembrance' may perhaps be legitimately counterbalanced by a certain Nietzschean 'forgetting'. A greater lightness of being may perhaps enable us to enter the strait gate of our brave new present.

Let me break off this tortuous dialogue with the revolutionary shades of the past to formulate a provisional conclusion. Benjamin is perhaps the last halfways theological thinker whose voice still speaks today to the disenchanted. The question of his actuality is, I am claiming, inseparable from the question – the *Gretchenfrage* – that our actuality asks of us. Where we stand in relation to Benjamin depends on where we stand vis-à-vis the present – assuming that we are still standing and not merely wobbling about. Just as Kierkegaard defined his concept of irony with constant reference to Socrates, so we may best define our actuality with constant reference to Benjamin. Far from merely belonging on today's agenda as a preliminary item to the real business at hand, the question is that of today's agenda. Somewhat like Kant's 'I think' which 'must accompany all my representations', and somewhat like the operations of Benjamin's hunchback dwarf, the present conjuncture is the synthesizing a priori which – whether we know it or not – effectively organizes everything we think. All this is to be learned from Benjamin. The question that remains is whether we can actually seize this specific historical now. Nothing seems more elusive, yet nothing is surely closer to hand.

* This is a revised version of a talk delivered at the opening of a conference held in Osnabrück in July 1992 to commemorate the centenary of Benjamin's birth.

NOTES

1. *Illuminations*, ed. Hannah Arendt, New York 1968, p258. (hereafter *I*)
2. R. Tiedemann and H. Schweppenhäuser (eds), *Gesammelte Schriften* (hereafter *GS*), Frankfurt am Main 1974-1988, 11/2 p691.
3. *GS* V/1 p819.
4. *GS* I/5 p1231.
5. *GS* III p281.
6. *GS* 11/2 p694.
7. Cf. Jürgen Habermas, 'The Rectifying Revolution . . .' *New Left Review* 183, September-October 1990.
8. *GS* I/3 p1242.
9. *GS* I/2 p658.
10. *GS* I/2 p681. These passages were intended as a comment on two sentences prominently displayed on the program of the Osnabrück conference: 'Walter

Benjamin war einer der wenigen Grossen. Ihm und seinem Andenken gegenüber haben wir eine bleibende Verpflichtung'. (Walter Benjamin was one of the truly great men. We have an enduring obligation to him and his memory) The author, the German President, was the 'patron' of the conference.

11. *GS* I/2 p677.
12. *GS* III p265.
13. *One-Way Street* [hereafter *OWS*], London, 1979, p238.
14. *GS* III p259.
15. *OWS*, p103.
16. Siegfried Unseld, (ed), Frankfurt am Main, 1972.
17. *GS* II/1 p241.
18. *GS*II/1 p245.
19. *GS* II/1 pp241-42.
20. *GS* II/1 p246.
21. *I* p257.
22. *GS* V/1 578 N 3,2.
23. *OWS*, 156.
24. 'That which is original is never recognizable in the naked manifest exigence of the factual' (*The Origin of German Tragic Drama* [hereafter *O*], London 1977, 45.
25. *GS* II/1 75.
26. *GS* I/1 27.
27. Gershom Scholem and T.W. Adorno (eds), 'To grasp actuality as the reverse side of the eternal in history and to take the impress from this concealed side of the medal'- this is how Benjamin describes *One-Way Street*, a book which, he claims, made 'no compromises with the currents of the time' (*Briefe*. [hereafter *B*], Frankfurt am Main 1966, I/459).
28. *GS* III 290.
29. As a non-arbitrary conjunction of two nows, true actuality has more in common, in Benjamin's eyes, with a Jewish-mystical concept of 'now-time' than with Platonic anamnesis. 'But this eternity is by no means a platonic or utopian one: it is rapturous. [. . .] The eternity of which Proust offers glimpses is bounded, not boundless time.' (I 212-13). Far from being a Platonic 'idea', the eternal is bound to a 'temporal kernel' (*Zeitkern*) which 'exists within' both the knower and the known' (*GS* V/1 578).
30. *I* p256.
31. *I* p258-59.
32. *GS* II/1 p219.
33. *I* p265.
34. *OWS* p158.
35. *GS* I/3 p1235.

36. Benjamin's work is, on the other hand, partly responsible for its own consecration. 'Among the peculiarities of Benjamin's philosophical prose [. . .] is the enormous extent to which it lends itself to canonisation, I would almost say to quotation as a kind of Holy Writ'. Gershom Scholem, 1983, *Walter Benjamin und sein Engel*, Frankfurt am Main, p35.
37. *B* 2, p659.
38. *I*, p256.
39. *B* 2, p762.
40. *GS* VI, p521.
41. *OWS*, p225.
42. In his book *L'Ange de l'Histoire* (Paris 1992), Stéphane Mosès claims that a Messianic conception of history shatters the foundations of 'historical reason' by locating the end of time at the heart of history (p20). Benjamin, however, maintains the exact opposite. Marx was right, he claims, to 'secularize' the notion of Messianic time by equating it with that of a classless society (*GS*, 1/3 p1231). From the perspective of a secularized Messianism, the end of time is, in other words, the end of what Marx had called 'prehistory', and not, as orthodox Messianism would have it, the end of history altogether.
43. *GS* III 97. Cf Adorno's plea for a 'radicalisation of the dialectic into its incandescent theological core' (*bis in den theologischen Glutkern hinein*) (*B* 2, p676).
44. *I* p257; *GS* I/3 p1243.
45. *I* p265.
46. *I* p256.
47. Cf., *GS* I/1 pp55-61.
48. Cf., *I* p265 and *GS* I/3 p1232.
49. *GS* III p259.
50. *GS*V/1 p491.
51. *GS* I p258.
52. *GS*VI p539.
53. *I* p257.
54. *I* p258.
55. *GS* V/2 p1057.
56. *I* p264.
57. *I* p257.
58. *B* 2 p690.
59. Whereas the good, materialist 'actualization'(*GS* V/l p574) of the past marks the interplay of two actualities, its false, historicist counterpart proposes actualization without actuality.
60. *I* p264.
61. *GS* V/1 p570 N 1,3.
62. *GS*V/1 p585.Cf. On the equipoise of the scale as a 'Messianic cessation of

happening' Henri Focillon's definition of the classical moment (*cit.* GS I/31 p229).

63. H.D. Kittsteiner, 'Walter Benjamin's Historismus', in Norbert Bolz und I Bernd Witte, *Passagen: Walter Benjamin's Urgeschichte des XLX. Jahrhunderts*, Munich 1984, pp163-197.
64. Where one side of the scales does not counterbalance the other, the result is either a lax, reactionary historicism which is more or less blind to the present or, conversely, a doctrinaire jacobinism which is too preoccupied with political abuses to see life as it is actually lived. Benjamin discusses this latter myopia in his review 'A Jacobin of today', which implicitly sets out to incorporate into the Enlightenment the critique to which the Historical School later subjected it (*GS* III pp260-265).
65. *GS* I/3 p1245.
66. 'A historical materialist cannot do without the notion of a present which is not a transition, but in which time stands poised and has come to a standstill' (*I*, p264).
67. *GS* V/1 p579, N3a, 4.
68. *OWS*, p45.
69. American Marxist feminists are among the few to have a prompt answer to this question: 'Race, Class and Gender'.
70. *I*, pp264-65.
71. Cf.*B* 2 p686.
72. Adorno reproached Benjamin for a 'lack of mediations' (*B* II p785). The 'dialectical image', as Benjamin conceives it, does not entirely skip the mediations; but it does - therein lies its beauty - skip through them: 'The dialectical image is a flash of ball lightning that covers the whole horizon of the past' (*GS* I/3 p1233) Benjamin saw in Marx's *Capital* an exemplary 'liquidation of the epic element' from historiography. (*GS* I/3 p1241). But he also wondered how to combine a Marxist method with 'increased visual expressiveness' (*Anschaulichkeit.* GS V/l p575). This, then, is the dilemma: can images, however dialectical, be adequate to the abstract structures of capitalist modernity? Consider, for example, the following substitution of one image for another: 'Marx says that revolutions are the locomotives of world history. But maybe the truth is quite different. Maybe revolutions are the moment when humanity - the passengers in the train - grasps for the emergency brake.' (*GS* I/3 p1232). But does not this image break down in turn? *Cf.* Kittsteiner's pertinent comment 'So here is the train. But where is the emergency brake? And who has the long arm to reach it and the strength to pull it?' (*loc.cit.* 196).
73. Adorno referred as early as the 1930s to the 'deeply romantic element in Benjamin's 'anthropological materialism'. (*B* 2, pp785-86).
74. *GS* I/3 p1223.
75. *I* p257.

76. Cf., *I* p220.
77. *I* p259.
78. *I* p262.
79. *I* p259.
80. Gershom Scholem, *loc.cit* 35. We are perhaps no longer quite (anti-) authoritarian enough to submit ourselves to this gesture. But the prevailing liberal consensus is hopefully not so authoritarian as to refuse Benjamin his tone. Benjamin's Messianic *promesse de bonheur* is hardly the 'life, liberty and happiness' inscribed in democratic constitutions. Hence indeed its attraction. It is not, however, *anti* - democratic. The gift is available to all, the authoritarian sentences are, after all, 'interpretable', and their esoteric dimension is, within the measure of the possible, reduced to a strict minimum: 'This means simply that [philosophical projects] possess a certain estoeric quality which they are unable to discard, forbidden to deny and which they vaunt at their own peril' (*O*, pp27-28).
81. *GS* IV/2 p1001.
82. A good translation is, according to Benjamin, a tangent which touches the original at the 'infinitely small point of its sense' before pursuing its own course. (*I* p80).
83. *B* I p425.
84. Benjamin's philosophy of language is likewise pitted against a 'bourgeois' enemy (*Cf. OWS* p111).
85. Both his life and his thought, Benjamin observed, moved between 'extreme positions' (*GS* II/3 p1369.) I finally explain [to Brecht]', he noted on another occasion, 'that to penetrate into the depths is my way of betaking myself to the antipodes.' (*GS* VI p528).
86. 'Rescue resides in the small leap in the continuous catastrophe' (*GS* II/1 p683).
87. *B* 1 p425.
88. Benjamin's piece *On the Mimetic Faculty*, for example, implicitly refuses to choose between an enlightened disenchantment and a Romantic re-enchantment of the world. Instead, it presents language as a medium in which the old forces of magic have been both liquidated and preserved. (*OWS* pp160-63).
89. *Loc.cit.*, p163.
90. *Cf.* Jürgen L Habermas 'The Rectifying Revolution' *loc.cit.*, n. 7.
91. The 'revisionist' reading of Benjamin was initiated in 1972 by Habermas's article 'Consciousness-Raising or Redemptive Criticism: The Actuality of Walter Benjamin' (originally published in *Die Aktualität von Walter Benjamin, loc.cit.*; translated in *New German Critique* 17, Spring 1979, pp30-59).
92. *GS* II/3,p1369.
93. *GS* VI, p535. Cf also the following remark of Brecht's: cited at the beginning of Benjamin's review of *The Mother* tr. as W.B., *Understanding Brecht* NLB,

London 1973, pp33-6: 'It isn't communism that is radical, it's capitalism' (*GS*, II/2 p511 tr. p33). The review ends by citing a line of Brecht's – 'Und aus Niemals wird: Heute noch!' (*ibid.*, p514 tr. p36) – which echoes the Jewish 'If not now, when?' Benjamin knew that the opposition between Brecht and Jewish theology was not as absolute as both Brecht and Scholem imagined.

94. *B* II p793. Benjamin is here declining Adorno's advice that he remain faithful to his theological impulses. These need, on the contrary, to be held in check and this is where Brecht comes in.
95. *GS* II/3 p1369.
96. *I* p256.
97. Benjamin's dwarf needs, in other words to outplay another one - that 'spirit of gravity' (*Geist der Schwere*) who confronts Zarathustra with the 'most difficult' (*das Schwerste*) of his tests. Benjamin called that heaviness 'the spirit of melancholy'. 'Péguy used to speak of that irredeemability of things, that recalcitrance, that heaviness of things, indeed of beings, which in the end allows a little ash to survive from the efforts of heroes and saints' (*cit. O* p157). Against that heaviness Benjamin and Nietzsche respectively pit 'salvation' and 'the eternal return'. The most we have are some residues of those faiths.
98. Cf.*OWS* p143.
99. *I*, p266.
100. *Cf. B* II, pp648-49.

From gender images to dialectical images in Benjamin's writings

Sigrid Weigel

I 'UNGRASPED SYMBOLISM'- THE ORIGINS OF THINKING IN IMAGES

> We are enslaved without ceremony by a symbolism that we have not grasped. – Sometimes we remember a dream as we are just waking up. So it is that moments of clairvoyance seldom illuminate the wreckage of our strength past which time had flown. (II. 1/91)[1]

These reflections on the moment of awakening that throws light on an ungrasped symbolism are not taken, as one might think, from Benjamin's entries relating to the *Passagen*-Project (*Arcades*-project), but are to be found in the first section of a text which the writer, then twenty-one years old, entitled 'The Conversation' (1913). Of the notes which go back to the time of his student activities and his association with the Youth Movement, this is not the only image, formulation or figuration which links his early writings with his last major project. The concept of experience (*Erfahrung*), reflections on the structure of time, including the concept of messianic time, nearness and distance, the movement and the gaze of things, the concept of revelation (*Offenbarung*), a non-instrumental language, the connection between eroticism and perception (*Erkenntnis*), various female figures, but particularly that of the whore (*Hure*), who is still called a prostitute (*Dirne*) here: all of these are motifs which already characterize the structure of the early essays, articles and notes and which we come across again in his writings of the 1930s. There is, however, one small, though very effective change in his mode of writing, a shift in his use of concepts and images of representation which lets them become dialectical images, i.e. images that are read – a 'tiny shift' which – to quote Foucault – has the effect of a 'small (repugnant) machinery that allows the coincidental, the *discontinuous*, and *materiality* to be incorporated into the very roots of thought.'[2]

Nevertheless, the conflicting relationship in which the 'I' is placed 'against the fathers' in the Benjamin text quoted above and which clearly identifies the perspective of the 'we' as that of youth, marks 'The Conversation' as obviously belonging to Benjamin's early writings. Other constellations, however – ones that do not refer to the position of the writer, but are to be read as *textual* constellations – foreshadow paradigmatic *Denkbilder* (thought-images) of the later writings in their scenic dramaturgy and in their topographical arrangement. So, for example, 'The Diary', which was to have formed a cycle along with 'The Conversation' and 'The Ball' and which is now published under the title of 'Metaphysics of Youth', anticipates a movement which Benjamin worked on over and over again, shaping it both philosophically and metaphorically. In the 'Theological-Political Fragment' (around 1920), he tried to capture this specific notion in a conceptual image,[3] namely in a counter-movement of the *dynamis* of the profane and of a messianic intensity, two forces moving in opposing directions but which still propel and reinforce each other (204). In the Kafka essay (1934), the same movement appears as a figure of reversal, as the 'direction of study that transforms existence into writing' (*II*.2/437) or in the image of this study riding against every storm 'that blows in from oblivion' (436). The same constellation later takes on the shape of a dialectical image as a philosophical-historical figure of thought to express the non-simultaneity between our way of looking at the chain of events and the way the angel of history looks at the catastrophe, at the wreckage of the past.

The very same constellation, however, already structures – perhaps as an as yet 'ungrasped symbolism' – his literary text 'The Diary' (1913). Here, the I is positioned in a metaphorical surrounding which anticipates the topographical setting of the later dialectical images. However, here it is still a mythical scenery because the I is positioned in the middle of a happening which 'surrounds (the I) *as* a landscape' (*II*.1199, italics S.W.). The I turns to face backwards, and the storm that rages in the troubled I, towards whom things approach, creates a 'countermovement of things in the I's time' (102). References to time, which we felt 'flooding mightily against us' (100), or a way of looking at things that propels us into what is to come (99) or phrasing that – '. . . all future is past' (102) – in the I's time, in which things happen to us: all these descriptions topographically outline that setting of the diary which is metaphorically condensed in its whole 'counterstriving disposition'[4] in the paradoxical image of the 'accession to the throne of one who abdicates' (101). The figure of the beloved woman, however, who steps towards the I out of the landscape of happening, or, rather, who is sent towards him out of it, makes it clear that it is gender-specifically organized.

The distance between this diary-landscape of the I and the landscape of collective wreckage in the ur-history of modernism – in other words, the transition from Benjamin's early writings about the I to his reading of the memory-images of modernism – could not be greater. Nevertheless, its specific constellation, which presents a counter-perspective to historical time, as well as the gender-dramaturgy of the early text ('Das Tagebuch'), mark a hidden connection with the *Passagen*-Project. The figure of the beloved woman, part of a mythical scenery, emerges from it – sometimes quite clearly, sometimes just as a shadow – to show the way through the labyrinth of texts in which that ungrasped symbolism is transformed into the mighty archive of a dialectical thinking in images. We encounter her here and everywhere in Benjamin's writings, like an Ariadne or guardian of the threshold.

And so, precisely because whenever the significance of gender difference in Benjamin's texts is paid any attention at all, the image of the 'whore as an allegory of modernism' – to be found in the *Baudelaire* book and in the *Passagen*-Project, for example – is always in the foreground, what I want to do here is follow the traces of that Ariadne figure in order to decipher the transformation of images into dialectical images throughout the labyrinth of Benjamin's texts.

II 'HOW DID SAPPHO AND HER FRIENDS SPEAK?' – LANGUAGE MAGIC AND GENDER DIFFERENCE

'The Conversation' already tries out that genre at the transition point between thinking in images and theoretical reflection that was to become as characteristic for *One Way Street* and *A Berlin Childhood around Nineteen Hundred* as it did for 'On the Concept of History': that is, a series of successive but self-contained short prose scenes or thought-images (*Denkbilder*). The eight parts of 'The Conversation' concentrate on the concept of another language, still called 'true language' here (92). This language beyond statements that tends towards prattle – in the text it says that the speaker mocks language – is not, however, independent of conversation but is, rather, made possible in and through conversation: that is, through the listener or through the silence that is produced as part of conversation. Silence as an 'internal limit of conversation' (92).

These reflections were to become integrated in the elaboration of Benjamin's language theory,[5] which was expressed programmatically three years later, in the well-known letter to Buber, in his formulations about 'what the word is denied', the 'unspeakable in language' towards which one 'must work within language and to that extent through it' (*Br.* 127).[6] What is important to me here is that this other language is not counterposed to conversation but located within it, thus manifesting the dialectical conception of Benjamin's language theory. This is a conception that perceives the sign-nature of language as being simultaneously 'a symbol of the non-communicable' (*OWS* p156)[7] – as in his essay on language of 1916 – or the semiotic nature of language as the bearer of the mimetic and thus as a condition for the possibility of a flashing appearance of 'non-sensuous similarities' (*OWS* p162) – as in 'On the Mimetic Faculty' of 1933. This marks an attempt to overcome the opposition between the model of arbitrariness in the 'bourgeois view of language' on the one hand and on the other, the notion in mystical language theory that the word is the essence of the thing (*OWS* pp 116/117).

In his essay on language of 1916, however, women are – with regard to the Adamite language of Genesis – completely absent. At most, one could think of Eve or women when reading the passage about the other muteness and sorrow of nature once it has been named and no longer speaks, since Eve or women are also predominantly in the position of the named:

> In all mourning there is the deepest inclination to speechlessness, which is infinitely more than an inability or disinclination to communicate. That which mourns feels itself thoroughly known by the unknowable. To be named – even when the namer is Godlike and blissful – perhaps always remains an intimation of mourning. (*OWS* 155/121)

Whereas in Benjamin's reading of Genesis[8] man is situated for the purposes of language theory as the speaker and at the same time at the source of language,[9] in 'The Conversation' productivity and the meaning of language originated from the listener, whose position almost immediately turns out to be female. A significant change in the cast of the text takes place in the fourth part. The neutral or male characters of the literary setting (the speaker and the listener in II., the unproductive character, the prattler – all *der* – and the genius – *das* Genie – in III.) become a male-female couple: that is, the male speaker and the female listener, which is then carried over in the fifth part into a conversation between genius and prostitute and in the sixth into general reflections on the difference between the sexes in language.

The fact that the female position is associated with silence here means that two different aspects are linked with it. As a listener, the woman is perceived as productive in terms of a 'true language'- the woman protects 'meaning from understanding, she impedes misuse of words and does not let herself be misused' (93) – and thus she marks a position, as it were, that is conceived as a female counterpart to the genius. In this text 'thinkers and women', namely, are what the author considers *Tätige* ('active participants') (92). Moreover, silence is linked to the obverse of language and to the sexual relationship between the sexes, as, for example, in the sentence: 'Silence's other conversation is passion (*Wollust*)' (93).

Nevertheless, the fact that Benjamin associates the female position in language with silence does not mean that he was indifferent to the issue of women's language. In the seventh and eighth parts of 'The Conversation', he addresses precisely this question. Both parts start with the same words – 'How did Sappho and her friends speak?'- deny the suitability of language for their conversation – 'For language denies them their souls' – and finally revolve around another kind of expression which is located between the corpus of language, the 'bodies of words', and body language. 'Women's language was left uncreated. Speaking women are possessed by an insane language.' (95). Reading this sentence, one cannot but be reminded of Luce Irigaray's psychoanalytical description of the notion that women do not have a place in established discourse and, consequently, only make use of that language in the form of a distorting mimesis, that is, that women: 'as lack, default, or as mime and inverted reproduction of the subject – show that on the feminine side it is possible to exceed and disturb this logic [an economy of the logos]' (S.W.).[10]

The moment of excess/exceeding is ascribed to women in Benjamin's 'Conversation' too:

> But women are silent. In whichever direction they listen, the words are unspoken. They draw their bodies closer and caress each other. Their conversation freed itself of topics and of language. . . . Silence and passion – eternally separated in conversation – have become one. (95/96)

We find the same impossibility of conceiving a simultaneity of discourse and the female body's pleasure which structures this description in the final chapter of Julia Kristeva's *About Chinese Women*, where – 'voice without a body, body without a voice'[11] – this non-simultaneity is described in a cultural-historical perspective as separating from and overcoming the maternal body through the male logos and as placed in the context of a history of monotheism, of the principle 'of a symbolic, fatherly super-ego community'.[12]

III 'THE FIRST-BORN MALE OF HIS WORK' – CREATION AND PROCREATION

However, the bodies of the Sapphic women in Benjamin's text are exempted from precisely this moment of the maternal, they are, rather, in a state of love for no specific purpose. 'Their bodies' love is without procreation, but it is beautiful to behold' (96). This motif of a Sapphic love without procreation, of an eroticism that is not bound to a specific purpose, anticipates a motif that will shift to the centre of attention in the *Passagen*-Project with the figures of the lesbian and the whore, the heroines of Baudelaire's poetry.

In the *Passagen*-Project, however, the figures of the lesbian and whore are reflected as allegories of modernism and as dialectical images in so far as Benjamin also discusses the preconditions that make them fascinating for a modernist author who compares himself with the hero of antiquity. These images are dialectically presented as a rejection of nature and the natural and as a reaction to the development of technology and the levelling of the differences between the sexes:

> It is part of the sacrificial path of male sexuality that Baudelaire has to perceive pregnancy to a certain extent as unfair competition. (1.2/p670)
> Male impotence – key figure of loneliness – in its sign the standstill of productive forces is completed – an abyss separates man from his kind. (p679)
> Baudelaire never wrote a poem about a whore from a whore's perspective (*cf.* Reader for City Dwellers 5). (p679)
> Baudelaire's readers are men. It was they who earned him his fame and whom he bought off. (V/p419)

In this way, taking Baudelaire's poetry as an example, Benjamin places the motif of love without procreation in the imaginary self-projection of an artist in the cultural-historical context of modernism. His readings of Baudelaire, however, could also just as easily be read as comments on his own early writings. There the motif of the prostitute (*Dirne*) as well as that of non-procreation acquire a central significance for the figure of the genius or for the concept of intellectual creation without procreation. Many of his early texts revolve around the connection between sexuality and intellectual activity, between procreation and creation and around the significance of gender difference for the 'community of the creative' (*II.* 1/p84). These images frequently alternate between the levels of bodily and intellectual creation. While the imagery of his texts bears evidence of a fascination with the transitions between the corporeal-erotic and the intellectual,[13] at the same time, in his argument, the author takes pains to prevent the two intermingling or one being subjugated by the other. This awareness is particularly emphasized with regard to the debate on traditional and contemporary myths concerning links between spirituality and creativity and on ideas of abolishing gender difference or, rather, the female as representative of the other sex, for example, in the topos of the 'spiritualization of the sexual'. In this vein, in a letter of 1913 to his friend Herbert Belmore, in which he accused the latter, by elevating the prostitute to the level of a symbol, of denying thousands of women their souls, Benjamin wrote:

> Let us be silent for a while on the subject of the spiritualisation of the sexual. This precious male inventory. And we will talk about the sexualisation of the spiritual: This is the morality of the prostitute. She represents culture in Eros, Eros which is the most vehement individualist, the most hostile to culture, it too can be perverted, it too can be of service to culture. (*Br.*6718)

Directing his criticism both at strategies which instrumentalize Eros in the intellectual field and at those which abolish or incorporate the female position in quasi super-sexual models (though represented by men) of contemporary cultural theory,[14] Benjamin accentuates the other, as it were invisible productivity of women – not without recourse, indeed, to traditional views of the gender relationship. This productivity he sees as linked to women's inaudible language which still has to function, however, as a precondition of cultural production – similar to the way in which Kristeva speaks of the productivity of women as 'an effect which has neither power nor a language system at its disposal, but which supports these mutely', a silent prop for the system which makes no appearance itself.[15] It is in this sense that Benjamin's marking of silence as a productive female position in 'The Conversation' is to be understood. In it, his concept of a *different* productivity of women, which played an important role in all the texts he wrote during these years, finds expression. However, it is hardly ever described positively, and nowhere more concretely than in 'The Conversation'. Rather, it is circumscribed by negation, for example by stressing the indispensability of this other productivity, as is the case in the representation of Socrates, whom Benjamin criticizes for degrading Eros as a means to an end:

> In a society of males there would be no genius; genius lives through the existence of the female. It is true: the existence of the female guarantees the asexuality of the intellectual in the world. (130)

Benjamin's emphasis on this other productivity of women could perhaps be read as a recuperative critique (*rettende Kritik*) which serves to rescue some differences between the sexes at the very historical moment of their disappearance. Except that women, then, are also banished to that mute region of another productivity.

These ideas, too, are to be found twenty years later transformed into dialectical images and can, therefore, be read in terms of their implicit phantasmagorical aspects, their cultural constructedness and their preconditions, especially by means of a de-montage or deconstruction of the concepts of the genius and the masterpiece. The *Denkbild* 'After Completion', for example, demonstrates this, as in it Benjamin describes a masterpiece as being constituted through consuming the female and as expressing a desire to conquer nature or to transcend one's own origin from the 'dark depths of the mother's womb'. In this way, the master becomes the 'first-born male of the work that he had once conceived' (*IV.l*/p438).

This *Denkbild*, in fact, directly takes up a phantasm that had been outlined in 'The Conversation' two decades previously. The theme of 'non-procreation' is developed in the fifth part, in the dialogue between the genius and the prostitute. Those who had no father and who do not want to procreate come to the prostitute – as a result of which they are given all the qualities characteristic of the genius. The genius, however, says of itself: 'They all became mother to me. All women gave birth to me, no man had begotten me' (*II.l*/p94).

This image places the genius in the position of competing with the Son of God by virtue of the notion of a virgin mother, thus citing a traditional myth of the genius. It is even further outdone by the fact that it proceeds to place the mother above and beyond competing, to deny her a body, as it were, by representing her as a woman whose births only result in failed intellectual products, dead poems: 'I can only think of my mother. May I tell you about her? She gave birth like you: to a hundred dead poems.' Whereas what is being expressed here is the idea of the genius competing both with God and with the woman's so-called reproductivity, representing a double claim on creation, so to speak, then in the later *Denkbild* this concept of the genius is illuminated from within. In the formulation of the 'first-born male of the work that he had once conceived,' we can see the process in re-verse: it is not the genius who creates the work, but the master who appears from the very same origin as the work that fancies itself as independent of nature.

Here we can observed the gradual transformation of an image with which the author seems to have been fascinated over a period of twenty years into a dialectical image; in other words, a shift which can be read as a disbandment and resolution of the misrecognized, imaginary structure of the image. This operation can be compared in this respect with Benjamin's work on his own history of fascination with Klee's *Angelus Novus*, also over twenty years, which he transformed into a reflection on the mythical rigidity of the image of the angel into the dialectical image of the 'Angel of History' in 1940.[16] And the thirteen sentences about books and prostitutes in Nr. 13 of *One-Way Street* (1928) could be read as an intermediate station between the myth of a procreationless creation in the 'Conversation' between genius and prostitute of 1913 and the *Denkbild* about the master that dates from the first half of the 1930s. Here, Benjamin comments ironically on the metaphorical status of books and prostitutes which arises through comparing them: 'Books and prostitutes (*Dirnen*) – they each have their own sort of men who live off them and plague them. Books have critics.' (*IV.1*/p109)

IV 'FOR EVERY WOMAN POSSESSES THE PAST AND, IN ANY CASE, NO PRESENT' – WOMEN AS THE GUARDIANS OF THRESHOLDS

Yet another trace leads from the women in 'The Conversation' to the later major projects. At the same moment, namely, as the gender changes in the cast in the fourth part of 'The Conversation', the topic of present and past is introduced in the text. While the speaker is obsessed by the present, women appear as the guardians of the past, which makes them superior even to the genius, who had been described as cursing his memory in the process of creation, as being poor in remembrance and at a loss as to what to do (93). It is exactly the opposite for women: 'For every woman possesses the past and, in any case, no present' (93). Their 'past is never concluded' (95). Instead, they lived in a time structure which forms, as it were, a re-verse counter-time to the *futur antérieur*, that 'shall-have-been' past that Lacan defined as the time structure of desire and as the historical time of the subject:[17] 'The present that eternally has been shall be again' (93). With regard to the past, however, the significance of gender difference becomes so dominant for Benjamin in this text that he synthesizes the two conceptually: by referring to the '*Weiblich-Gewesenes*' (the female-has-been) (95).

Twenty years later, we come across the interlacing of recurrence and what is past, which in the earlier text formed a mythical structure of the feminine – 'The present that eternally has been shall be again'- but is later shaped in a figuration of conflict used to circumscribe the structure of the desire for happiness as the longing for a repetition of the never-has-been. We encounter this structure in the veiled or coded text 'Agesilaus Santander' which Benjamin wrote on Ibiza in 1933 as a birthday present for a women he loved.[18] It links the Talmudic legend of the endless number of angels created anew every instant with the motif of the New Angel fixed to the wall, the *Angelus Novus*:

> He wants happiness: the ecstasy of the unique, new, as yet unlived conflicts with the bliss of the once-more, the having-again, what has been lived. That is why he has nothing new to hope on any path except

> that of the return home if he takes a new person with him. Just as I, no sooner had I seen you for the first time, travelled back with you to where I came from. (*VI*/p532)

Here, the woman is no longer situated in the past, nor does she possess the past; instead, she opens the approach to what is past, or, rather, to the recurrence of what has been. It is in this sense that we encounter women as guardians of the past in several texts of the late 1920s and the 30s. However, their position is then clearly transposed onto the writing-scene and becomes decipherable against the foil of a signature of the feminine in the imaginary. This is elaborated in the context of the motif of *flânerie*, which projects the script of the city as the scene of memory, as is the case in the thought-images of the *Berlin Childhood around Nineteen Hundred*. There, the structure of memory and the significance of female-connotated locations in the imaginary were always interconnected.[19] In this context, memory appears as the muse of *flânerie*, of a memorizing while strolling:

> She walks ahead on the streets, and each one of them is precipitous for her. She leads downwards, if not to the mothers, then to the past, which can be all the more spell-binding in that it is not only the author's own, private one. (*III*/p194)[20]

By following the images and traces of memory, Benjamin worked on reconstructing the genealogy of the function of the feminine as an image and sign: in the *Berlin Childhood* he elaborated this through a series of childlike primal scenes, in the *Passagen*-Project through reading collective dream-images and ruins of the culture of modernism. In this way, a semiotics of different female loci in writing becomes apparent: for example, the magic function of those household spheres (sewing box, wardrobe) associated with the feminine, the underground of presymbolic areas circumscribed by mothers, the mythical figure of Ariadne, who mingles with the desired female friend; furthermore, the stone allegories functioning as incorporations of a memory of myth and wilderness in cities that Benjamin calls *Schwellenkundige* (versed in thresholds), thereby alluding to their metaphorical function as replacements for the presymbolic in the order of the city.

This links the imaginary function of the female with its position as guardian of the past in writing. Thus the reference to the 'female has-been' acquires its significance not only by virtue of the fact that real women belong to the forgotten realm of culture, but also because the images of the female, the female figures in cultural memory predominantly represent what has been, represent the forgotten and the repressed. Though they are still marked by their origins in the sphere of the forgotten, they no longer inhabit that sphere but, through the figure of the return of the repressed, they come to incorporate what represents the forgotten in the imagistic archives of modernity.

As opposed to these representations of femininity, Benjamin interprets Kafka's female figures as *Vorwelt* (primeval) figures in his Kafka essay (1934) in which one can see clear traces of his reading of Bachofen at around the same time, although he was less interested in Bachofen's 'Golden Age' of matriarchy than in his prehistoric *Vorwelt* of Hetaerism, the very earliest stage of development of an 'unwedded motherhood', described in Bachofen's image of a swamp vegetation.[21] Thus he describes the location of Kafka's novels:

> His novels are set in a swamp world. The creature appears in them at the level Bachofen describes as the Hetaeric. That this level has been forgotten does not mean to say that it does not protrude into the present. On the contrary: it is present by virtue of its being forgotten. (*II.2*/p428)

This is why Benjamin describes the female characters in Kafka's writings as swamp creatures that belong to a sphere of 'unregulated lushness' (*regellose Üppigkeit*). If he refers in this connection to the strangeness of the 'whore-like-women' (413), however, these differ enormously from the whores of the arcades in so far as their character is not associated with the motif of the negation of procreation. On the contrary, for in Bachofen's primeval world of Hetaerism, the positions of whore and mother are not yet distinct. The figure of distortion in the Kafka essay does, however, link them with the whores of the arcades, the allegories of modernism.

When Benjamin makes use of the Freudian term *Entstellung* (distortion) in his Kafka essay, namely, first and foremost as a mnemonic category – distortion as a 'form which things take on when they have been forgotten' (431) – and when, in addition, he assumes that what Kafka's texts are actually about is oblivion and that everything forgotten mingles 'with the forgotten of the primeval world' (430), then Kafka's female figures are not only creatures of the primeval world, but they also have a part in the form of the distortion.

V 'DISTORTION INTO THE ALLEGORICAL' – WHORES AS BODY – AND IMAGE-SPACE FOR THE ALLEGORIES OF MODERNISM

Of the figures in Benjamin's imagistic archive in the 1930s, that of the whore emerges more and more clearly, soon to take over the same role as the one played by the prostitute (*Dirne*) in his early writings.[22]

While she is of great significance in the preliminary work on the *Berlin Childhood*, she more or less disappears from the later elaborations of this text, which is then primarily governed by the sign of the maternal.[23] The whore makes her way at last and completely into the *Passagen*-Project or the *Baudelaire* book. In the text of the 'Berlin Chronicle' (1932), the whores turn up both as 'guardians of the past' (*VI*/p472) and as threshold-dwellers:

> But was it really a transgression, is it not far more a wilfully lustful persistence on the threshold, a hesitation which has its most pertinent motive in the fact that this threshold leads into nothingness? In the large cities, though, the places where one stands on the threshold to nothingness are countless, and the whores are the Lares of this cult of nothingness, as it were, and stand in the entrances to tenement houses and on the more softly resounding asphalt of the *perrons*. (472)

Although in this context the topography of the threshold is primarily linked to the motif of sexual awakening, the description of the scene as a ritual does, nevertheless, refer to that significance of the *rites de passage* in the collective imaginary represented by the architecture of the arcades in Benjamin's ur-history of modernism. Along with the constellation of awakening as the prime case of 'dialectical thinking' and with the conception of the dialectical image, the whore entered the scenery of the *Passagen*-Project as an allegory of modernism. Here we find her chiefly on the threshold: she has, then, moved out of the primeval world into that sphere of the transition between dreaming and wakefulness which appears as a condition for the possibility of awakening. As threshold-dwellers (*V*/p617), the whores thus occupy a position in Benjamin's late works to which his efforts to decipher the phantasmagorias, the wish-symbols and the materialized images of the collective return over and over again. It is not the fact that they are associated with the past or with the forgotten that primarily characterizes his interest in women here, but rather the nature of the expression which links representations of the feminine with that of the past in the very aspect of distorted representation that Freud analysed as the structure of the language of the unconscious.

> Its distortion into the allegorical resists the deceptive transfiguration of the world of commodities. The commodity tries to look itself in the face. It celebrates its incarnation in the whore. (*I.2*/p671)

This incarnation of the commodity is substantiated for the purposes of Benjamin's reading of the imagistic archive of modernism above all through the fact that the whores confronted him with images become flesh, as it were. They are not only 'seller and commodity in one', they are both image and body at once. The figuration of looking-oneself-in-the-face, after all, describes both an incarnation or personification of the image and a self-reflection of the image or of its embodiment in real bodies. This formulation also recalls leitmotif-like attempts by Benjamin to make the relationship between nearness and distance productive for reflection on various modes of representation – such as trace and aura, for example – and not only the familiar Kraus quotation about the word that, the closer you look at it, the further it looks back (*I.2*/p647). This figuration also plays a role in the outlines of the plans for the category of body and image space:

> . . . in all cases where an action projects its own image and is this image, absorbing and consuming it, where nearness looks with its own eyes, the long-sought image sphere is opened, the world of universal and integral actualities . . . (*II.1*/p309)

This image space is a body space in that it comes to representation in the form of bodily innervations, that is, through the bodies of the collective. Such a coincidence of representation and perception, of image and body space predestinates the whore as the central figure of the *Passagen*-Project. Through reflection on her, it is not only the images that become dialectical images, the allegories that become distorted representations in which the imaginary structure of representation is dispersed from within. But the whores are also the figures on which the materialistic reversal in Benjamin's thinking in images was completed, a reversal in which the primary material, the corporeality and the organic in man and things entered the foreground, thus forming the concept of 'body and image space'.

(Translated by Rachel McNicholl)

NOTES

1. All quotations from Benjamin which are not taken from English publications come from Rolf Tiedemann and Hermann Schweppenhäuser, '*Walter Benjamin: Gesammelte Schriften*', Frankfurt-am-Main, 1972, 180ff. and are my own translations. The numbers in parentheses refer to volume and page of this edition.
2. Michel Foucault, *L'Ordre du discours*, Gallimard, Paris 1971, p61.

3. This attempt to imagine and represent a philosophical figure of thought (*Denkfigur*) by means of arrows in different directions or by depicting opposing forces moving in one direction has, as it were, the representability of a geometrical or topological image. Here one can recognize efforts to capture dialectics in an image, which, however, was only really successful with images that were read or written.
4. See Anne Duden's text with the same title ('Gegenstrebige Fügung') about Carpaccio's paintings in: *Denkbilder, Selbstbilder, Zeitbilder. Literaturmagazin* 25, Reinbek bei Hamburg 1990, pp83-89. On the technique of 'dialectical images' in Duden's reading of images see my essay on the 'Judasschaf' in Sigrid Weigel, *Bilder des kulturellen Gedätchtnisses. Beiträge zur Gegenwartsliteratur*, Dülmen 1993.
5. Whether it is called language magic or language theology, both aspects, that of magic and that of theology, are already contained in 'The Conversation'. 'The conversation of the genius is prayer, however. . . . The speaking genius is more silent than the listener, just as one who is praying is more silent than God.' (93)
6. Quotations marked with *Br.* come from Gershom Scholem and Theodor W. Adorno (ed), 'Briefe', Frankfurt-am-Main, 1978.
7. Quotations marked with *OWS* come from the English translations in *One Way Street and Other Writings*, Verso, London 1979.
8. Benjamin points out that in the second version of the story of the Creation there is a reference to the material from which man was made, but he himself refers to the first story of the Creation in order to discuss 'the relation of the creative act of language'. (*OWS* p115).
9. On the debate concerning Stoessel's thesis of the forgotten human dimension and of the oedipal structure in the essay on language see my essay 'Passagen und Spuren des Leib- und Bildraums in Benjamins Schriften' in Sigrid Weigel (ed), *Leib- und Bildraum. Lektüren nach Benjamin*, Cologne 1992, pp49-64.
10. Luce Irigaray, 'Ce sexe, qui n'en est pas un', Minuit, Paris 1977, pp75-6. (Here Eng. trans. from Toril Moi, *Sexual/Textual Politics: Feminist Literary Theory*, Methuen, London/New York 1985, p139.)
11. Julia Kristeva, *About Chinese Women*, Marion Boyars, New York 1986.
12. *Ibid.*, p242.
13. For example in the images of silence giving birth, of the deflowering gaze (*II.1*/p92), of the conceiving landscape (p99), of the womb of time (p102) or of being pregnant with knowledge (p131).
14. The crassest example being the model of the 'Junggesellenmaschinen'(Bachelor Machines), cf. Jean Clair/Harald Szeemann (eds.), *Junggesellenmashinen/Les Machines Célibataires*, Zürich 1975.
15. Kristeva, Julia, 'Die Produktivität der Frau. Interview by Elaine Boucquey', in *Das Lächeln der Medusa. Alternative* Nr. 108/109, 1976, p167.

16. For more precise detail on this subject cf. my article 'Problems and Representability of a female Dialectic of Enlightenment' in *Australian Feminist Studies* (Adelaide) No.11 Autumn 1990, pp1-15.
17. Cf. Samuel M. Weber, (*Return to Freud: Jacques Lacan's Dislocation of Psychoanalysis*, Cambridge University Press, Cambridge 1991).
18. This was the Dutch painter Tut EnCate, cf. Walter van Gerwen 'Walter Benjamin 1932/33 auf Ibiza', lecture held at the Benjamin Symposium in Osnabrück, June 1992.
19. Cf. the chapter 'Traum, Stadt, Fraut in Sigrid Weigel, *Topographien der Geschlechter: Kulturgeschichtliche Studien zur Literatur*, Reinbek bei Hamburg 1990.
20. Thus in the Hessel Review; also, with slight deviation, in the early drafts of the *Passagen* written from 1927 on (*V*/p1052).
21. Johann Jakob Bachofen, *Das Mutterrecht*. Ed. v. Meule. Basle 1948, p36. Cf. also Gerhard Plumpe 'Die Entdeckung der Vorwelt. Erläuterungen zu Benjamin's Bachofenlektüre.' in *Walter Benjamin: Text und Kritic* 32/32, Munich 1979, pp19-27.
22. Though the *Dirne* is predominant in his early writings, which also allude to student experiences, and the *Hure* in the later works, it is quite clear that the term *Hure* refers to the whore's status as an image. However, Benjamin's choice of vocabulary is not uniform; although he refers exclusively to the *Dirne* in the texts up to *One Way Street* (1938), the *Hure* turns up in the same time in the first drafts of the *Passagen* (e.g. *V*p1023 and *V*p1057). Then again, he refers to the *Dirne* in his letter to Horkheimer of 1938 about the plan for the *Baudelaire* book (*Br.* p752) and also in the first schematic plans for it (*VII.2*p739).
23. Cf. note 19.

The City in Pieces

Victor Burgin

In her book about Walter Benjamin's Paris Arcades project, Susan Buck-Morss tells the story of how, in 1924, Benjamin traveled to Italy: 'in order to bring to paper his [thesis] *The Origin of German Tragic Drama*, with which he hoped to secure an academic position at the University of Frankfurt'.[1] This was the year of Lenin's death, and the year of the first Surrealist manifesto. An eventful year in politics and art, it was no less eventful for Benjamin's personal life. In Italy he met, and fell in love with, Asja Lacis: 'a Bolshevik from Latvia, active in post revolutionary Soviet culture as an actress and director, and a member of the Communist Party since the Duma revolution'.[2] In 1928, having failed to win the approval of the university, *The Origin of German Tragic Drama* was nevertheless published.[3] Benjamin dedicated it to his wife, from whom he separated that same year. In this same year Benjamin also published *One Way Street*, a montage of textual fragments in which he juxtaposes observations on everyday life with descriptions of his dreams. One of the longer fragments is titled: 'Teaching Aid—Principles of the Weighty Tome, or How to Write Fat Books'.[4] *One Way Street* is not a Weighty Tome. No academic monument, it has more the appearance of a city-plan: avenues of open space cross its pages, between compact and irregular blocks of text. Benjamin's dedication to *One Way Street* reads:

> This street is named
> Asja Lacis Street
> after she who
> like an engineer
> cut it through the author

I

When, in 1924, Benjamin first told Lacis about the academic thesis he was working on, her horrified response was: 'Why bury oneself with dead literature?'[5] In Benjamin's subsequent production, funerary construction gives way to a lighter and more open textual architecture. When, in 1925, he and Lacis wrote an essay together about the city of Naples, the central image (which Susan Buck-Morss tells us was 'suggested by Lacis') is that of 'porosity'. Naples rises where sea meets cliff. Lacis and Benjamin write: 'At the base of the cliff itself, where it touches the shore, caves have been hewn [. . .] As porous as this stone is the architecture. Building and action interpenetrate in the courtyards, arcades, and stair-ways. In everything they preserve the scope to become a theatre of new, unforeseen, constellations. The stamp of the definitive is avoided. No situation appears intended forever, no figure asserts its "thus and not otherwise." This is how architecture, the most binding part of the communical rhythm, comes into being here'.[6] Benjamin and Lacis find that: 'Buildings are used as a popular stage. They are all divided into innumerable, simultaneously animated theatres. Balcony, courtyard, window, gateway, staircase, roof are at the same time stages and boxes.'[7] Or, again: 'Housekeeping utensils hang from balconies like potted plants. [. . .] Just as the living room reappears on the street, with chairs, hearth, and alter, so, [. . .] the street migrates into the living room'.[8] The permeability which Lascis and Benjamin saw in the streets of Naples is also to be found in *One Way Street*, a street which will eventually lead to the *Passagen-Werk*. We will remember that Benjamin named this street *Asja Lacis Street*, 'after she who, like an engineer, cut it through the author'. Just as Benjamin recounts his dreams in *One Way Street*, so his laconic dedication to the book is itself a dream image: the image of a book which is a city street, cut through the body of the author by his lover. Benjamin's written body is penetrated by Lacis, just as the body of what might have been *his* text on Naples became porous, translucent, permeable to her voice. The lapidary inscription commemorates an erotic event in which the categorical distinctions which separate body, city and text dissolve.

The (con)fusion of representations of body and city has a history. In the third book of Vitruvius, dedicated to the design and construction of temples, the Roman architect describes how the outstretched limbs of a 'well-formed man' subtend the circle and the square. The purpose of the description – the basis of a widely-known drawing by Leonardo da Vinci – is to urge that buildings should display the same harmonious relation of parts to whole as Vitruvius found in the human form. We may moreover recall that the circle and the square are the diagrams of, respectively, the *orbis terrarum* and the *castrum* – the subject territories of the Roman Empire and the Roman military camp. The body is not simply that which is to be contained by a building, the body *contains* the very generating principle of the building. In an article of 1974,[9] Françoise Choay describes how, in the work of Alberti and other architect-theorists of the Italian Renaissance, the Vitruvian doctrine was woven into a mythology of origins. For example, Humanist authorities wrote that the first men derived their units of measurement from the palms of their hands, their arms and their feet. Or again, that Adam, driven from the Garden of Eden, protected himself from the rain by joining his hands above his head – a gesture which subsequently led him to construct the first roof. That the human body is seen as the origin not only of the building, but of the entire built environment, is apparent from the descriptions and drawings of anthropomorphized cities which appear in illustrated books during the Renaissance. Choay describes an image from a book by Francesco di Giorgio Martini as showing: 'a personnage whose head is adorned with a fortress which he supports with his arms. His body is inscribed in a rectangle marked *città*. His legs are spread, and his feet and elbows are figured by towers. His navel marks the center of a circular public place, on the periphery of which is situated the principle church'.[10] Such fantasy constructions were already implied in the writings of Alberti, who had found that, 'The city is like a large house and the house like a small city', but that ultimately, 'every edifice is a body'.[11]

If, in Renaissance Italy, the city could be conceived of as a body, it was because the city had recently coalesced from a condition in which it was virtually undifferentiated from the countryside. In a book of 1974, translated in 1991 as *The Production of Space*, Henri Lefebvre observes: 'The city in Vitruvius is conspicuous by its absence/presence; though he is speaking of nothing else, he never addresses it directly. It is as though it were merely an aggregation of "public" monuments and "private" houses. [. . .] Only in the sixteenth century, after the rise of the medieval town (founded on commerce, and no longer agrarian in character), and after the establishment of "urban systems" in Italy, Flanders, England, France, Spanish America, and elsewhere, did the town emerge as a unified entity – and as a *subject*'.[12] The text in which Alberti inaugurates the concept of the corporeal city[13] postdates, by about fifteen years, his treatise on painting, *De Pictura*, which contains the first written description of a method of drawing in linear perspective. Perspective provided, quite literally, the 'common ground' on which the identification of architectural space with corporeal space could 'take place'. In the Renaissance, the inaugural act in constructing a painting was to lay out the horizontal plane which united the illusory space of the image with the real space of the viewer. This is the familiar grid of receding squares, accelerating towards a vanishing point, which in many paintings rises to the finished surface thinly disguised as a tiled floor. The side of each square in the underlying perspective grid represented a common unit of measurement, the *braccio*, equivalent to one third of the height of a standing man. By this means, the correct stature of a depicted figure could be determined relative to any point in the illusory depth of the represented space. The size of all other objects – not least the built environment – could then be determined by reference to this common corporeal measure. Man, here, is literally 'the measure of all things'. For all that the erect male body may have been at the origin of this space, however, it quickly ceded its place to its disembodied metonymic representative, the eye – in what Lefebvre has called, 'the spiriting-away or scotomization of the body.'[14] As a consequence, as Luce Irigaray has remarked, 'Man no longer even remembers that his body is the threshold, the porch of the construction of his universe(s)'.[15]

At the dawn of modernity, disembodied geometric and mathematical principles came to dominate all visual representational practices. The same abstract order which informed painting and architecture was brought to enhance the instrumentality of such things as navigational charts, maps and city plans. In conformity to the exigencies of a militant and expansive mercantile capitalism, the image of the convergence of parallel lines towards a vanishing point on the horizon became the very figure of Western European global economic and political ambitions. This optical-geometric spatial régime – the panoptical-instrumental space of colonialist capitalist modernity – would govern Western European representations for the ensuing three centuries. It has been widely remarked that this representational space, inaugurated in the Renaissance, entered into crisis in the early part of the twentieth century. We have become familiar with the arguments from industrialization, urbanization and technology: Fordism and Taylorism, factory town and garden city, steam train and airplane, telephone and radio, all were implicated in a changed 'common sense' of space. On the basis of the 'artistic' evidence, also, few would disagree that the early twentieth century was a time of major change in Western representations of space, and space of representations. Exhibits presented in evidence here typically include such things as Analytical Cubism, the Twelve-tone Scale, Jazz and Bauhaus design. It is in terms of such arguments that I understand Lefebvre when he writes: 'around 1910 a certain space was shattered. It was the space of common sense, of knowledge (*savoir*), of social practice, of political power, [. . .]; the space, too, of classical perspective and geometry [. . .] bodied forth in Western art and philosophy, as in the form of the city and town'.[16] Lefebvre also observes, however, that: ' "common sense" space, Euclidean space and perspectivist space did not disappear in a puff of smoke without leaving any trace in our consciousness, knowledge or educational methods'.[17] A certain space was shattered, but nevertheless it did not disappear. The 'nevertheless' does not signal that disjunction between knowledge and belief to which Freud gave the term *Verleugnung*, 'disavowal'. For our terminology here, we might better turn to Mao Tse-Tung: the relation between the existing instrumental space of political modernity and the emergent space of aesthetic modernism is one of 'non-antagonistic contradiction'.

II

Benjamin and Lacis, themselves out of place in Naples, found all things in Naples to be dis-located, as when 'the living room reappears on the street'. This particular image, retrospectively determined by a short history of Surrealism, returns in Benjamin's long essay of 1938 about Paris at the time of Baudelaire. Here, Benjamin remarks on the tendency of the flâneur to, 'turn the boulevard into an *intérieur*'. He writes: 'The street becomes a dwelling for the *flâneur*; he is as much at home among the façades of houses as the citizen is in his four walls. To him the shiny, enameled signs of business are at least as good a wall ornament as an oil painting is to a bourgeois in his salon.'[18] This passage, in retrospect, helps to reveal a fundamental ambiguity both in Lacis and Benjamin's essay about Naples, and in Benjamin's dedication to *One Way Street*. The *flâneur* who turns the street into a living-room commits an act of transgression, which reverses an established distinction between public and private spaces. By contrast, Benjamin and Lacis saw the porosity of urban life in Naples as the survival of pre-capitalist social forms which had not yet succumbed to the modern segregation of life into public and private zones. Again, Benjamin's terse dedication to *One Way Street* pictures a fusion of spaces in the same instant that- through the image of penetration – it asserts the individual integrity of those spaces. Like an arrested filmic lap-dissolve, which refuses to decide either origin or destination, the image forms through condensation. It also forms through displacement to, or from, the image of Haussmann's infamous *percements* which ripped through working-class districts of Paris like the cannon-fire they were designed to facilitate. An ambivalence inhabits this textual fragment: as if two different spaces – one sealed, the other permeable – compete to occupy the same moment in time. In both the essay on Naples and the dedication to *One Way Street*, the metaphor of porosity competes with a dialectic of interior and exterior which belongs to a different register. This ambivalence marks the representational space of modernism in general.

One of the most visible images of the modern dialectic of interior and exterior is the wall of steel and glass, of which the glass and iron structures of the Paris arcades are a prototype. We may take the specific example of the Administrative Office for a model factory complex built by Walter Gropius and Adolf Meyer for the Werkbund exhibition in Cologne in 1914. As Richard Sennett has described it: 'in this building you are simultaneously inside and outside. [. . .] From the outside you can see people moving up and down between floors. [. . .] You can see through walls, your eyes move inside to outside, outside to inside. The confines of the interior have lost their meaning. [. . .] Gropius and Meyer have used glass in and around the doors so that you can literally look through the building to people entering from the other side. [. . .] Inner and outer become apparent at once, like the front and side of a cubist portrait.[19] It is no doubt this sort of 'image of the modern' that Benjamin has in mind when he celebrates, 'the twentieth century, with its porosity, transparency, light and free air'.[20] The modernist architect to whom he pays explicit hommage, however, is not Gropius but Le Corbusier, the designer of the 'radiant city'.[21] Le Corbusier's project of 1930 for the Ville Radieuse is the source of the now cliché perspectivist vision of urban modernity as made up of evenly spaced towers rising from a limitless expanse of park land. The project evolved from Le Corbusier's plan for the Ville Contemporaine, to contain three million people, which was exhibited in Paris in 1922. Kenneth Frampton describes the Ville Contemporaine as, 'an élite capitalist city of administration and control with garden cities for the workers being sited, along with industry, beyond the "security zone" of the green belt encompassing the city'.[22] We may remember, then, that as much as modernity is the locus of transparency in architecture, it is also at the origin of the social isolation in and between high-rise apartment houses, the death of the street as a site of social interaction, and the practice of 'zoning', which establishes absolute lines of demarcation between work and residential areas, and between cultural and commercial activities. The transparent wall, used by such socialist modernists as Gropius to unite interior with exterior, was destined to become the very index of capitalist corporate exclusivity.

III

Lefebvre finds both that, around 1910, 'a certain space was shattered' and that 'it did not disappear'. The phallocentric abstract space of capitalist modernity survived to inhabit the representational space of aesthetic modernism. Indeed, it survives into the present day. It is not that one spatial formation was replaced by another. It is rather as if a superior 'layer' of spatial representations itself became permeable, 'porous', and allowed an inferior layer to show through. Lefebvre himself supplies the appropriate analogy. He notes that early in the genesis of a biological organism, 'an indentation forms in the cellular mass. A cavity gradually takes place [. . .] The cells adjacent to the cavity form a screen or membrane which serves as a boundary [. . .] A closure thus comes to separate within from without, so establishing the living being as a "distinct body".' This 'closure', however, is only ever relative: 'The membranes in question remain permeable, punctured by pores and orifices. Traffic back and forth, so far from stopping, tends to increase and become more differentiated, embracing both energy exchange (alimentation, respiration, excretion) and information exchange (the sensory apparatus)'. Closure, then, rather than belonging to the natural order, is a creation of the social order. Thus, Lefebvre writes: 'A defining characteristic of (private) property, as of the position in space of a town, nation or nation state, is a closed frontier. This limiting case aside, however, we may say that every spatial envelope implies a barrier between inside and out, but that this barrier is always relative and, in the case of membranes, always permeable.'[23] The transgressional magic of the *flâneur* is to make the interior appear on the 'wrong sides of its bounding wall, the wrong side of the façade. Certainly, the transformation is an illusion, but then the interior itself is an illusion – in a double sense. First, Benjamin points out that the bourgeois interior emerges into history, in the nineteenth century, as a reified fantasy: 'For the private person, living space becomes, for the first time, antithetical to the place of work. [. . .] The private person who squares his accounts with reality in his office demands that the interior be maintained in his illusions. [. . .] From this springs the phantasmagoria of the interior. For the private individual the private environment represents the universe. In it he gathers remote places and the past. His drawing room is a box in the world theatre.'[24] In an essay about the domestic architecture of Adolf Loos, Beatriz Colomina writes: 'In Loos's interiors the sense of security is not achieved by simply turning one's back on the exterior and become immersed in a private world – "a box in the world theatre", to use Benjamin's metaphor. It is no longer the house that is a theatre box; there is a theatre box inside the house, overlooking the internal social spaces, so that the inhabitants become both actors in and spectators of family life – involved in, yet detached from their own space. The classical distinction between inside and outside, private and public, object and subject, are no longer valid'.[25] It is not, however, that these distinctions are no longer valid, it is rather that they have been displaced – as in the Paris arcades, which pierce the façade only to reproduce the façade in the form of glass entrails within the body of the building.[26] Further, Lefebvre's example of the biological organism would indicate that, in any real sense, the absolute distinction between interior and exterior can never be valid. It will always belong to 'reality', never to the order of the Real. Here, then, is the second sense in which the interior is an illusion. Extending the analogy of the biological organism to the social space of the built environment, Lefebvre reminds us that an apparently solid house is, 'permeated from every direction by streams of energy which run in and out of it by every imaginable route: water, gas, electricity, telephone lines, radio and television signals, and so on', and that similar observations apply in respect of the entire city. Thus, he writes: 'as exact a picture as possible of this space would differ considerably from the one embodied in the representational space which its inhabitants have in their minds, and which for all its inaccuracy plays an integral role in social practice.'[27] If the built environment is conceived of in terms of the body, then a different body is at issue here.

An Arnold Newman photograph from 1949 shows the components of a prefabricated house laid out on what appears to be the concrete runway of an airfield. Every shape in the intricate pattern of this carpet of components is equally visible. No hierarchy, formal or functional, governs the relations between the parts. Contiguity alone links wood, metal and glass; frames, planks and pipes. This is nothing like a house, yet nothing but a house. If the houses destined to be its neighbours had been laid out alongside, it would have been impossible to tell where one ended and the other began. At the beginning of his book of 1974, *Économie Libidinale*, Jean-François Lyotard similarly lays out the surfaces of the body. In a long and violent passage, glistening with mucus and blood, he unfolds not only that which is seen, 'the skin with each of its creases, lines, scars. [. . .] the nipples, the nails, the hard transparent skin under the heel', but also the most intimate and deep interior linings of the body. Moreover, as nothing but proximity links one surface to another, we pass indiscriminately to other contiguous bodies. We pass, for example, from these lips to other lips, and to the lips of others. We pass from the palm of the hand, 'creased like a yellowed sheet of paper', to the surface of an automobile steering wheel. Even further, Lyotard reminds us, we must not forget to add colours to the retina, or to add to the tongue, 'all the sounds of which it is capable', including, 'all the selective reserve of sounds which is a phonological system'. All of this, and more, belongs to the libidinal body. This 'body' bears no allegiance to what Lyotard terms the 'political economy' of the organic. The 'political body' is a hierarchically organized assembly of constituent organs – jointly ruled by mind and heart – which seeks to resist death, and to reproduce itself. It is a body clearly differentiated from other bodies, and from the world of objects. It is this body under the Law which may become the site of 'transgression'- illustrated, for Lyotard, by a Hans Bellmer drawing in which a fold in a girl's arm stands in place of the crease of the vulva. It is not such transgressive metaphor which is at issue, but a more corrosive metonymy. Lyotard writes: 'We must not begin with transgression, we must immediately go to the very end of cruelty, construct the anatomy of polymorphous perversion, unfold the immense membrane of the libidinal "body", which is quite the inverse of a system of parts'. Lyotard sees this 'membrane' as composed of the most heterogeneous items: human bone and writing-paper, steel and glass, syntax and the skin on the inside of the thigh. In the libidinal economy, writes Lyotard: 'All of these zones are butted end to end [. . .] on a Moebius strip, [. . .] a moebian skin [an] interminable band of variable geometry (a concavity is necessarily a convexity at the next turn) [with but] a single face, and therefore neither exterior nor interior'.[28]

Gropius and Meyers' design for the 1914 Werkbund Exhibition may render interior and exterior mutually visible, but it does not thereby abolish the hierarchical distinction between the two: it is, after all, an administration building. The glass walls of the corporate towers which follow may be transparent, but they are no more porous than are their 'glass ceilings'. Such façades retain their Classical function of both leading the eye towards a vanishing point, or point of interest, and of marking a boundary. Lefebvre seems to leave the transparent walls out of account when he notes: 'A façade admits certain acts to the realm of what is visible, whether they occur on the façade itself (on balconies, window ledges, etc.) or are to be seen *from* the façade (processions in the street, for example). Many other acts, by contrast, it condemns to obscenity: these occur *behind* the façade. All of which seems to suggest a "psychoanalysis of space".'[29] The façade of which Lefebvre speaks here is opaque. By his account, if nothing is concealed then there is no need for psychoanalytic theory. This would be to reduce psychoanalysis to a theory of repression, but modern psychoanalysis is no more *necessarily* concerned with repression than the modern façade is necessarily opaque. Lefebvre's observation about the façade is the only passage where he suggests the possibility of a psychoanalysis of space. There are nevertheless many points in Lefebvre's complex and densely argued book where his ideas invite development in terms of psychoanalytic theory. Most fundamentally, he writes that space is: 'first of all *my* body, and then it is my body counterpart or "other", its mirror-image or shadow: it is the shifting intersection between that which touches, penetrates, threatens or benefits my body on the one hand, and all other bodies on the other'. The full psychoanalytic implications of such a remark – most obviously, in relation to Lacan's idea of the 'mirror stage' – remain to be developed. Indeed, in so far as they apply to considerations of space, they are as yet little developed within the field of psychoanalysis itself.

IV

The problematic of space is encountered from the beginning of Freud's therapeutic practice and metapsychological theory: both in real terms, as in the question of the therapeutic setting, and in metaphorical terms, as in his topographical models of mental processes. It is perhaps because of this early ubiquity that the topic of space as such came to receive little, and late, direct consideration in psychoanalysis. To my knowledge, Paul Schilder's essay of 1935, 'Psycho-Analysis of Space', is the first to address the topic explicitly and exclusively. Schilder finds that: 'Space is not an independent entity (as Kant has wrongly stated) but is in close relation to instincts, drives, emotions and actions [. . .].'[30] His remarks here anticipate an isolated work-note made by Freud in 1938: 'Space may be the projection of the extension of the psychical apparatus. No other derivation is probable. Instead of Kant's *a priori* determinants of our psychical apparatus. Psyche is extended; knows nothing about it.'[31] Schilder's findings in respect of psychical space emerge from his work on, in the title of his book of 1935 (a book which is one of the sources of Lacan's idea of the mirror stage), *The Image and Appearance of the Human Body*.[32] In 'Psycho-Analysis of Space' Schilder writes: 'There is at first an undifferentiated relation between an incompletely developed body-image and the outside space. Clearer differentiations take place around the openings of the body. There is a zone of indifference between body and outside world which makes distortions of body-space and outside-space by projection and appersonization possible.'[33]

'Appersonization' is the process in which: 'We may take parts of the bodies of others and incorporate them in our own body-image'.[34] In a pathological setting, such interchange of body-parts is a characteristic of the 'psychoses'. Amongst what Freud calls the 'defence psychoses', autism and schizophrenia bear most directly on the corporeal relation to external reality. In her book of 1972 on *Autism and Childhood Psychosis*, the British psychoanalyst Frances Tustin notes that: 'The common psychiatric division of psychotic children [is] into those suffering from Early Infantile Autism and those suffering from childhood Schizophrenia'.[35] Tustin finds this distinction 'too rigid'. For expository clarity however, outside of a clinical setting, it is convenient to retain the distinction. Schematically, the terms 'autism' and 'schizophrenia' name the opposing extremities of a continuum of modes of psycho-corporeal relation to external reality. The middle range of this schematic continuum would encompass 'normal' socially acceptable ways of relating to the world. At one extreme limit, autism represents a total closing down of that relation: the autistic subject may appear 'dead to the world'. At the opposite extreme, schizophrenia represents a total opening of the relation: to the extent that the schizophrenic body is scattered in pieces throughout its world. Both autism and schizophrenia are normal states of very early infancy, the time when there is as yet little substantive distinction between an outer world of 'real' objects, and the inner world of those 'objects' which are the psychical representations of sensations from, primarily, bodily organs and the mother's body. Pathological autism and schizophrenia represent a fixation at, or regression to, such early object relations. We should however remember that, as Freud remarks: 'the frontier between the so-called normal states of mind and the pathological ones is to a great extent conventional, and [. . .] is so fluid that each one of us probably crosses it many times in the course of a day'. As Octave Mannoni succinctly puts it: 'we are all more or less healed psychotics'.[36]

A book of drawings by Antonin Artaud, published in France in 1986,[37] is accompanied by an essay by Jacques Derrida which is, in effect, an extended reflection upon the rarely used French word *subjectile* – a word which appears, appropriately rarely, in Artaud's writings. The 1978 edition of the *Petit Robert* dictionary defines *subjectile* as, 'Surface serving as support (wall, panel, canvas) for a painting'. This is not how the term functions for Artaud. Rather, as Derrida notes, the *subjectile* is that which lies, 'between the surfaces of the subject and the object'.[38] It is the place where may be traced: 'the trajectories of the *objective*, the *subjective*, the *projectile*, of the *introjection*, the *interjection*, the *objection*, of *dejection* and *abjection*, etc.'[39] Derrida describes a graphic work by Artaud in which, 'with the aid of a match, Artaud opens holes in the paper, and the traces of burning perforation are part of a work in which it is impossible to distinguish between the subject of the representation and the support of this subject, in the layers of the material, between that which is above and that which is below, and thus between the subject and its outside, the representation and its other.'[40] Reading this, I was reminded of a recurrent television news image: the image of a house, or apartment, whose walls have been pierced by rocket-fire, or shells. For all its repetitions, the image never fails to 'pierce' me. This has nothing to do with Barthes' *punctum*, nor the *stadium*. This is neither a private nor an ethical reaction. Something quite different is at issue. Discussing the child's anxiety at being separated from its mother, Freud notes that at the origin of the distress is the child's perception of the mother as the one who will satisfy its needs. Thus, rather than being reducible simply to object loss: 'The situation [. . .] which [the child] regards as a "danger" and against which it wants to be safeguarded is that of a [. . .] *growing tension due to need*, against which it is helpless'(italics in the original). Even more fundamentally, regardless of need, anxiety derives from, 'the economic disturbance caused by an accumulation of amounts of stimulation which require to be disposed of. It is this factor [. . .] which is the real essence of the "danger".'[41] In the contemporary environment of mass-media, particularly television, we are all of us subject to anxiety arising from, amongst other things, exposure to pain we are helpless to alleviate. The helpless distress we may feel – comparable to infantile 'transitivism' – bears witness to the congenital instability of psycho-corporeal boundaries which is at the source of both empathy and jealousy, compassion and aggression. It indicates the fragility and permeability, the porosity, of the layers between one embodied subject and another. In the physical encounter, the porosity is of the boundary of skin which contains the body ego, the 'skin ego'.[42] In the mediatic encounter, there is permeability between 'layers', such that interior and exterior, here and there, are simultaneously affirmed and confused. I am thinking of the corneal and retinal layers which both receive and transmit the image; the phosphor-coated layer of glass which – in receiving the bombardment of electrons which encode the image – effectively pierces the layer, the screen, which is the wall of my living room; the pierced layer of the wall *in* the image within or behind the television screen – within that building, behind that wall, where someone in their living room perhaps once watched television.

V

The Paris arcades of which Benjamin spoke, and the modernist buildings which they presaged, did not mark the emergence of an historically unprecedented space. Such examples rather represent the imperfect partial development of an image of space latent in all of us: the pre-oedipal, maternal, space: the space, perhaps, that Benjamin and Lacis momentarily refound in Naples. In this space it is not simply that the boundaries are 'porous', but that the subject itself is *soluble*. This space is the source of bliss and of terror, of the 'oceanic' feeling, and of the feeling of coming apart; just as it is at the origin of feelings of being invaded, overwhelmed, suffocated. The generation of Europeans to which I belong grew up in a world of fixed borders, of glacial boundaries: frozen, it seemed for eternity, by the Cold War. Now, in the time of thaw, borders everywhere are melting, sliding, submerging, re-emerging. Identities – national, cultural, individual – are experiencing the exultant anxieties which accompany the threat of dissolution. Benjamin's Europe was one of strong borders, a fact which was to prove tragically fatal to Benjamin himself. Today's national borders are largely inconvenient to world capitalism, they have long been routinely ignored by transnational corporations, and by a money market become a global computer network, operating at the speed of light. As weak and emergent nations struggle to maintain their faltering identities by drawing their borders more tightly around them, stronger established nations are losing the political will to effectively police their uncertain limits. The boundaries of today's Europe are increasingly porous. The recent history of Germany is an example. A space in transition, it represents the economic and political equivalent of 'osmosis' – the movement of a fluid through a semi-permeable membrane, from the weaker to the stronger solution. However, as 'The Wall' crumbled inside Germany, osmosis at Germany's borders – fluid transmissions from the weaker to the stronger economy – has reawoken a pathological horror of mixing, the modern history of which has been so effectively catalogued by Klaus Theweleit.[43] The rhetoric of neo-fascism, by no means unique to Germany, sounds familiar – but it now resounds in a different space. Rhetoric, we may remember, was originally an art of space – of gesture and of staging – as well as an art of speech. The space of the stage, the Antique source of perspectival space, has changed.

In explaining the principle of drawing in perspective, Leonardo da Vinci asked his reader to imagine he were looking through a window and tracing the outline of what he saw upon the surface of the glass. Virilio describes the television screen as 'an introverted window, one which no longer opens onto adjoining space.'[44] Today, the perspectivist's 'window on the world', and proscenium arch, remain the habitual frames of our representations – even in television. But such means of circumscribing the *mise-en-scène* appear out of their time; dislocated survivors from another time, a sort of nostalgia. The truth of this is nowhere better seen than in the images of computer-generated 'virtual' realities with which we have recently become familiar. Their impeccably Euclidean 'wire-frame' spaces invoke nothing so much as illustrations from seventeenth-century treatises on perspective, creating much the same uncannily nostalgic effect as a polystyrene bowl which has been molded to bear the impression left in wet clay by a potter's fingers. Benjamin remarked that the arrival of photography in the nineteenth century 'gave the moment a posthumous shock'. Much of this shock was the shock of the uncanny: the strangeness of the automaton, the android, the replicant; the shock of the unfamiliar familiarity of this new old representational space. The photograph, we are now accustomed to observe, lends itself easily to fetishism: the preferred commodity form of capitalism, the most favored psycho-aesthetic form in which modernity and 'post-modernity' alike are traded. Photographs, therefore, are most amenable to 'disavowal' as the mechanism by which we may defend ourselves against their more distressing (un)realities. As Mannoni expresses the form of disavowal, 'I know very well, but nevertheless':[45] 'I know very well that this (unpleasurable) reality exists/existed, *but nevertheless* here there is only the beauty of the print.'[46] Since Laura Mulvey's influential essay, 'Visual Pleasure and Narrative Cinema',[47] we have also become accustomed to the idea that fetishism is also a predominant psycho-sexual structure of cinematic representation. The television image is rarely 'beautiful' in the way of a photograph, or a cinematic shot (I am thinking of the type in which a Sternberg frames a Dietrich), nor does its evanescent mobility allow the petrification necessary for fetishistic investment. The regressive unconscious defence mechanisms invoked by television, as it funnels suffering and excitation into our box in the world theatre, as it pours all the world's broken cities into our *interior*, are different from those invoked by photography and cinema-photography. They produce a different space.

For all its 'thick-skinned' stupidity, television is also a fragile permeable membrane of near-global extension. Its web of instant mutable satellite links, indiscriminately crossing fixed meridians and old frontiers, has turned global space from a graph paper into a palimpsest. Paul Virilio has remarked that both Benjamin and René Clair compared architecture to cinema, in that both address what Benjamin termed 'simultaneous collective reception'.[48] What Virilio finds of particular interest in this comparison is the implicit recognition of a historical transition from the representational priority of 'surface' to that of 'interface'. Benjamin notes that Baudelaire described the inhabitant of the modern city as, 'a kaleidoscope equipped with consciousness,' and that with the coming of film, 'perception in the form of shocks was established as a formal principle.'[49] The subsequent arrival of television – also, like architecture, a technique of 'simultaneous collective reception' – has massively consolidated this principle. In his essay of 1936, 'The Work of Art in the Age of Mechanical Reproduction', Benjamin wrote: 'Our taverns and our metropolitan streets and offices and furnished rooms, our railroad stations and our factories appeared to have us locked up hopelessly. Then came the film and burst this prison-world asunder by the dynamite of the tenth of a second, so that now, in the midst of its far-flung ruins and debris, we calmly and adventurously go travelling.'[50] Today, for more anxious, less adventurous, armchair travellers, the 'far-flung ruins and debris' of exploded towns is routinely projected into our living rooms through the aperture of television. Television, 'the box', is today's 'box in the world theatre' – so often a theatre of war. For Virilio, it is television which has definitively marked the end of perspectival space, the orderly concatenation of façades. He writes: 'The blind alley disappears into the superimposed vision of a [. . .] television that never turns off, that always gives and receives [...] all surfaces and all the pieces of a tele-topological puzzle [. . .],'[51] All the surfaces and all the pieces of the body form a complex puzzle we were once required to solve in order to become human. Like the elements of a building, the completed puzzle-picture holds together more or less provisionally: here, cracks may run wild under a calm façade; there, they may shatter a transparent carapace; and other structures may endure only in mute and fearful isolation. Today, the autistic response of total withdrawal, and the schizophrenic anxiety of the body in pieces, belong to our psycho-corporeal forms of identification with the tele-topological puzzle of the city in pieces.

NOTES

1. Susan Buck-Morss, *The Dialectics of Seeing: Walter Benjamin and the Arcades Project*, MIT, Cambridge, Mass 1989, p8.
2. *Ibid.*, p11.
3. Benjamin submitted his completed dissertation im 1925 and was, 'advised to withdraw his petition [. . .] rather than suffer the embarrassment of rejection.' [*Ibid.*, p22.]
4. Walter Benjamin, 'One Way Street', in *Reflections*, Harcourt, New York and London, 1978, p79.
5. Asja Lacis, *Revolutionär im Beruf: Berichte über proletarisches Theater, über Meyerhold, Brecht, Benjamin und Piscator*, Regner & Bernhard, Munich 1971, pp43-44; quoted in *The Dialectics of Seeing*, p15.
6. Walter Benjamin and Asja Lacis, 'Naples', in *Reflections*, pp165-6.
7. *Ibid.*, p167.
8. *Ibid.*, p171.
9. Françoise Choay, 'La ville et le domaine bâti comme corps dans les textes des architectes-théoriciens de la première renaissance Italienne', *Nouvelle Revue de Psychanalyse* (Paris) no 9, Spring 1974.
10. *Ibid.*, p248.
11. *Ibid.*, p244.
12. Henri Lefebvre, *The Production of Space*, Basil Blackwell, Oxford 1991, p271.
13. *De Re Aedificatoria*, written about 1450 and published after his death, in 1483.
14. *The Production of Space*, p201.
15. Luce Irigaray, *Éthique de la différence sexuelle,* quoted in Margaret Whitford, *Luce Irigaray: Philosophy, in the Feminine* (London: Routledge, 1991) p53.
16. *Op.cit.*, Lefebvre, pp25-6.
17. *Ibid.*, pp25-6.
18. Walter Benjamin, *Charles Baudelaire: A Lyric Poet in the Era of High Capitalism* (London: NLB, 1978) p37.
19. Richard Sennett, *The Conscience of the Eye: The Design and Social Life of Cities* (New York: Knopf, 1990) p104.
20. Walter Benjamin, *Gesammelte Schriften* (Frankfurt am Main: Suhrkamp Verlag, 1972-, v. V) p292, quoted in *The Dialectics of Seeing: Walter Benjamin and the Arcardes Project*, p303.
21. 'How are we to imagine an existence oriented solely toward Boulevard Bonne-Nouvelle, in rooms by Le Corbusier and Oud?' [Walter Benjamin, 'Surrealism:

The Last Snapshot of the European Intelligentsia', *Reflections*, New York: Harcourt, 1978, p189.]

22. Kenneth Frampton, *Modern Architecture: a critical history*, (London: Thames and Hudson 1987) p155.
23. *Op.cit.*, Lefebvre, pp175-6.
24. Walter Benjamin, *Reflections*, p154.
25. Beatriz Colomina, 'Intimacy and Spectacle: The Interiors of Adolf Loos', *AA Files*, 20, 1990.
26. My thanks to Peter Wollen for suggesting this metaphor.
27. *Op.cit.*, Lefebvre, p93.
28. Jean-François Lyotard, *Économie Libidinale* (Paris: Editions de Minuit, 1974) pp10-11.
29. *Op.cit.*, Lefebvre, p99.
30. Paul Schilder, 'Psycho-Analysis of Space', *International Journal of Psychoanalysis*, v. XVI, 1935, p295.
31. *The Standard Edition of the Complete Psychological Works of Sigmund Freud*, London; (Hogarth, 1953-74, v. XXIII), p300.
32. Paul Schilder, *The Image and Appearance of the Human Body* (New York: International Universities Press, 1950).
33. 'Psycho-Analysis of Space', p295.
34. *The Image and Appearance of the Human Body*, p172.
35. Frances Tustin, *Autism and Childhood Psychosis*, 1972, Science House, p106.
36. Octave Mannoni, 'La Part du Jeu', *L'Arc*, n 69 (Special issue on Donald W. Winnicott).
37. Paul Thevenin and Jacques Derrida, *Antonin Artaud - Dessins et portraits*, Paris: (Gallimard, 1986). My thanks to Lindsay Waters for having brought this essay to my attention.
38. *Ibid.*, p79.
39. *Ibid.*, p63.
40. *Ibid.*, p70.
41. Sigmund Freud, 'Inhibitions, symptoms and anxiety' (1926), *The Standard Edition of thc Complete Psychological Works of Sigmund Freud*, London: (Hogarth, 1953-74), v. XX, p137.
42. See Didier Anzieu, *The Skin Ego*, New Haven: (Yale, 1989).
43. Klaus Theweleit, *Male Fantasies* (Minneapolis: Minnesota, 1987,v.1; 1989, v.2.).
44. Paul Virilio, *Lost Dimension* (New York: Semiotext(e), 1991) p79.
45. Octave Mannoni, 'Je sais bien, mais quand même', in *Clefs pour l'imaginaire ou l'autre scène* (Paris: Seuil, 1969).
46. Victor Burgin, 'Photography, Phantasy, Function', in Victor Burgin, (ed.), *Thinking Photography* (London: Macmillan, 1982) pp190-91.
47. Laura Mulvey, 'Visual Pleasure and Narrative Cinema' (1975), in *Visual and*

Other Pleasures (London: Macmillan, 1989).

48. *Lost Dimension*, op. cit., pp69-70.
49. Walter Benjamin, *Charles Baudelaire*, p132.
50. Walter Benjamin, 'The Work of Art in the Age of Mechanical Reproduction', *Illuminations* (London: Fontana, 1973) p238.
51. *Lost Dimension*, p71.

WALTER BENJAMIN, THE INTELLECTUAL

Zygmunt Bauman

> Nobody excluded the possibility that things could proceed in other, entirely different ways. You would have said that now each individual was ashamed of being the way he was expected to be.
>
> Italo Calvino, *Time and the Hunter*

To say that Benjamin was an intellectual, is not, of course, to explain Benjamin. One cannot explain the unknown by an unknown. Neither is it to classify him. To classify is to determine, to close, but the state of being an intellectual is one of indetermination and opening, and refusal to be determined and closed. To say 'Benjamin, the intellectual' is, rather, to admit that explanation and classification are bound to remain forever elusive. It is to point out that we can only speak of Walter Benjamin the way we speak of the state of being an intellectual, the two narratives being virtually inter-changeable. In both narratives, the failure to explain and classify are the explanation and classification one would find in the end, were there such an end. In both, the end is never to reach an end. In both, forever escaping fixation is for the constituted subjects the sole 'fixing' there is and can be. If Benjamin invites the attribute of intellectual more than any other thinker or writer aspiring to the same, it is because he made that general fate of the intellectual, with its grandeur and misery, hope one cannot do without and blunders one cannot escape, into his consciously embraced private destiny; into his life programme. Benjamin's life, and Benjamin's death, were about the refusal (or was it incapacity?) to be fixed.

Not that Benjamin sought a life in the ivory tower; that stands for a solitude one enjoys. Benjamin's abode was one shared with most intellectuals – that of the exile. Exile is the solitude one resents and wants to escape from. Exile is the condition of a perpetual escape act, so perpetual and so prospectless that, as in the case of Kafka's *hunger artist*, it turns sooner or later into the only life one is good at and the only one one can bear. Exile is the kind of being whose purpose is to be elsewhere.

> I heard the sound of a trumpet, and I asked my servant what it meant. He knew nothing and had heard nothing. At the gate he stopped me and asked: 'Where is the master going?' 'I don't know', I said, 'just out of here, just out of here. Out of here, nothing else, it's the only way I can reach my goal.' 'So you know your goal?' he asked. 'Yes,' I replied, 'I've just told you. Out of here – that's my goal.'[1]

'He knew the impossibility of fitting in and yet never renounced the desire to do so'- wrote Benjamin's fellow exile Theodor Adorno.[2] More than anything else, Benjamin wished to belong and yet this state was the one he was least capable of and found the most repulsive. Wherever he approached in his life-long effort to escape from exile, through a perverse Midas touch, he turned belonging into a new exile. It is as though the function he performed best, without fail in all domiciles on whose doors he knocked, was, to quote Jabés, to make the residents feel at home.[3] More than anyone who shared his fate, Benjamin knew that his condition, like the modernity of which it was a part and a paragon, is 'under the sign of suicide'- it lives by the effort to cancel itself, this self-cancellation being the only life it could have, this suicide being 'not a resignation but a heroic passion'.[4] More than anyone Benjamin believed that exile is a condition that will never end, though it consists in the incessant labour to end it, and that believing that the end is nigh is a disaster as complete and irrevocable as abandoning efforts to make that belief true. ('In our wanderings,' wrote Maurice Blanchot, 'impatience is the fundamental sin because it ignores the reality of wandering which requires, as law, that we should never believe the goal is at hand or that we shall ever reach it.'[5]) Sketching his portraits of Krauss, Kafka or Brecht, which like all genuine portraits were self-portraits in part,[6] he found the defeat of all efforts to reconcile, the impossibility of bringing together what fate decreed should stay apart, to be the most eloquent colours in his palette. Walter Benjamin reproached Gershon Scholem, his friend in captivity and adversary in the search of escape: 'I almost believe that you desire this in-between state, yet you ought to welcome any means of ending it'. To which Scholem replied: 'You are endangered more by your drive for community . . . than by the horror of loneliness that speaks from so many of your writings.'[7]

It is, perhaps, this suicidal attraction for the twin horrors of community and loneliness that endeared Benjamin to so many of his intellectual readers. For the same reason Benjamin was fascinated by Kafka or Brecht. Far and wide, Benjamin had been defined as he who escapes all definition. '*Messianique et désespéré, juif et non-juif . . . poète rejetant l'intuition, théologien sans Dieu, communiste sans parti, flâneur stakhanoviste, collectionneur de citations sans bibilothèque . . . , obsédé de la langue mais pas philologue*': this is how Genevieve Brisac recently described him.[8] Despite collating the lists so many others before her set out to compile, she still stops far short of completing the inventory of incongruities which made Benjamin the enigma that haunts the intellectual dreamers of integrity, while brutally thrusting upon them the prescience few seek and fewer still cherish. Benjamin sought many homes, but he was nowhere at home. Or, rather, he made a home of his homelessness. He threw the doors wide open, but would run away if too many accepted the invitation. It was his luck, and his tragedy, that not many did.

To describe Benjamin, is to describe the intellectual. One inconceivability compounds the other. Both are containers, rather than contents; whirlpools, that exist solely by not holding the stuff that flows through them, by having the power of setting that stuff in accelerated motion, putting paid to all stillness and rest. Pretending otherwise, trying to describe them by what they *have* rather than by what they *do*, and by what they do rather than by how are they doing it, and then to fix whatever remained of them in a psychic or social chain of causes and effects – would be, as Adorno warned us, 'to postulate precisely the standard image of a living being' which Benjamin's speculation, and even more so his life practice, exploded, 'and to which the general consensus clings all the more obdurately the less of a life life becomes.'[9]

To heed this warning is to resign ourselves to a narrative without a centre. Or rather – to borrow Pascal's simile – to a narrative whose circumference is nowhere, and thus the centre is everywhere. The centre is where we place it; and this is a right place for the centre to be, as long as we accept that this is not the only place where it is or may be placed. This is precisely what I propose to do when suggesting that Walter Benjamin be considered as the philosopher and practitioner of possibility. To consider what the possibility is, or rather what it is not, and better still when it stops being what it is, is one way to grasp what being Walter Benjamin, and more generally being the intellectual, is about.

> '*La réponse est le malheur de la question*' – wrote Blanchot, and explained it: '*dans le Oui de la réponse, nous perdons la donnée droite, immédiate, et nous perdons l'ouverture, la richesse de la possibilité . . . L'espoir dit la possibilité . . . La possibilité, ce n'est pas ce qui est seulement possible et devrait être regardé comme moins que réel. La possibilité, en ce nouveau sens, est plus que la réalité . . . La possibilité établit la réalité et la fonde.*'[10]

This is why response is the bad luck of the question. It disembowels and mummifies the possibility; it reduces it to mere reality. Then the possibility is no more; what comes instead, is so much inferior, poorer, ill founded, robbed of hope and waiting.

What we watch, with our eyes, like those of *der Angelus Satanus*, turned away from where we go and what is, because we go there, in front of us – and what we then call 'history' – is a graveyard of possibilities; coffins scattered all around the field; coffins precariously, never as neatly as one would wish, arranged in rows by the burial ground attendants called historians. Each coffin has a name attached, a singular name, but what it contains is a bundle of possibilities that had been murdered when the bearer of name died. The name belies the coffin's content: it speaks of death, not life, of fixation, not hope, not of that time of the possibility, the time in which possibility lives, which is *noch nicht geworden*. Graveyard – the celebration of death which is the ultimate response, the ultimate bad luck of the question of the life.

Benjamin – who in one of his escapades in search of belonging wished to be called a historical materialist and even tried hard to retell his philosophy in a form that would make this label, at least in his own eyes, credible – was moved by one emotion more than any other: by the spirit of rebellion against history as a graveyard of possibilities. He resented the idea of the historical narrative as a story of what has been and could not have been any other way, a story of disenchantment showing hope to be vanity; he rejected the idea of history as *Schadenfreude*, as a gleeful 'I told you so', or as a feast held on the grave of forlorn chances. It was this emotion which had drawn Benjamin, simultaneously, to Jewish messianism (in which, to quote Gershon Scholem, transcendence is 'breaking in upon history, an intrusion in which history itself perishes'[11]) and Marxism (described by Ernst Bloch as the 'billeting officer of the future', as a philosophy that 'sets hope squarely in the front' and 'does not exclude any perspective except one that would lead to a situation without good fortune').[12] It was the same emotion that made Lev Shestov, another contemporary of Benjamin's, construe a God out of the trust that 'everything is possible', that history can be annulled, so that the shameful act of poisoning Socrates would 'never have existed';[13] a God able to cancel 'all the horrors of the history of humanity', make them 'cease to exist', show the 'fact', the 'given', the 'real' not to dominate us, not to 'determine our fate either in the present, in the future or in the past', so that 'what has been becomes what has not been; man returns to the state of innocence.'[14] A God who declares that everything is possible,[15] and thereby renders history, complete with the ill-famed finality of its verdicts, irrevocability and determination, null and void; a God who cancels the responses and throws the questions wide open again.

The same emotion . . . it inspired Scholem or Rosenzweig to seek feverishly for life still smouldering in a tradition killed by indifference or ridicule;

it prompted Bloch or Lukács to allow himself to be seduced by the promise that tradition be disempowered and its hold on the future broken; it goaded Shestov to draw on the fresh experience of Russian *God-seekers* in custom-making God, in his case a God mighty and resolute enough to invalidate man-made nightmares, past and future. Benjamin must have spotted family resemblance; no wonder he was tempted, no wonder he played with all three themes, only to put them aside again – perhaps because he found them too constraining still: they all refused to allow for *all* possibilities, most notably for the possibility that possibilities are also mortal, that they may be killed and killed they are, history being the name of their mass murder.

Benjamin had no illusion that hope is immortal. Quite the contrary. Killing of hopes is the most common of human pastimes. The life of hope is brief; hope fades away before it could recognize itself as hope. Possibilities are so vulnerable, their extermination is so easy, precisely because they do not know of themselves as possibilities as long as they stay alive. One knows of them as possibilities only when they are possibilities no more. They can come to life only posthumously, in the act of resurrection – and then it will be only a spiritual resurrection, a sort of galvanization in thought of what has been extinct in the 'material world'. Possibilities come into their own only as imagined possibilities, and in this incarnation they come complete with their obituaries and gravestones. Before they are killed, they drift, plankton-like, in the carefree innocence of the *an sich*; but once they have been killed, it is too late for the *für sich*.

It is the awesome power and the exhilarating task of imagination to recapture the past possibilities, to recapture them in a mode which was not their lot ever before: in the self-conscious mode, the *für sich* mode, which they themselves never experienced when alive. The task is to 'fan the spark of hope in the past',[16] to chronicle victories which could be where the defeats were, to re-live the past as it *could be lived* – that is, in a way different from the way it was lived, in a way that cancels the present in the form given to it by those defeats. In direct contradiction to common sense, which is nothing but compliance with the accomplishment of the victors, it is the past which is, for Benjamin, the true abode of possibilities. It is in the past that they can be uncovered in the act of rebellion against historical necessity, which is then shown to be but a hideout and apology for the crimes that made the victors into victors. Historical narrative as exhumation of lost (or murdered) possibilities (an act of *construction*, rather than restitution, by Benjamin's own admission) was Benjamin's version of revolutionary action. To undermine the present where it feels most secure, in the allegedly once-for-all recorded past ('*réassaisir le rapport là où le rapport est perdu*', in Blanchot's words), to challenge the authority of latter-day verdicts, and thus to sap the arrogance of those who rule today by annulling the irrevocability of their triumphs of yesterday is the task of the historian-as-a-revolutionary. This is revolution not as binding the not-yet-gained future, but as redemption of the lost past; revolution not as mortgaging the living, but manumitting the dead.

What are the consequences of that revolution? For one, it ends any distinction between 'major' and 'minor' events, the historical and the non-historical, acts worth recording and acts unworthy of record: 'nothing that has ever happened should be regarded as lost for history'. The redemption of lost possibilities means that no event, however minute and however thoroughly forgotten, can be ignored. There are no rules to guide the historian's attention, and no excuses to relieve his conscience in case of intentional neglect. Trying to grasp a hidden order in the cheerful disorder of his legacy, Hannah Arendt defined Benjamin as a 'collector'. And a collector he was, but only because the task of redeeming missed chances dissembled history into a collection – of episodes, fragments of a yet-unwritten and never-to-be-fully-written narrative, of stories without clear origin, infinite connections and uncountable sequels. Writing history was to Benjamin the work of a collector, ever unearthing new pieces, measuring them against others already unearthed, arranging and re-arranging them on the shelves of glass cabinets where they can be examined on all sides, never being fully sure what is the right place and company for any of them. And each piece was precious, every one shimmering in the anticipation of that luminescence which is the reflection of the collector's attentive gaze, each full of expression precipitated by the collector's empathy. In the collection that wants to pass itself as history, everything is potentially a collector's item. This potentiality is one of its possibilities first denied, then lost, and now to be redeemed.

And redeemed it must be – through the historian/collector's empathy. But what is empathy? Emphatically, it is not to be achieved by following Ranke's recipe of recreating the past *wie es eigentlich gewesen ist*. Empathy is not reliving the past as it was once lived, nor forcing one's way into experiences as they were once experienced. This is not what redemption is about; this would amount to reproducing the unfreedom that ended in defeat, the suicidal innocence of the fleeting moment, the impotence of the act unaware of its chance. The actor in the focus of an historian's eye is, as Blanchot put it, 'the ephemeral character who is born and dies each evening in order to make himself extravagantly seen, killed by the performance that makes him visible.'[17] He who comes later knows what has happened after that evening, after that performance. That, because of this advantage, he can grasp the import of the performance better than the actor could, is banal. That, because of this advantage, he can grasp the performance as it never was but could be, is not at all banal; it is also, appearances apart, excruciatingly difficult. It aims at nothing less than redeeming the possibility from its inborn blemish: its inability to live its lightning-brief existence self-consciously.

The entry into the past is guarded by more than one trap. The best known (which does not mean the most innocuous or the easiest to avoid) is the trap discovered by Proust: 'he who has once begun to open the fan of memory never comes to the end of its segments; no image satisfies him, for he has seen that it can be unfolded . . . remembrance advances from small to smallest details, from the smallest to the infinitesimal, while that which it encounters in these microcosms grows ever mightier.'[18] When visited at leisure, in the land of memory time stands still, no longer hurried past by clocks. Objects, once elusive and flicking by, now become docile: they can be handled, turned around, closely examined. The past is thus a quicksand that sucks in the unwary visitor, a pit with no bottom, a landscape with no horizon. There is nothing by which to orient oneself, nothing to guide one in the choice of direction. Or, rather, each object – each sight, smell, touch, sound – vies with every other to drive and orient the wanderer, each beckoning in a different direction.

This is a trap which Proust explored for us to the bottom, finding that in the world *remembered* there is no bottom to be found, even if we remember that world as shapely, slick and neat, cut to our size, streamlined by what Alfred Schutz called 'topical relevances'- now evident, vivid and sprightly, now fuzzy, limp and puzzling. And yet there is another trap – less expected, more formidable – which was of particular concern to Benjamin. 'Transformation of material content into truth content', he observed, 'makes the decrease in effectiveness, whereby the attraction of earlier charms diminishes decade by decade, into the basis of a rebirth, in which all ephemeral beauty is completely stripped off, and the work stands as a ruin.'[19] Can the beauty of the past, that beauty which has lured us on the memory trip, be reborn and relived? That beauty was ephemeral, it shot by in one dazzling moment – no wonder that we wish to catch it in its flight, hoping that this time we will make it stand still, stay with us forever. What we find out, however, is that the beauty of that beauty lay precisely in its ephemerality. It was, indeed. the beauty of the ephemeral, the unfinished, the elusive, the not-fully-defined; the beauty of anticipation still a long way away from turning into certainty; the beauty of the *possibility* that did not know yet, and did not care to know, whether it would ever become the truth. This happy-go-lucky innocence of possibility may be lived only once. It cannot be recaptured on a memory trip. You set out on this trip in search of the lost hope: what you find out is the graveyard, the ruin, the frustration called the truth. 'The images, severed from all earlier associations . . . stand . . . like precious fragments or torsos in a collector's gallery – in the prosaic rooms of our later understanding . . . It is to cheat oneself of the richest prize to preserve as a record merely the inventory of one's discoveries, and not this dark joy of the place of the finding itself'.[20] *Dark* joy: will it be preserved, or killed, when drawn into the 'prosaic rooms of our later understanding'? And is there a way, any way at all, to preserve it without killing it? 'Prosaic rooms of our later understanding' are the second, redoubtable trap guarding the entry into the past. And how difficult, if not impossible, it is to bypass this trap, since 'the medium in which alone such images take form' is 'the present in which the writer lives'.[21] The same medium that allows you to look makes you blind to what you wished to see. But you will be totally blind if not for that medium; and there is no other medium you may take on your voyage with you. It is probably this Tiresias-style clarity of vision bought at the price of blindness, understanding obtained at the expense of hope, order purchased in exchange for beauty, which constitutes the past in its unique modality: the promised land of wisdom, the graveyard of possibilities.

The point is, though, that knowing all that does not change anything. The job is difficult, formidably so, yet it has to be done. Or, at least, one must go on doing it. More often than not the scalpel kills the very thing one wished to set free – that yet-unfulfilled possibility one wanted to liberate from the prison of history – but it still remains the only chance of keeping the possibility alive and making history a little less of a prison.

Of Edward Fuchs, whom he described as collector and historian (in that order) Benjamin wrote, with approval: 'He breaks the epoch away from its reified *historical continuity*, and the life from the epoch, and the work from the life's work'. Benjamin proceeds to lay the pragmatic rules and the apology for such practice:

> Historicism presents an eternal image of the past, historical materialism a specific and unique engagement with it. The substitution of the act of construction for the epic dimension proves to be the condition of engagement. In it those powerful forces that lie bound in the 'once-upon-a-time' of historicism are set free . . . Historical materialism conceives historical understanding as an after-life of that which is understood, whose pulse can still be felt in the present.[22]

Let there be no mistake: the 'historical materialism' of Benjamin has been made entirely to his own measure. Certainly, it was only loosely related to the historical materialism of the party that was to be one more room in the long gallery of rooms too prosaic to accommodate the ebullient solitude of Benjamin, the intellectual. Leaving party badges aside, the strategy proposed here is to go for the 'eruptive immediacy' of the moment of creation still unsure of what it is about to create and what of its work will be recorded – mummified, ossified – as history. For that voyage to what is no more, Benjamin offers the present wisdom as the guide. This self-same wisdom grew out of a history notable more for what it consigned to silence than for what it made to speak with a digitally recorded, electronically cleansed voice; a history born of forgetting, though claiming remembrance as its parentage. What is demanded here makes Munchausen's feat, pulling himself from the bog by his hair, pale in comparison. Yet nothing short of such a feat will do.

Whether such a feat could or would ever be performed is not at issue here. What matters is the way in which the very demand for such a feat, presenting its pursuit as the strategy of intellectual work, rewrites the values, shifts the priorities, and in the end transforms the concept of that material which is preserved in the flow of time as ruins made picturesque, beautified, adorned and varnished by historical narrative as heritage. This material is seen by Benjamin as the creative act, and the act of creation is the act of disruption, an unruly act, an act that rejects constraints called causal determination while being unsure of its destination; an act that breaks, simultaneously, the rule of the Law and the laws spun by the theoretical rule-seekers. This vision is in direct conflict with that other vision, the victorious vision, the vision of the victors – one promoted in theory, and above all in practice, by the political law-makers, as well as by the courtier-scholars who re-issue their practices as history and their intentions as historical laws.

The paradox is that the victorious law-makers, as far as they are successful in mortifying the flow of time into a history with a pointer, create by the same token the hope of the progress, of a movement-toward a redemption; a closely supervised and managed hope, condensed out of the now expropriated, once self-propelled hope diffuse in free creation. This practice which murders hope parades as the guardian of hope. But the two hopes could not be more different. One is the hope of infinite possibility, of making the impossible possible; the other is the hope of extinguishing the possibility that stands in the way of certainty, of rendering that possibility impossible. Benjamin's strategy is, first and foremost, concerned with unmasking this opposition and the paradox which sustains it. But unmasking it means exploding the carefully cultivated myth of time-as-progress. It means the disenchantment of history as a telos-guided movement, movement with a pointer – but in order to re-enchant it as a site of infinitely potent creation. It means consigning progress to where it truly belongs: to history as the slaughter-house and graveyard of possibilities, to historical narrative as a catalogue of the museum. But it also means replacing the false certainty of progress with the unprocessed, untamed, undomesticated hope of free creation.

To disenchant history as progress means to disavow the self-proclaimed history-makers: 'Not to take sides, but to stay outside the arena where sides are drawn and taken; not to rebel against this or that claim to the guardianship of history and the execution of its laws, but to dismiss the very act of claim-making'. This refusal to join in the fray is also taking sides of sorts, though none of those 'standing on the side of history' would recognize it as such. It is taking the side of freedom which shares the fate of possibility, which lives as long as possibility stays alive and dies the moment possibility is incarcerated or killed. The disengagement from history-making as the closure of possibilities is the one and only engagement the intellectual is capable of without turning into the courtier, and the one and only intellectual commitment Benjamin would approve of without caveats, and practice through his life. In his suicide, he embraced what seemed to him the last possibility in a world that was to cleanse itself of possibilities once and for all. He refused to survive his freedom.

Taking the side of possibility, enthroning possibility as the supreme value, means to mock the dreams of certainty, foundation, destiny. It means irony. In Hans Sahl's words, 'unmasking reality' by unmasking 'the impotence of the word worn by reality as a façade'.[23] Sahl does not think much of such a strategy. The 'unmasking of reality', he says, 'remained only an interpretation, limping behind reality'. *Only* an interpretation; to say this is to misunderstand Benjamin's strategy at its core. Far from being a weak and inferior substitute for the real 'blasting off' of reality, interpretation is the supreme, most formidable of weapons freedom may wield in its never fully won, never fully lost struggle with the paralysing and immobilizing powers that strive to build reality on its grave. To interpret, to re-interpret, to unmask the impotence of the word, to demonstrate the non-finality and inconclusiveness of all interpretation, to show all and any interpretation as 'one of many': these are ways to re-empower freedom against reality which founds its pretence on belief in the opposite. 'There is no alternative', 'there is no choice', 'this is the truth'; such phrases belong to the rhetoric of power eager to announce the death of possibility so that it can wear the ceremonial dress of reality unmolested.

Pierre V. Zima found a striking parallel between the role Benjamin assigns to the intellectual as intrepid interpreter, and Bakhtin's model of the carnival culture. 'À l'inverse de la culture officielle qui ne reconnait que la *différence absolue* et le *monologue*, le carnaval met en scène la coincidence des contraires et la pluralité des voix: la *polyphonie*.'[24] In a blatantly polyphonic, carnival-like world (unlike the humourless world of official culture which leaves differences the choice between the finality of estrangement or a death sentence, and which views all polyphony as a short interruption in the normality of monologue) the Hegelian *Aufhebung*, the Hegelian *bestimmte Negation*, that bridge to a new affirmation and new positivity, is not a plausible prospect. In this world, the *Aufhebung* is itself *aufgehoben*, and in a Nietzschean, rather than Hegelian, fashion. In this world, differences are neither absolute nor temporary. To show them like that, to unmask that ambivalence which is reality's most closely guarded secret, is to shock; hopefully, to shock into freedom. This is what Benjamin's *Chokerlebnis*, like Bakhtin's *laughter* or Adorno's *negativity*, is about. This is what the defence of freedom is about: the defence against the twin dangers of the absolutization of differences and the temptation to sacrifice the dialectics of opposition at the altar of the new affirmation.

As Ferenc Fehér pointed out, in Benjamin, as in Brecht (whose art was Benjamin's unfading fascination)[25] the traditional aesthetics of catharsis has been replaced by that of shock and astonishment. Cartharsis implies the presence of a moral order in the world surrounding the drama. Shock implies its absence: the shock is the discovery of its absence. Catharsis means the domestication of the bizarre. It leads back to the normal and the familiar, and it lends the normal all the allurements of safe haven. Shock promises nothing but more turbulence and navigation that never ends. Since history does not move, self-propelled, towards an end that is the salvation – working towards redemption that may never come can be done only, as Richard Wolin suggested, by obtaining and sharing the insight into the complexity and endemic ambivalence of the world that prevails.[26]

In a history without evolution, life becomes a disrupted continuum; or, rather, a continuum of disruptions. In Fehér's opinion,[27] Benjamin 'was the perfect embodiment of the principle of Adorno formulated in his aesthetics as the maxim of our age: where there are no certitudes, experiments are legitimate'. They are the only legitimate actions, as the possibilities life entails are not known and cannot be known in advance; nor are they guaranteed or foreclosed beforehand by preordained destiny of historical evolution. Benjamin's 'indifference to canons and certitudes' was consistent with his notorious inconsistency, manifested in 'the parallel pursuit of clearly irreconcilable paths of research' and, let us add, his treating as complementary philosophies that wished to be mutually exclusive and finish each other off. Benjamin, the intellectual, stubbornly refused to partake of the game of exclusion, which always is but a thinly disguised game of monopoly. Benjamin's famed eclecticism, for which players of that game could never forgive him, was but recognition of the close affinity between freedom and ambivalence.

The strategy of Benjamin, the intellectual, is not a strategy of redemption. It is, instead, a strategy of keeping the ground ready for redemption, if the redemption comes; and of making sure that, if it comes, it is recognized for what it is (the Messiah, as Kafka suggested, comes only the day after his arrival . . .). Contrary to many opinions, this strategy does not detract from the importance of intellectual work; nor does it deprive it of urgency. If anything, the contrary is the case. In a history without a telos and a pointer, without a deterministic chain pulled ahead and thus kept straight by its still invisible, yet fully defined end, without a pragmatically correct programme for what is to be done to assist that end in its effort – in such a history, every moment, every 'now' becomes pregnant with significance, a non-contrived and not borrowed significance, a significance all of its own. Benjamin's time has no logic nor preordained consistency, as Stephane Moses admirably shows in a recent study.[28] It is a fractured, fragmented time, in which every instant carries a weight escaping all advance measure: the 'impossible' may arrive every moment, hiding its determination to the last second. In that time, the most important departures happen without apparent rhyme or reason. All decisive blows, we remember Benjamin saying, have been delivered with the left hand . . .

NOTES

1. 'The Departure', transl. Tania and James Stern; in: *The Collected Short Stories of Franz Kafka*, ed. Nahum N. Clatzer, Harmondsworth: Penguin 1988, p499.
2. 'Introduction to Benjamin's *Schriften*'; in: *On Walter Benjamin, Critical Essays and Recollections*, ed. by Gary Smith, Cambridge Mass.: MIT Press 1988, p15.
3. Edmond Jabès, *The Book of Dialogue*, transl. Rosemarie Waldrop, Middleton: Wesleyan UP 1987, p55.
4. Walter Benjamin, *Charles Baudelaire: A Lyric Poet in the Era of High Capitalism*, transl. Harry Zohn, London: Verso 1983, p75.
5. Maurice Blanchot, *The Siren's Song: Selected Essays*, transl. Sacha Rabinovitch, Bloomington: Indiana UP 1982, p139.
6. Rainer Rochlitz, 'De la philosophie comme critique littéraire', in: *Revue d'Esthétique*, 1981, No.1, p43.
7. Gerschon Scholem, *Walter Benjamin: The Story of Friendship*, New York: Faber & Faber 1982, pp229, 234.
8. Geneviève Brisac, 'Le grains de blé de Benjamin', in: *Le Monde*, 6 March 1992, p25.
9. 'Benjamin the Letter Writer', in: *On Walter Benjamin....* p330.
10. Maurice Blanchot, *L'Entretien infini*, Paris: Gallimard 1969, pp14, 59.
11. Gershon Scholem, *The Messianic Idea in Judaism*, London: Allen and Unwin 1971, p10.

12. Ernst Bloch, *On Marx*, transl. John Maxwell, New York: Herder & Herder 1971, pp34, 41.
13. Lev Shestov, *Umozrenie i Otkrov'enie* (Contemplation and Revelation), Paris: YMCA Press 1964.
14. Lev Shestov, *Athens and Jerusalem*, transl. Bernard Martin, Athens: Ohio UP, p68.
15. Nicolai Berdiayev's introduction to Lev Shestov's *Umozrenie i Otkrovenie*; also his *Tipy religiarnoi mysl v Rosii* (The Types of Religious Thought in Russia), Paris: YMCA Press 1989, p400.
16. Walter Benjamin, 'Theses on the Philosophy of History', in: *Illuminations: Essays and Reflections*, transl. Harry Zohn, New York: Schocken Books 1968, p255.
17. Maurice Blanchot, *Vicious Circles*, transl. Paul Aster, New York Station Hill 1985, p60.
18. Walter Benjamin, 'A Berlin Chronicle', in: *One Way Street and Other Writings*, transl. Edmund Jephcott, London: Verso 1985, p296.
19. Walter Benjamin, *The Origin of German Tragic Drama*, transl. John Osborne.
20. Walter Benjamin, 'A Berlin Chronicle', p314.
21. *Ibid.*
22. Walter Benjamin, 'Edward Fuchs, Collector and Historian', in: *One Way Street*, p352.
23. Hans Sahl, 'Walter Benjamin in the Internment Camp', in: *On Walter Benjamin....* p347.
24. Pierre V. Zima, 'L'ambivalence dialectique: entre Benjamin and Bakhtin', in: *On Walter Benjamin*, p131.
25. Ferenc Fehér, 'Lukács, Benjamin, Theatre', in: Agnes Heller and Ferenc Fehér, *The Grandeur and Twilight of Radical Universalism*, New Brunswick: Transactions Publishers 1991.
26. Richard Wolin, *Walter Benjamin, An Aesthetic of Redemption*, New York: Columbia UP 1982.
27. Ferenc Fehér, 'Lukács and Benjamin: Parallels and Contrasts', in: *The Grandeur and Twilight....* p303.
28. Stéphane Mosès, *L'Ange de l'Histoire: Rosenzweig, Benjamin*, Scholem, Paris: Seuil 1992.

WALTER BENJAMIN – OUT OF THE SOURCES OF MODERN JUDAISM

Gillian Rose

'There is nothing as whole as a cleft heart.'
(Rabbi Menachem Mendel of Kotsk)[1]

I

In a review of Robert Alter's recently published book, *Necessary Angels: Tradition and Modernity in Kafka, Benjamin and Scholem*,[2] S.S. Prawer subtly questions the wisdom of understanding Kafka, Benjamin and Scholem without looking beyond Judaism, with what Alter calls its 'classic triad' of revelation, law, and commentary,[3] to the German tradition, especially Goethe and romanticism, which 'they did not shake off when they turned to French literature or to Jewish mysticism, and further, to the concerns of 'the wider gentile world of tradition and modernity.'[4]

In the case of Benjamin, however, Prawer's understated scruple against reductionism is otiose, not only in the face of Alter's own nuanced approach to the paradoxes of language and identification (a central chapter in his book is entitled 'On Not Knowing Hebrew'),[5] but also in view of the rich and substantial body of criticism already in existence in which reference to the Jewish dimensions of Benjamin's life and work helps to clarify precisely the tremendous scope of his interests – from the mourning play to Marxism to messianism. Moreover, this body of criticism has not assumed that Judaism is itself secure as tradition but has problematized the 'crisis' of Judaism and of Jewish identity. With different emphases, this approach is evident in Scholem's own essays on Benjamin and his Angel, and in his remarkable account of their friendship;[6] in Hannah Arendt's famous essay on Benjamin in *Men in Dark Times*;[7] in T.W. Adorno's essay on Benjamin in *Prisms*;[8] in Jürgen Habermas's essay on Benjamin's 'redemptive criticism';[9] and, more recently in Iriving Wohlfarth's aptly named study, 'On Some Jewish Motifs in Benjamin.'[10]

Nevertheless, it could be argued that none of these studies have distinguished clearly enough how Benjamin related fundamental elements of Judaism – tradition, commentary, Messianism – to specifically modern

Jewish philosophical reflection on tradition and modernity. While Benjamin's relation to Franz Rosenzweig's great *Star of Redemption* and to Rosenzweig's philosophy of language have received attention from Stéphane Mosès and others,[11] there exists little study of Benjamin's relation to neo-Kantianism, especially to his reception of Hermann Cohen's platonizing neo-Kantianism.[12] Cohen's mathesis of the origin (*der Ursprung*), developed in the *Logic*, which forms the first part of his three part System, also provides the mathesis of his late work, *Religion of Reason out of the Sources of Judaism*.[13] While he sought to overcome the structure of neo-Kantianism, it is this grammar of origin which Benjamin opposes to the logic of idealism in the 'Epistemo-Critical Prologue' to *The Origin of German Trauerspiel*. And this is why the title of this paper alludes to Benjamin's inheritance from Cohen's great work – 'out of the sources of Judaism.'

In this paper, written to celebrate the centenary of Benjamin's birth, I hope to develop a new approach to assessing Benjamin's thought 'out of the sources of modern Judaism.' Here it will not be a question of referring to Judaism, whether traditional or modern, in order to demonstrate the patterning of Benjamin's complex work; on the contrary, I shall propose a way of understanding the complexity of Benjamin's work which will itself yield the difficulty of his relation to Judaism. This illumination of Benjamin's thinking will make it possible *to derive the meaning that Judaic categories exhibit in it*. Since Benjamin's thinking will be engaged comprehensively, the emergence of the Jewish question cannot diminish the focus of Benjamin's vision. This should also satisfy Prawer's discretion.

II

At the heart of Goethe's novel, *Wilhelm Meister's Apprenticeship*, lies the story of 'the beautiful soul.'[14] Borrowing from Goethe's novel within a novel, Hegel makes her story the pivot of the section of the *Phenomenology of Spirit*, 'Conscience. The "beautiful soul," evil and forgiveness,'[15] which concludes the path of objective spirit. 'The beautiful soul' is a learned but sickly female, who comes to reject marriage, aristocratic courts and the activities of the new class of Burghers. She retires from the world to cultivate her deepening religious piety, but, in spite of her perspicacity, she fails to find any means of public expression, or any bridge back to ethical and political life. In both Goethe's and Hegel's recounting, she pines away in consumption and dies.

This *image* of 'the beautiful soul' (who cannot, in fact, be pictured because her 'beauty' is not aesthetic but *ascetic*) is *dialectical*, for it captures the impotence that results from excessive religious zeal, which opposes the world in the name of an inner, individual Protestantism, or, collectively, in the name of the brethren of the common life – a pre-Reformation community of lay celibates, women and men, whose idea and organization were adopted in the eighteenth century by Pietist communities, especially the community of Herrnhut, led by Count Zinzendorf, to which Goethe refers by name in his novel in connection with 'the beautiful soul'.[16] The concentration on the image of 'the beautiful soul' exhibits what Benjamin called *dialectics at a standstill*, for she bears no fruit – her body disintegrates as her soul swells – and she returns in death to fallen nature, neither realized nor redeemed. This zealous and melancholy profile, caught in a narrative, forms a constellation with earlier and later times.[17]

What Goethe, Hegel, Kierkegaard,[18] Weber and, I shall argue, Benjamin, have in common is probably most familiar from Max Weber: the investigation of *the unintended consequences* of the Protestant Ethic.[19] Protestant legitimation of one's worldly vocation – a vocation which may demonstrate but which may never earn individual salvation – results in 'worldly asceticism.' The Lutheran doctrine of 'the calling' and the Calvinist doctrine of predestination produce the sober, methodical organization of everyday life. Weber explored the connection between the Protestant ethic and 'the spirit of capitalism:' the worldly asceticism which establishes the preconditions for the development of rational, capitalist accumulation and investment. Goethe, Hegel and Kierkegaard, and, I shall argue, Benjamin, explored further *the unintended psychological and political consequences* of Protestant *Innerlichkeit* (inwardness) and worldly asceticism. They followed the way in which the Protestant doctrine of salvation creates hypertrophy of the inner life. Hypertrophy of the inner life is correlated with atrophy of political participation. Eventually, the interest in salvation itself atrophies, but the inner anxiety of salvation persists and is combined with worldly opportunity and ruthlessness; this combination of anxiety and ruthlessness amounts to the combination of inner and outer violence.

To Goethe, Hegel and Weber, the eighteenth-century German Pietism represented the attempt to establish a reformation of the Reformation, which, alas, resulted in yet another set of paradoxical or 'unintended' outcomes. In its reaction to burgeoning bourgeois legality with its excessively autonomous individuality as well as in its reaction to the remnants of the aristocratic ethic, Pietism produces a more extreme asceticism – more emotional inwardly, and organized outwardly to render 'the invisible Church of the elect visible on this earth.'[20] In Goethe and Hegel, 'the beautiful soul' offers the image of this kind of piety: intelligent, bookish, and intense, she mourns a world which she cannot and will not join; her increased subjective freedom represents a decrease in objective freedom, an incapacity for and a refusal of political participation. She mourns a world which she has no reason to mourn – because it is not lost: it is beginning.

III

Walter Benjamin, it will be argued here, investigates 'the Baroque Ethic and the Spirit of Fascism.' He extends the exploration of the Protestant ethic from Protestant or Pietist inwardness to the inwardness of the Protestantism of the Counter-Reformation, to nineteenth-century French Catholic inwardness, and to the inwardness of Jewish modernity. These forms of inwardness are correlated with the transition from *worldly asceticism to worldy aestheticism*, from worldly renunciation to worldly ornamentation (the Baroque ethic of worldly aestheticism persists from the seventeenth century to the twentieth century). They are also correlated with the transition from the end of politics in the spirit of capitalism to aestheticized politics in the spirit of Fascism. While the Protestant Ethic leads to *the withering of the interest in salvation without loss of the anxiety of salvation*, the Baroque ethic evinces a created and creaturely world with the aspiration but *without the promise of redemption*. In Judaic categories, this spiritual condition gives rise to the messianic fixation. For the Messianic fixation in Judaism always indicates *a disgrace or disorder in the relation to revelation*. ('Revelation' in Judaism means the Written and the Oral Law, the teaching and its interpretation, not the redeeming death of Christ which effects individual salvation.) Benjamin expresses this disgrace of revelation as 'the decay of aura' or 'transmission without truth'.[21] The object, style and mood of Benjamin's philosophy converge, not in the Christian mournfulness or melancholy, discerned from the Baroque *Trauerspiel* to Baudelaire, but in the Judaic state of desertion – in Hebrew, *agunah* – the stasis which his agon with the law dictates.

In philosophical terms, the spirit of Fascism does not mean that spiritual value is accorded to Fascism, but that Benjamin derives the meaning of 'Fascism' from the violence of its relation to actuality – this is spirit in Hegel's sense of misrecognition of otherness. Fascist violence is itself derived from the change in the structure of experience – the subjectivity which issues from and responds to the atrophy of substance.

Benjamin is the *taxonomist of sadness*, and he adds figures of melancholy to the philosophical repertoire of modern experiences: the repertoire which includes stoicism, scepticism, the unhappy consciousness, resignation and *ressentiment*. But his figures of melancholy – baroque, Baudelaire, Kafka, 'left-wing,' the angel of history – are not counterposed to recognition, love, forgiveness or faith: and therefore their mourning is not completed; it remains *aberrated* not *inaugurated*. The figures of melancholy are counterposed instead to the Divine, which is characterized by pure violence or pure language, and is approachable in mimesis or correspondences. The accessibility of the Divine in mimesis and correspondences eschews law or mediation or representation. As a result, subjective, fallen, melancholy judgement can only be overthrown by the expiation of bloodless violence of a new, divine immediacy – the general strike, the distracted cinema audience, a Socialist emergency law (to oppose the Fascist emergency), the Messiah.

If the dialectical image of Pietist melancholy is 'the beautiful soul,' then the dialectical image of the baroque melancholy is the *agunah* – the deserted wife, who has not been sent a bill of divorce and who does not know if her husband is still alive; she may not remarry nor does she even know whether she may embark on mourning. In the tales of the modern Hebrew writer, S.Y. Agnon, which Benjamin cherished, everybody is in a state of desertion, including the *shekhinah*, the Divine Presence in the world.[22] The aim of this centenary reflection is to move from *aberrated to inaugurated* mourning to break the hard heart of subjective judgement; to soften the rigid stare of the *Angelus Novus*, the angel of history.

Strictly speaking, there is no Judaic theology[23] – no logos of God – because Rabbinic Judaism, formed in post-biblical times, is the creation of the Rabbis, who, claiming to be the rightful heirs of the prophets, established *Talmud Torah* at the focus of Jewish life. *Talmud Torah* means the teaching of the teaching, or the commentary on the law. Its validity derives from the tradition that the Oral Law as well as the Written Law were revealed to Moses on Sinai. The Oral law was handed down to the Elders, and thence to the Rabbis, who eventually wrote it down, first in the *Mishnah* and then in the *Talmud*.[24] The Oral Law is also called 'the commandment' and 'the interpretation.'[25] Now, if there is, strictly speaking, no Judaic theology, there can be no theological notions of creation, revelation and redemption. However, to characterize Judaism philosophically, it is often necessary to resort to these notions. The key to the three must be 'revelation,' for it is only according to revelation that nature can be seen as created, and that redemption is either proclaimed or promised. In Christianity, the Redeemer lives and the repentant, individual soul is saved. In Judaism, the Messiah is promised and life is lived in view of this deferment; redemption, when it comes, will be universal – it is promised to the whole world, not just to the Jews.

Scholem has shown in many of his studies that while Messianism in its deferment is always an ingredient of Judaic self-definition, it only tends to become urgently and exclusively definitive of Jewish peoples in emergencies when they are politically and mortally endangered – by expulsion, pogrom, or persecution. Settled and relatively secure communities are not intensely eschatological; they live within the repetition of the liturgy and the study of the law.[26] Similarly, the Kabbalistic, or mystical tradition, redefines the meaning of the Written and Oral Law so as to bypass the rigorous complaisance of life lived according to *Talmud Torah*. The black letters of the Written Law are themselves understood as a specification of the whiteness between the letters, so that the Written Law itself is already an interpretation of God's unknowable name. The former divine word is already oral, already transmission.[27] Scholem points out how Martin Buber and Franz Rosenzweig approach this Kabbalistic antinomianism when, in a now famous correspondence, they agree that the meaning of revelation is not ritual, not law – even if understood as commandment – but the sheer event of revelation itself – 'I am I.'[28]

IV

From the early philosophical and short essays to the *Arcades* work and to the so-called theses on the concept of history, I shall argue, Benjamin expounds 'the Baroque Ethic and the Spirit of Fascism' – the mournful character, equally creature of subjective judgement and sovereign of the violent politics of law-abolishing emergency. *The disgrace of revelation*, by which I mean a revelation which stamps the creature and the creaturely world of nature as forever lacking grace, that is, with no hope of redemption, this disgrace of revelation, is evident from the beginning in Benjamin's essays on language and mimesis. These essays develop the neo-Kantian metaphysics which unifies religion and philosophy for which Benjamin called,[29] by bypassing the notion of law – whether understood as regularity, imperative (normative), or lawlikeness without law.

In the essay 'On Language as Such and the Language of Man,' language is defined as naming, not as verbal, grammatical, propositional, judgemental or logical. 'Linguistic being' consists in the communicability of naming, the unfallen language of man to God.[30] This idea of the universality and intensiveness of names as the condition of communication precedes *meaning*: 'There is no such thing as a meaning [*einen Inhalt*] of language.'[31] 'Meaning' assumes a problematic relationship between the inexpressible and unexpressed mental entity and language, while the thesis of the communicability of names defines *revelation*: 'the inviolability' of the name is 'the only and sufficient condition and characteristic of the divinity of the mental being that is expressed in it.'[32] Revelation, on this argument, is encompassed by the second story of the Creation in the first chapter of the book of *Genesis* in the gift of language: 'In God name is creative because it is word, and God's word is cognizant because it is name. "And he saw that it was good;" that is He had cognized it through name.'[33]

Created from God's word, the thing in itself is known in its name by a human word which effects the translation of things into the language of man. Through translation God's unspoken word becomes the naming word in the knowledge of man. However, 'knowledge of good and evil abandons name, it is a knowledge from outside, the uncreative imitation of the creative word.'[34] The Fall is the fall of 'the eternal purity of names' into 'the sterner purity of the judging word':[35] it gives rise to a new immediacy, the magic of judgement, to language as a means, as mere sign, to abstraction. Judgement is ambiguous: both a new immediacy and the mediation of abstraction: 'This immense irony marks the mythic origin of law.'[36] After the Fall, the tree of knowledge of good and evil becomes the emblem of language fallen into judgement.

After the Fall, the original bliss of mute nature, now named by man, turns into a deep sadness:

> After the Fall, however, when God's word curses the ground, the appearance of nature is deeply changed. Now begins its other muteness, which we mean by the deep sadness of nature. It is a metaphysical truth that all nature would begin to lament if it were endowed with language.[37]

'This proposition has a double meaning.' It means that nature would lament language, and that nature would lament. Lament, Benjamin comments, is 'the most undifferentiated, impotent expression of sadness.' Nature mourns because she is mute but it is her sadness that makes her mute:

> In all mourning there is the deepest inclination to speechlessness, which is infinitely more than inability or disinclination to communicate. That which mourns feels itself thoroughly known by the unknowable. To be named – even when the namer is Godlike and blissful – perhaps always remains an intimation of mourning. But how much more melancholy to be named not from the one blessed, paradisiac language of names, but from the hundred languages of man, in which name has already withered, yet which, according to God's pronouncement, have knowledge of things . . .
>
> In the language of men, however, [things] are over-named . . . over-naming as the deepest linguistic reason for all melancholy and (from the point of view of the thing) of all deliberate muteness.[38]

Benjamin's distinctions and elisions between 'melancholy,' 'mourning' and 'lament' indicate *several specific challenges* to the Judaic tradition apparently recovered here. To the tradition (the Oral Law) the Fall is the occasion of loss and gain; it delineates the precondition of human passion and action. Lamentation over the condition of exile is not 'impotent': on the contrary, it is the strongest thing: it is the recovery of strength by moving from refusal of loss to acknowledgment and acceptance, 'receiving everything back.' Revelation is not creation, not naming, but commandment and love, the commandment to love the Lord with all one's might. To the tradition, the dominion of the tree of knowledge marks the transition from unitary, unrestrained life to the duality of good and evil. The distinctions of good and evil, commandment and prohibition, holy and profane, pure and impure, are the appearance of *Torah* in this aspect of revelation which prevails prior to regaining the unity of life.[39] For Benjamin, however, the birthing of law is absolute loss, so he employs Greek terms for its *adventus*: 'This immense irony marks the mythical origin of law.' 'Myth' belongs to Greek religion, 'irony' to Greek philosophy. This inaccessibility of revelation as God's silent language is far more nugatory and abandoned than the secret of revelation in antinomian, apocalyptic Kabbalistic Messianism. No wonder, in sooth, it is so sad. However, to fulfil the promise of the taxonomy of sadness, it is sad in the sense of the mournfulness of desertion, *agunah, aberrated* mourning, not the sadness of true mourning and lamentation, of being 'thoroughly known by the unknowable,' *inaugurated* mourning.[40]

Torah has its origin in God. According to Maimonides, the *Torah* exists with God in eternity before the creation of the world. To Benjamin, the origin of law in the Fall either provokes the melancholy response of nature and man, the creaturely world, in the face of inexorable judgement; or the response of heroic genius, the speechlessness of the hero in Greek tragedy, who breaches 'the demonic determination of legal statutes'; or the response of comic genius of character in Greek comedy who breaches, in his amoral persistence, the fate of guilt by which the law makes the impersonal into the measure of the personal, the individual.[41] The only complete response to the violence of law-making and law-preserving, the violence in law, would be divine, the law in violence, which is only conceivable as God's anarchy.

Since the Epistles of Paul and the Gospels, Judaism has borne the opprobrium of the evangelical opposition of Christian love to pharisiacal law. In the modern period, the further connotations of 'positive' or 'human' law (without the Christian criterion of natural law) can accrue to *Torah* if it is translated as *law*, when it would be more accurately translated as *teaching* or *instruction*. These inherited difficulties in the presentation of Judaic motifs, as well as their ambivalent relation to the tradition of cultural orthodoxy, lead Buber and Rosenzweig to dissociate the idea of the divine from the idea of law. In their thought, the divine is *dialogue*, or *love* in opposition to the fallen world of law; God is diadic not triadic – divine anarchy. As a result, the difference between modern and pre-modern law cannot be conceived by these apologies for Judaism. As boundary-destroying agapic love, this conception of God falls to Nietzsche's criticism of Pauline love: that it is violent in its annihilation of bonds and boundaries.[42]

Benjamin displays the same unease with the traditional conceptuality of *Torah*. He, too, conceives all law as pagan, mythic violence, as law-making and law-preserving violence; but, to my knowledge, he is the only modern, Jewish thinker who is consistent enough to realize that this violence in law has implications for the idea of God. To avoid transferring the world's violence in law to God's violence in love, Benjamin defines divine sovereignty not as love but as law-abolishing *violence*.

In his essay the 'Critique of Violence,' it is not violence which is criticized, but any notion of the rule of law, the law of the constitution or representative institutions. All visible law is mythic law-making violence which posits and changes boundaries and laws even as it claims to be policing established ones. State power is 'legal violence,' 'bloody power over mere life for its own sake.' Only the violence of God or the general strike, which is invisible because total, can counter the partial and bloody violences of the law. This divine or sovereign violence abolishes law by destroying boundaries without making new ones. It is boundlessly expiatory; without demanding sacrifices, it accepts them.[43]

Benjamin comes near to the idea of *Talmud Torah* when he contrasts the commandment as a guideline (not a criterion) and its educative potential[44] with the versatility of mythic law-making violence, which invests people with guilt not punishment. But he maintains the strict opposition between the pagan feast of law-making violence, ranging from the Greek to the modern state, the violence in law, and divine violence, either invisible in act, visible in outcome, or in the general strike effecting the suspending of violence because it has no programme, no utopia, no law-making.[45] Consequently, the idea of mediation or negotiation which lights up in the idea of commandment is quickly extinguished. There is no way to distinguish law-abolishing violence from law-making violence that *decides* in the state of emergency to usurp divinity, because there is no recognizable rule of law and no benign or wise judgement, no *phronesis*. The Tower of Babel triumphant is conceivable.

This outline of the baroque ethic and the spirit of fascism is drawn in these early, seminal pieces. The mournfulness of creaturely being, set in language and deserted by God, experiences the world as *excess of signification without salvation*, which is the meaning of worldly aestheticization, not truth as beauty but ornamentation without truth – *the baroque ethic*. Restricted by its mythic origin to law-making and law-preserving violence, subjective judgement beholds itself in the phantasmagoria of soulless personifications of this mythic law. Seeking in desperation the unobtainable redemption, *the spirit of fascism* usurps divine violence in the spectacle of war which is to abolish the boundaries of the world. The invisible Church of the elect is to be visible on earth.

To express this in the terms of Benjamin's so-called 'Theologico-Political Fragment,' the Messianism prefigured in the cosmic violence of total passing away and the inner man's suffering of misfortune in isolation[46] is appropriated by Fascism for a theocracy of imminent and immanent end. To strive to accept eternal transience is 'the task of world politics,' that is, the politics that would abolish the fallen world, a method that 'must be called nihilism.'[47] This politics presupposes the inner man in isolation, able to bear a suffering that promises neither realization nor redemption. *E contrario*, it implies misfortune which is unable to bear this suffering, a thirst for the realization of entreated redemption, for the politics of the world, and total perdition.

V

> The baroque writer felt bound in every particular to the ideal of an absolutist constitution, as was upheld by the Church of both confessions.[48]

The Origin of German Trauerspiel explores the transition from the Protestant ethic to the Baroque ethic, from Lutheran and Calvinist salvation, with its ethic of worldly asceticism and its outcome in the rational spirit of capitalism, to the loss of salvation, characteristic of German Protestantism and Spanish Catholicism of the Counter-Reformation, with its ethic of worldly aestheticism and its outcome in the violent spirit of Fascism. This is to propose three, potentially disturbing theses: that Benjamin's account of the origin of Fascism is contained in his exploration of seventeenth century Baroque drama; that our tendency to melancholy, however intellectual and passive, is violent; that Benjamin analyses, or breaks down, but he also fixes what he discerns.

If the Reformation delivered religion from the hands of the Pope to the hands of the Prince, then the Baroque inherits the Princely sovereign, recipient of this absolute power. The double dangers of political authority and of religious authority are concentrated in the Prince, whose melancholy autocracy results in the rule of tyrant, martyr or, most dangerous of all, the intriguer. The complementary Lutheran doctrines of salvation, 'justification by faith alone,' and 'the priesthood of all believers,' have turned into *the Princedom of all believers*; every unscrupulous action is justified in a world where signification has been separated from salvation. This excess of signification is baroque ornamentation, worldly aestheticization. The powerless melancholy of the contemplative and feckless Prince bestows on the intriguer the licence to exploit his own melancholy. The loss of salvation, of 'value rationality,' together with the instrumental rationalization of the world, transformed the initial Protestant release of worldly energy into what Weber called 'the iron cage', (*ein stälhartes Gehäuse*), and 'the house of bondage' (*ein Gehäuse der Hörigheit*) – the biblical phrase for the captivity and enslavement of the Jews in Egypt, who were liberated in the Exodus, in the redemption of hostages by God. The difficulty or end of politics which ensues when that redemption does not obtain was the stasis which preoccupied Weber's authorship; the violence of aestheticized politics which ensues when that redemption does not obtain was the stasis, 'the pile of debris,' which preoccupied Benjamin's.

Both the method and the content of *The Origin of German Trauerspiel* display the logic of baroque mournfulness. The famously difficult 'Epistemo-Critical Prologue' to the book is best read as the text to which the rest of the book provides the introduction. For the 'Prologue,' couched in the Platonizing neo-Kantianism of Cohen, speaks of the salvation and redemption of the world of phenomena in a way which *presupposes* the loss of salvation and disgrace of revelation in a world of beings who know themselves to be creatures, not natural beings. This presupposes the account of *Trauerspiel* to come. Both Kantian deduction and Platonic derivation of the phenomenal world are disqualified in the 'Prologue'; method and anamnesis are to be replaced by the truth of names. Names, 'unimpaired by cognitive meaning', are linguistic displays of Ideas, which are not prototypes but 'constellations,' 'Faustian mothers.'[49] They 'do not make the similar identical, but they effect a synthesis between extremes.'[50] The name of names is 'the Origin' (*der Ursprung*) which has nothing to do with genesis (*die Entstehung*):

> The term origin is not intended to describe the process by which the existent came into being, but rather to describe that which emerges from the process of becoming and disappearance.[53]

Not fully factual, 'its rhythm is apparent only to a dual insight' of singularity and repetition.[52] This dual insight bears the hallmark of Cohen's 'logic of origin,' for Benjamin's 'Idea' and 'phenomena' are not synthesized, but, no longer distinguished from the noumenal world (unknowable things in themselves), they hold in an asymptotic relation whose tenability is giving by the origin or mathesis – what Benjamin calls, 'the Faustian mothers.' Cohen's System also abolishes epistemology and Kantian *Kritikismus* for an ultimate logic of redemption. The methodological nihilism of names has the same origin as *Trauerspiel* itself – 'the instrument of lamentation and its resonance.'[53]

> The baroque knows no eschatology . . . no mechanism by which all earthly things are gathered in together and exalted before being consigned to their end. The hereafter is emptied of everything which contains the slightest breath of this world, and from it the baroque extracts a profusion of things which customarily escaped the grasp of artistic formulation and, at its high point, brings them violently into the light of day, in order to clear an ultimate heaven, enabling it, as a vacuum, one day to destroy the world with catastrophic violence.[54]

In the seventeenth century, *Trauerspiel* referred to historical events as well as dramas; it presupposes the new concept of absolute sovereignty which 'marked the final collapse of the theocratic concept of the state,' and the need for kings and princes to maintain power, resist harmful counsel and avert the state of emergency power.[55] The tyrant, the martyr and the intriguer, the three faces of the monarch, are the characters this sovereignty may take when regal action 'is no longer integrated into the process of redemption.'[56] The persistence of religious aspiration in spite of the increasing worldliness of Protestants and Jesuits of the Counter-Reformation and the absence of a divine plan of salvation 'lead to a complete revolution of the content of life, while orthodox ecclesiastical forms were preserved.'[57] The king 'proves to be a secularized redemptive power' who may resolve 'the conflicts of a state of creation without grace.'[58]

> As its vocational ethic so emphatically proclaims, Lutheran moralism was always intent on bringing together the transcendence of the life of faith and the immanence of everyday life; it therefore never permitted the decisive confrontation between human-earthly perplexity and princely-hierarchical power on which the conclusion of so many of Calderon's dramas depends.[59]

This ethic of the Spanish Counter-Reformation comes to prevail over the original German Protestant ethic. Lutheran moralism, which correlated inner faith with the everyday world brings about the rise and fall of Princes. The tyrant, arbitrary and emotional, combines absolute power of decision with severe indecisiveness;[60] while the martyr is a 'radical stoic' who 'fortifies [herself] against a state of emergency in the soul' and acts regardless of her own downfall – for the martyr is frequently a chaste woman.[61] However, the most dangerous face of sovereignty is the intriguer, 'all intellect and will-power.'[62] This is the baroque ethic *par excellence*, 'the unique ambiguity of . . . spiritual sovereignty,' which requires 'both strict inner discipline and unscrupulous external action.'[63] This strict discipline in a creature 'stripped of all naive impulses'[64] may produce a saint or an evil genius. The combination of 'icy disillusion' and 'the fierce aspiration of the will to power . . . awakens a mood of mourning,' in the intriguer, which is infernal in the Protestant dramas, tranquil in the Spanish Catholic dramas.[65]

The silence of the tragic hero is defiant. It is 'designed not only to bring about the restoration but above all the undermining of an ancient body of laws in the linguistic constitution of the renewed community.'[66] *Trauerspiel*, by contrast, 'are not so much plays which cause mourning [*traurig macht*], as plays through which mournfulness finds satisfaction [*die Trauer ihr Genügen findet*]: plays for the mournful [*vor Traurigen*].'[67] It is the absence not only of salvation but also of revelation which makes not for mourning, which would acknowledge the law, but for mournfulness and melancholy, perplexed by the created world which lacks both law and redemption: 'For all the wisdom of the melancholic is subject to the nether world; it is secured by immersion in the life of creaturely things, and it hears nothing of the voice of revelation.'[68] And 'Melancholy betrays the world for the sake of knowledge. But in its tenacious self-absorption it embraces dead objects in its contemplation, in order to redeem them.'[69]

Melancholy is the logical outcome of Protestantism; in particular, of the antinomic relation to the everyday of Lutheranism: the denial of good works in the doctrine of justification by faith alone affirmed the secular and the political world as the demonstration of obligation, 'but in its great men it produced melancholy.'[70] For life is deprived of all value. Distinct from stoical refusal of emotion, and also from the unhappy consciousness which regards itself as a degraded creature, separated from transcendent actuality, mourning becomes the state of mind which tries to revive the world of alienated objects and deadened emotions.[71] Benjamin summarizes: 'the ethical subject' has 'lost its heart in the beautiful soul.'[72]

Allegory is the *prodigious* outcome of this mournfulness, since 'the most simple object appears to be a symbol of some enigmatic wisdom because it lacks any natural creative relation to us.'[73] If the symbol means the immanence of the moral world in the world of beauty and therefore of perfected individual action within redemption, allegory is the contemplative claim immersed in the depths which separates the visual world from meaning:[74]

> Whereas in the symbol destruction is idealized and the transfigured face of nature is fleetingly revealed in the light of redemption, in allegory the observer is confronted with the *facies hippocratica* of history as a petrified, primordial landscape. Everything about history that, from the very beginning, has been untimely, sorrowful, unsuccessful, is expressed in a face – or rather in a death's head . . . This is the heart of the allegorical way of seeing, of the baroque, secular explanation of history as the Passion of the world; its importance resides solely in the stations of its decline . . . The greater the significance, the greater the subjection to death, because death digs most deeply the jagged line of demarcation between physical nature and significance.[75]

In allegory, nature is emblematic: torso, rune, ruin, fragment, monument, piled up with no goal, significations without realization, sacrament or salvation, present the physiognomy of history as decay not as bloom.[76] Lutheran *Heilsgeschichte*, the presentation of history as the fall and salvation of man, becomes the allegory of soulless nature eternally separated from the story of salvation.[77] The meaning of baroque, allegorical personification is not the spiritualization of the physical, the ensouling of things, but, on the contrary, allegorical personifications deprive nature of a soul while imposing a gravid body on emblems which 'offer themselves to view in desolate, sorrowful dispersion.'[78] Banal objects arise from allegory with 'the overbearing ostentation [which] is soon displaced by its disconsolate everyday countenance . . . succeeded by that disappointed abandonment of the exhausted emblem.'[79]

Trauerspiel in its extreme allegorical forms demands a theological understanding not an aesthetic one, but this theology would be a dynamic theology of history not 'a guaranteed economics of salvation.'[80] For mourning in *Trauerspiel* is really the mournfulness which will not soften and weep in the meekness of genuine grief,[81] but remains rigid and petrified. It belongs to the theology of evil: 'the absolute spirituality, which is what Satan means, destroys itself in its emancipation from what is sacred.'[82] The figures of the tyrant and of the intriguer show this at work in 'three original satanic promises . . . spiritual in kind: What tempts is the illusion of freedom – in the exploration of what is forbidden; the illusion of independence – the secession from the community of the pious; the illusion of infinity – in the empty abyss of evil.'[83] These are indeed the features of the spirit – of the spirit which issues from the baroque ethic of worldly allegory – the spirit of fascism, or, *what fascism means*.

Yet Benjamin offers two unexpected intimations of salvation before his masterpiece concludes: the allegorical emblems of Golgotha reinforce the desolation of human existence, the world abandoned to the spirit of Satan, but, reversing the direction of allegory, melancholy immersion in the contemplation of bones 'faithlessly leaps forward to the idea of resurrection,' which 'clears away the final phantasmagoria of the objective,' and rediscovers itself – without mourning, violence or play – 'seriously under the eyes of heaven.'[84]

This *seriousness* exposes the theatricality of the Baroque altogether. For the final reminder returns to the substitution of subjective judgement of good and evil for God's initial beholding of creation and his benison, 'And God saw everything that he had made, and, behold it was very good.' 'This knowledge [of evil] as the triumph of subjectivity and the onset of arbitrary rule over things, is the origin of all allegorical contemplation.'[85] While the earthly courts are uncertain in their judgements, 'in the heavenly court the illusion of evil comes entirely into its own.'[86] But there is the rub – for the whole topography is engineered: 'the display of manifest subjectivity becomes a formal guarantee of the miracle, the divine action itself'; just as in the baroque balcony, 'the constant reference to the violence of the supporting and supported forces . . . emphasize the soaring miracle above, by drawing attention to the difficulty of supporting it from below.'[87]

In the Counter-Reformation, Protestantism has become melancholy and mournful in the face of a world without salvation. This rigid mourning gives rise to the baroque ethic of violent display and contemplation of the allegorical, aestheticized world and to the evil genius of the intriguer – the spirit of fascism, hierarchical and absolute sovereign – who, having destroyed his own impulses and unscrupulous towards the world, rules by emergency and the frenzy of destruction. In developing this *genealogy of morals*, Benjamin insinuates 'seriousness,' 'meekness' of the heart that grieves, the actualities abused by the Baroque ethic, but he knows no divine or human law, no *Torah*, revelation, or democracy, beyond the ancient violence of law in Greek tragedy and the arbitrary subjective rule over things of the judgement of man from the biblical Fall, to the Christian Baroque, and I argue, to the spirit of Fascism.

The *genealogy* of the Baroque Ethic and the Spirit of Fascism in the *Trauerspiel* book forms a constellation with later times. Benjamin's shorter studies offer further explorations of mournful sovereignty. These figures of melancholy in his gallery of sadness exhibit different qualities and degrees of the disgrace of revelation, of the law which is presupposed and rigified in allegory or in the phantasmagoria of commodities.

VI

From the early study of Goethe's late novel, *Elective Affinities*, to his general article on Goethe's life and work, commissioned by a Soviet Encyclopedia but rejected by it, Benjamin argues that Goethe's opposition to Christian remorse and to Jacobi's Pietist metaphysics according to which nature conceals God is belied by the baroque ethic of his works.[88] The presentation of marriage as the mythic law and the implication that Ottilie's death displays the muteness of mythic sacrifice in *Elective Affinities* are undershadowed by the emblematic world of fallen nature; and the violence released in the decay of marriage reveals history as *Trauerspiel*.[89] The second part of Faust, the summation of Goethe's experience as a courtier, is not set in an eighteenth-century court but in an idealized Baroque Court and it ends in a vision of Catholic penitence, which arises out of its 'innermost political necessity.'[90] Benjamin derives this necessity from Goethe's unease with bourgeois culture, 'Become what you are,' for which he is ostensibly the most lyrical and assiduous advocate. Bourgeois risk is effectively reprieved by the secret *Turmgesellschaft*, the society of the tower, in *Wilhelm Meister's Apprenticeship*, and by feudal artisanship and utopian-socialist pedagogy in *Wilhelm Meister's Wanderings*.[91] According to this comprehension, Goethe never overcame the strain of Pietism in himself, so that Herrnhut, the Pietist community, located by the entrepreneurial spirit in the heart of action in opposition to 'the beautiful soul,' who withdraws from the world, is, nevertheless, subsequently realized in the *Turmgesellschaft*.

The very form of the novel also represents profound baroque perplexity. The intrinsic difficulty of communicability in the novel arises from the unravelling of counsel from the fabric of life. Only sects can tell Tales – the Russian legends of Leskov, Buber's reinventing of Hassidic Tales – because only sects retain a vision of salvation which confers meaning on death, so that life can be related with its weave of wisdom.[92] But when sects, too, lose their faith, and relinquish the delicate intimation of redemption in order to attempt realization – to make the invisible Church of the Elect visible on earth – they exhibit the *spirit of fascism*.

Proust proves a fellow taxonomist of sadness for he found a law for his malady. By submitting to 'the laws of night and honey,' he conquered the hopeless sadness within himself.[93] Proust transformed existence into the preserve of memory and overcame 'the incurable imperfection in the very essence of the present.'[94] Out of this abyss of loneliness, Proust recognized Baudelaire's acquiescence in his own distress, his immoderate garrulousness in the face of death.[95]

It is, however, in his commentaries on Kafka's solitariness that what

Benjamin calls 'the sickness of tradition,' the disgrace of revelation, is most fully diagnosed.[96] 'Tradition' means the Oral Law, the commentary on the Written Law, its transmissability and hence its truth. Kafka's prose pieces have 'a similar relation to doctrine as the Haggadah does to Halalakah,' that is, they tell stories and anecdotes to illustrate the meaning and outcome of the laws and statutes.[97] Wisdom is inherent in tradition, 'it is truth in its haggadic consistency.'[98] Kafka's genius lies in his response to the loss of this consistency of truth: 'he sacrificed truth for the sake of clinging to its transmissability, its haggadic element.'[99] The misery and beauty of his parables arise from their witness of the vacuum at the heart of the tradition. Benjamin's equation of haggadah and the Oral Law indicates his strange relation to the tradition he seeks to witness in the stations of its decline. For the Oral Law or commentary is not necessarily haggadic; haggada, stories or anecdotes, constitutes a small proportion of it.

To capture Kafka's world, Benjamin introduces two versions of the aetiological Talmudic legend which explains the preparation of the Sabbath meal. On receiving a letter from her fiance, who has not forgotten her, and is on his way to her, a princess, languishing in exile in a village whose language she does not speak, prepares a meal – the only way she is able to express her joy.[100] Benjamin argues that this Messianism (which, to him, will be without law because it is mute) indicates ignorance of the law; this tallies with his emphasis on the predominance of uncompleted grace in *The Castle*.[101] True to the tradition, Benjamin stresses that Kafka is not asserting law against myth: not the law but the learning is lost – the gate to justice.[102] However, Odradek, Joseph K. and the victim in the Penal Colony, are taken to be engrossed in deciphering the nature of their unknown and unincurred guilt.[103] Benjamin does not raise the possibility that Joseph K might be guilty (as Orson Welles implies in his film of *The Trial*) and is punished, not because he has lost access to the doorway of the Law, to learning, but because of his refusal to keep his promise to life, to struggle with the doorman who seems to bar the access to the Law, in the parable 'Before the Law', which is included in *The Trial*.

In his introduction to his translation of Baudelaire's *Tableaux Parisiens*, 'The Task of the Translator,' Benjamin argues that pure language, which is without the learning and work of law and is mute in the languages of man, is the only mode of access to God: 'In the original [language], language and revelation are one without any tension.[104] The languages of man represent supplementary intentions towards the pure language.[105] The task of the translator is to find how far the hidden meaning of languages is from revelation.[106] Revelation is here hidden, mysterious, not discernible from surface transmissability.[107] Benjamin has changed the relation of the Written to the

Oral Law by understanding all human signification as removed from revelation so that even the 'original' language is not original, but an interlinear interpretation of pure language.[108] Approach to this pure language is highly charged and dangerous. If the translator succeeds in making two languages proximate to pure language, he will perish; like Holderlin, who went mad, 'the gates of a language . . . may slam shut and enclose the translator with silence.'[109]

VII

If Protestant salvation gives rise to the ethic of worldly asceticism and its unintended outcome, the spirit of capitalism, then Counter-Reformation Protestant and Catholic loss of salvation gives rise to the Baroque ethic of worldly aestheticization and its unintended outcome, the spirit of Fascism. To Baroque melancholy, the world is allegorical, the phantasmagoria or personification of soulless things. Hyper-disciplined interest in this sorrowful projection results in the destructive rule of the tyrant or the intriguer. In the capital of the nineteenth century, Paris, these two genealogies, the Protestant and the Baroque, form a *constellation*, for the sovereignty of the commodity fetish, expanded form of the spirit of capitalism, becomes the allegorical personification of soulless things. Baudelaire's melancholy lyric is the new Baroque ethic of the commodity fetish, while the Fascist total mobilization of war is its eschatological consummation.

Baudelaire manages to be the last, successful lyric poet in the face of 'the increasing atrophy of experience.'[110] The prevalence of shocks, which characterize collective life and cut it off from remembrance and tradition, and which individual consciousness cannot absorb (unless ready for anxiety) are made into the matter and form of his poetry.[111] This is captured by the shock of love at last sight, as it were, in Benjamin's understanding of Baudelaire's poem to a passer-by. The unknown woman, who passes by, arouses the sexual shock that can beset a lonely man: not the rapture suffused with eros which could lead to loss or mourning, but the distraught response to a pale ghost of a woman, who is dressed in mourning.[112] Benjamin's commentary implies desertion, aberrated mourning, not inaugurated mourning; not fulfilment and loss, even if only for a rapturous moment, but the inability to engage the other, to know her desire and to be known by her. The woman in mourning is phantasmagorical; embellished by her flounces, to the soulless voyeur, she is without soul.

This melancholy desertion of the shocked poet on the passing of the phantasmagorical woman is the *baroque ethic* – the mournful fixation on the aesthetic of the untouchable world. The *flâneur*, by contrast, accepts the condition of phantasmagoric allegory, the deathless but dead-pale other, and, recognizing himself in this fate, yields the position of observer and 'succumbs to the fascination of the scene which finally lures him outside into the whorl of the crowd.'[113] Baudelaire's theory of correspondences represents his attempt to overcome shock and resume assimilable experience by regaining access to remembrance without any mediation of law or representation. The attempt to bypass law issues in rage: 'it is the very inability to experience that lies at the heart of rage.' This rage gives a sense of 'unfathomable desolation' to Baudelaire's verse.[114] The opposition of *spleen* and *idéal* in *Les Fleurs du Mal*, it might be argued, displays the same mutual implication as the baroque balcony: violent, tortured supports theatrically emphasize the supervenient miracle.

The loss of the ability to know and be known (which would define the ability to mourn or inaugurated mourning), to look and to have one's gaze returned, even nostalgically, by conjuring up lost love in old photographs, is what Benjamin means by 'the decay of aura': 'To perceive the aura of an object we look at means to invest it with the ability to look at us in return.'[115] A look exchanged presupposes the unique manifestation of distance, a ceremonial barrier which entices approach. This separation would be effaced by blank, unseeing eyes, which abolish the distance necessary for relating. In the idea of the repetition of exchanged looks which manifest distance, Benjamin offers a visual image of recognition as repetition: acknowledgement of the relation of the other to herself in my relation to myself. In Baudelaire, *sexus* is detached from *eros*: the eyes of the other are void, without distance, they have no familiarity, no resemblance, and hence no family, no ethical life.[116] This emphasis on the visual is itself derived by Benjamin from the nature of modern life – the decline of listening and the importance of sight to negotiate one's solitary way among the public conveyances of modern transport. Yet Benjamin accepts the terms of Baudelaire's complaint, his desertion by the dead look of the female other, because he shares with Baudelaire the inability to hear the commandment.

> '*Fiat ars – pereat mundus*', says Fascism, and, as Marinetti admits, expects war to supply the artistic gratification of a sense perception that has been changed by technology . . .[117]
>
> In big parades and monster rallies, in sports events, and in war, all of which are nowadays captured by camera and sound recording, the masses are brought face to face with themselves.[118]

In the essay 'The Work of Art in the Age of Technical Reproduction', the new technology has two contrary implications for Benjamin, which are equally derivable from the destruction of distance. Technology may result in total violence, or in the complete abolition of violence – this was the ambiguity in the idea of 'law-abolishing violence' in the 'Critique of Violence.' Mankind's 'self-alienation has reached such a degree that it can experience its own destruction as an aesthetic pleasure of the first order.'[119] On the other hand, the new technology has 'burst our prison world asunder,'[120] and its destruction of traditional boundaries may lead to the general and mild politics of distraction. In the second case, the politics of distraction, the technological abolition of distance bases art on a different practice – politics; but, in the first case, the witness of mankind's own destruction as an aesthetic pleasure, the technological abolition of distance bases politics on another practice – art.

The 'decay of aura' means not just the loss of authenticity or authority, but the loss of the distance from any other, so that one cannot even see oneself looking back. This may result in sublime violence, which, seeking to restore grace, does not even recognize itself as the object as well as the subject of destruction. Benjamin prefers to argue that this law-abolishing violence will resemble the general strike in his depiction of the cinema audience, half-hungry for an artistic medium which will embellish shock experiences, yet discovering that their change in apperception can be satisfied by the mode of distraction in the cinema – rather than by retreating into melancholic, judgemental concentration.[121] Yet he seems to realize, too, that the old cult has been replaced by the new, as the old religious ritual is recreated in the spell of movie stars, the phony spell of commodities.[122]

What Benjamin wants to imply is that 'the tremendous power of bourgeois autonomy,' specifically, the Protestant ethic, 'being alone with one's God,'[123] free to shake off clerical bondage, and the sad legacy of melancholy which that liberation imposes, has been overcome by technological change. Yet he is equally aware that this overcoming of mournfulness has not occurred. The violence released from baroque sovereignty would explain why the two contrary outcomes of distraction and destruction emerge, but not solely from changes in technology.[124] Benjamin has taught us better concerning the Baroque ethic and the spirit of Fascism. The Baroque ethic is not superseded; and Benjamin's *oeuvre* ends not with Messianic redemption but with another baroque *Trauerspiel*, which is staked on transforming aberrated mourning into inaugurated mourning in order to overcome the spirit of fascism: this *Trauerspiel* takes the form of the so-called 'Theses on the Philosophy of History.'

VIII

These eighteen theses, entitled in German 'On the Concept of History', seek urgently to replace the Fascist state of emergency, which (as has been learnt from the tradition of the oppressed), 'is not the exception but the rule,' by 'an actual state of emergency.'[125] Real emergency is imagined as a sovereign, divine, law-abolishing violence, which will awaken and boundlessly expiate the dead. This is what the Messiah means: the conception of the present not as homogenous, empty time but as the 'time of the now'; the past is referred to redemption, to a unique not an eternal image of the past, 'a constellation' with the present, both 'shot through with chips of Messianic time.'[126] This attempt to revitalize the struggle of historical materialism against Fascism *exhorts remembrance as both method and outcome* of the revolution: 'it means to seize hold of a memory as it flashes up at a moment of danger.'[127] A great revolution will introduce a new calendar, a sequence of holy-days, recurring 'days of remembrance,' by contrast with clock-measured time.[128]

The theses on the concept of history grapple with the insinuation and exhortation of divine law-abolishing violence against the partial, pagan, mythical, emergency rule of Fascism, which decides to become sovereign. Unlike law-making and law-preserving violence, which displays the semblance of the rule of law, Fascism exposes its predatory nature. However, the theses on the concept of history grapple even more profoundly with the law judging violence of Social Democracy, which displays the features of *Trauerspiel*. To overcome this Social Democratic *Trauerspiel*, Benjamin must transform baroque mournfulness into mourning, *aberrated mourning* into *inaugurated mourning*. However, without a divine law that can appear, he risks deepening the despair he would overcome. This lack of visible law accounts for the mood of exhortation; and the theses culminate in the commandment that is at the heart of Judaism: *Zakhor*, the commandment to remember. This Judaic commandment to remember, which Benjamin would enlist for the method and outcome of revolution, is utterly different from contemplative, Platonic anamnesis.

> Consider the darkness and the great cold
> In this vale which resounds with mystery.
> Brecht, *The Threepenny Opera*[129]

These two lines, with which the seventh thesis on history begins, express the perception, which is characteristic of *Trauerspiel*, of history as fallen and allegorical nature. The second thesis introduces 'the secret [*heimlich*] index which refers the past to redemption,' the Messianic idea. As a result of this arcane calibration, the fixed contemplation of the angel of history is all the more mournful; while the presentation of history as a single catastrophe, driven by a storm from Paradise, and the image of the ever-mounting pile of debris, which 'we call progress,' reinforce the most remorseless image of a world without redemption: '*even the dead* will not be safe from the enemy if he wins. And this enemy has not ceased to be victorious.'[130] Social Democracy is directly associated with medieval *acedia*, or sadness, 'the indolence of heart which despairs of possessing the genuine historical image as it flares up briefly.'[131] Social Democracy has inherited 'the old Protestant work ethic;' 'it recognizes only the progress in the mastery of nature, not the retrogression of society; it already displays the technocratic features later encountered in Fascism;' and it believes in 'the infinite perfectibility of mankind.'[132] The combination of sadness with this brutal optimism leaves Social Democracy resourceless to oppose Fascism, while it shares some of the most destructive features of Fascism.

This political melancholy is blasted against Messianic mourning, not the *work* of remembrance but its eschatology: history is exilic not universal; and thinking as well as its object – history – should be arrested not flowing. A 'constellation saturated with tensions' should be shocked into monadic form, which is a sign of 'a Messianic cessation of happening, or, put differently, a revolutionary chance in the fight for the oppressed past.'[133] This is the point at which the argument in this paper might reopen the debate with Adorno. For, to Adorno, 'universal history must be construed and denied.'[134] Instead of crystallizing 'the configuration pregnant with tensions" into a Messianic monad, Adorno would unravel the antinomies of realization before staking everything on the flash of redemption – which could leave everything as it is; restore the old regime; or inaugurate a greater violence.

Benjamin's peroration to the theses on the concept of history acknowledges that the future cannot be entreated 'but reminds us that 'the Torah and the prayers instruct [the Jews] in remembrance'. This final reminder becomes the approximation to transforming homogenous, empty time into 'the strait gate through which the Messiah might enter.'[135]

However, in Judaism, the politics of *Zakhor*, remembrance, are equivocal. The ancient commandment of remembrance, the annual renewal of awareness of the exilic condition and of the redemption, has the consequence of devaluing historiographical discernment in different times and places. It encourages eschatological repetition in the place of political judgement.[136] But, for Benjamin, all political judgement is melancholic and violent. Even Benjamin's reference to *Zakhor*, the commandment to remember, has been given an idiosyncratic mystical and messianic twist. There are six *Mitzvot*, injunctions to remember, in Biblical and Rabbinic Judaism: Remember the

Angelus Novus by Paul Klee

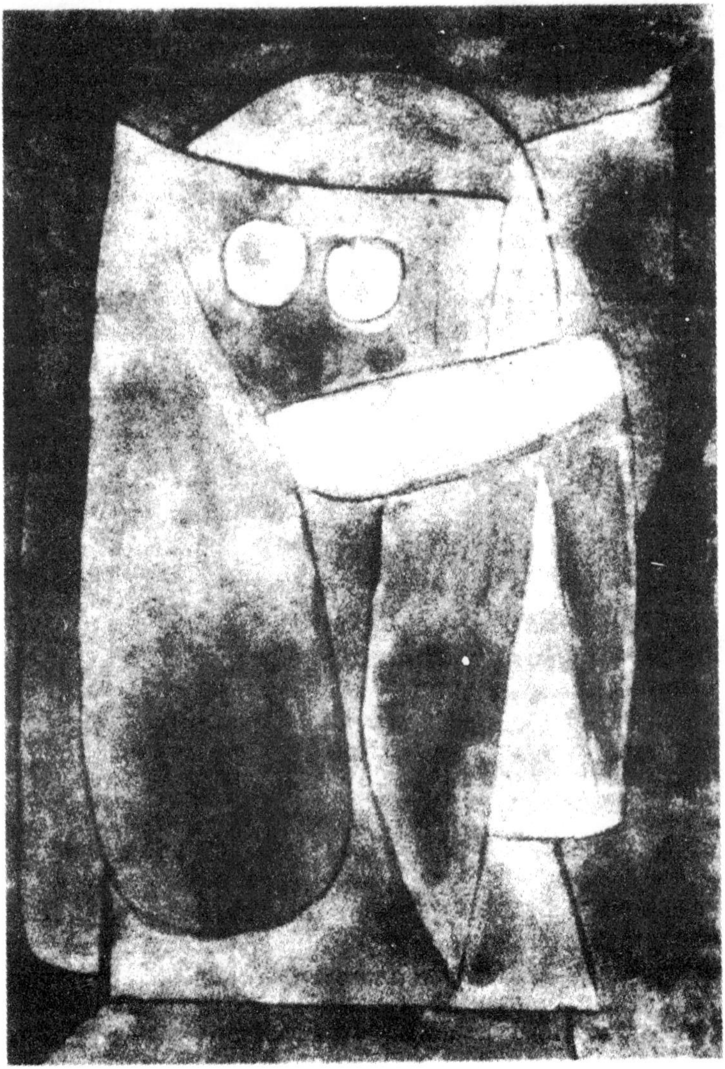

Angelus Dubiosus by Paul Klee

day you came out of Egypt;[137] Remember the Sabbath and keep it Holy; Take heed lest you forget the things your eyes saw at Horeb (this commandment refers to the Golden Calf, and the giving of the Second Tablets of the Law, with Moses as mediator); Remember the wrath of the Lord in the desert; Remember what the Lord did to Miriam (she slandered her brother and was smitten with leprosy); Remember what the Amalekites did to you (they attacked from the rear).[138] There is, however, a crucial difference between the first five and the last of these commandments. The first five are not restricted: they may be remembered on any day, because they are constructive; the sixth may only be remembered on a special Sabbath once a year, because it is soul-destroying and destructive. This last commandment, therefore, affords rest from one's enemies, and that is what is not to be forgotten. For Benjamin the enemy – Fascism – had not ceased to be victorious, and must be remembered every instant. Yet, in the 'Critique of Violence', Benjamin emphasized that the commandment, 'Thou shalt not kill,' relates to God and the doer, and may be abused neither to justify the ends of killing over the means, nor, on the contrary, to sanctify mere life rather than just existence.[139] The need for Talmud Torah, local jurisprudence, the complex contextuality of the commandment, seems to have been forgotten in his invocation of *Zakhor*:[140]

> the idea of happiness . . . resonates with the idea of redemption. This happiness is founded precisely upon the despair and the forsakenness which were ours.[141]

Agunah, the deserted wife, is the Judaic category and Messianic image of this forsakenness, which I have suggested by analogy with the Christian, baroque image of melancholy. In Judaic terms, I would argue that, in spite of his emphasis on creating new holy days, Benjamin knew no Day of Atonement, no *Yom Kippur*, although this date is already in the liturgical calendar. In his work, the hard heart of judgement does not melt into grief, into forgiveness, or into atonement.

In philosophical terms, I would argue, Benjamin only knew the dialectical image as a lightning flash, 'the Then . . . held fast', in the Now of recognizability. The rescue that is thus – and only thus – effected, can only take place for that which, in the next moment, is irretrievably lost.'[142] It is this unequivocable refusal of any dynamic of mutual recognition and struggle which keeps Benjamin's thinking restricted to the stasis of desertion, *aberrated* mourning, and the yearning for invisible, divine violence. This yearning for divine annihilation finds expression in his lament at being excluded from the ranks of the New Angels, which God creates in immense numbers, and which have the sole purpose of singing His praise before His throne for a moment before they dissolve into nought.[143] Unable to praise God, this is Klee's traumatized Angel, who appears in the ninth thesis – the New Angel. Propelled backwards into the future by a storm from Paradise, he cannot stay and he cannot dissolve, but must impotently watch in horror the single catastrophe of History, the infernal raging caused by the same paradisical storm, as it piles up its debris at his feet.

I prefer another angel of Klee's, *Angelus Dubiosus*. With voluminous, blue, billowing and enfolded wings in which square eye-holes are cut for the expanse of rotund, taupe flesh to gaze through, this mole-like angel appears unguarded rather than intent, grounded and slack rather than backing up and away in rigid horror. To me, this dubious angel suggests the humorous witness who must endure.

To celebrate Benjamin is to lament his aberrated mourning. *Inaugurated* mourning bears the fruits of forgiveness: it may become silent. I conclude by reading from Agnon's novel *A Guest for the Night*: 'I do not remember whether we walked and talked, or whether we walked in silence. Perhaps we were silent, perhaps we talked. When the heart is full the mouth speaks, but when the soul is full a man's eyes look with affectionate sadness, and his mouth is silent.'[144]

NOTES

1. From Ruth Nevo's 'Introduction' to her translation of *Chaim Nachman Bialik: Selected Poems*, Jerusalem: Dvir and The Jerusalem Post, 1981, pvii.
2. Harvard University Press, Cambridge, 1991.
3. *Op.cit.*, p17. Alter also refers to 'language, interpretation, tradition and revelation' (p23).
4. *Times Literary Supplement*, 2.8.1991.
5. Alter prefaces the second chapter, 'On Not Knowing Hebrew', with a dream from Benjamin's *One Way Street*: 'In a dream I saw myself in Goethe's study . . . Goethe rose to his feet and accompanied me to an adjoining chamber, where a table was set for my relatives. It seemed prepared, however, for many more than their number. Doubtless there were places for my ancestors' (p25).
6. 'Walter Benjamin', 1964 and 'Walter Benjamin and his Angel', 1972 in *On Jews and Judaism in Crisis: Selected Essays*, trans. Lux Furtmüller and Werner J. Dannhauser, Schocken, New York 1978 pp172-197, 198-236; *Walter Benjamin: The Story of a Friendship*, trans. Harry Zohn, Faber and Faber, London 1982.
7. 'Walter Benjamin: 1892-1940', 1968, in *op.cit.*, trans. Harry Zohn, Penguin, Harmondsworth 1973, pp151-203.

8. 'A Portrait of Walter Benjamin', 1950 in *op.cit.*, trans. Samuel and Shierry Weber, Neville Spearman, London 1967, pp227-42.
9. 'Consciousness-Raising or Redemptive Criticism: The Contemporaneity of Walter Benjamin', 1972, trans. Philip Brewster and Carl Howard Buchner, in *New German Critique*, 17 (Spring 1979), pp30-59.
10. In Andrew Benjamin (ed.), *The Problems of Modernity: Adorno and Benjamin*, Routledge, London 1989, pp157-216.
11. 'Walter Benjamin and Franz Rosenzweig', *The Philosophical Forum*, Volume XV Nos 1-2, (Fall-Winter 1983-4), pp188-205. Moses's argument that Rosenzweig's dialogism is fundamentally different from Benjamin's lapsarian view of communication overlooks the way in which both Rosenzweig and Benjamin defend a divine 'grammar' of names in opposition to idealist logic of universals.
12. Bernd Witte mentions Benjamin's knowledge of Cohen's book on Kant (p42); of the third part of Cohen's *System, Aesthetic of Pure Feeling* (p52); of Cohen's *Religion of Reason out of the Sources of Judaism*, (p.54) in *Walter Benjamin: An Intellectual Biography*, trans. James Rolleston, Detroit, Wayne State, 1991; see too, the discussion of neo-Kantianism in Witte, *Walter Benjamin – Der Intellektuelle als Kritiker: Untersuchungen zu seinem Frühwerk*, Stuttgart: Metzler, 1976, pp6-14.
13. See Gillian Rose, 'Kant among the Prophets: Hermann Cohen', in *Judaism and Modernity*, Blackwell, Oxford 1993, pp111-25.
14. Book Six is entitled, 'Confessions of a Beautiful Soul', Thomas Carlyle, in the first English translation of 1824 (still to be recommended) translated *schöne Seele* as 'fair saint', Chapman and Hall, London 1899.
15. *Op.cit.*, trans. Miller, Clarendon, Oxford 1979, pp383-409.
16. Max Weber discusses the connection between the brethren of the common life and Pietist sects in one of the many long footnotes to *The Protestant Ethic and the Spirit of Capitalism* (trans. Talcott Parsons, Unwin, London 1968), pp240-2 note 108; he also discusses Goethe's *Wilhelm Meisters Wanderjahre and Faust*, on the relation between deeds and renunciation, pp180-1.
17. In Goethe's novel, 'the beautiful soul', other-worldly asceticism, is contrasted with the ethic of worldly asceticism; in Hegel's *Phenomenology*, 'the beautiful soul' is contrasted with 'the hard heart of judgement' and forgiveness. For further discussion of 'the beautiful soul' see Rose, *The Broken Middle: Out of our Ancient Society*, Blackwell, Oxford 1992, pp153-246.
18. Adorno represents Kierkegaard in terms of Benjamin's notion of baroque melancholy (*Kierkegaard: Construction of the Aesthetic*, trans. Robert Hullor-Kentor, University of Minnesota Press, Minneapolis, pp62-4, 54). For a criticism of Adorno's reading of Kierkegaard, see Rose, *The Broken Middle*, pp8-9, 13-16.
19. The method employed in this paper, which construes the continuity, first, between Max Weber and Benjamin, and, equally, between Benjamin and Carl

Schmitt's theories of sovereignty and emergency, which are crucial from the *Ursprung des deutschen Trauerspiel* (where Benjamin links the concept of the baroque and the state of emergency with reference to Schmitt's *Political Theology* (trans. pp65-6, and see note 55 *infra*)) to the so-called 'Theses on the Philosophy of History' (where Benjamin calls for 'a real state of emergency' to oppose the Fascist norm of emergency (see note 125 *infra*)). should be compared with the recently published, major study by G.L. Ulmen, *Politischer Mehrwert: Eine Studie über Max Weber und Carl Schmitt*, trans. Ursula Ludz, G.L. Weinheim, VCH, Acta Humaniora, 1991: and with Norben Bolz, 'Charisma und Soveränität: Carl Schmitt und Walter Benjamin im Schatten Max Webers', in Jacob Taubes (ed.), *Religionstheorie und Politische Theologie*, Band 1, *Der Fürst dieser Welt: Carl Schmitt und die Folgen*, Wilhelm Fink, Munich 1993, pp249-62. Schmitt wrote a response to Benjamin's *Trauerspiel*, 'On the Barbaric Character of Shakespearean Drama: A Response to Walter Benjamin on the Origin of German Tragic Drama', which is an Appendix to 'The Source of the Tragic', ch. 3 of *Hamlet oder Hecuba: Der Einbruch der Zeit in das Spiel* (1956), trans. David Pan in *Telos* (Special Issue) 'Carl Schmitt Friend or Foe?' 72 (Summer 1987), pp146-51.

20. Weber, *The Protestant Ethic and the Spirit of Capitalism*, p130.
21. According to Scholem, 'it must be emphasized that later on when he had turned to historical materialism, out of those two categories of Revelation and Redemption only the latter was preserved *expressis verbis* but not the former, closely though it was bound up with his basic method of commenting on great and authoritative texts' ('Walter Benjamin', *On Jews and Judaism in* Crisis, p194). In my view, this was true at all times.
22. See 'Agunot', 1908, Agnon's first major tale (in *Twenty-One Stories*, New York: Schocken, 1970, pp30-44).
23. Even Scholem uses 'theology' loosely when discussing Benjamin's thought.
24. The *Mishnah* was the first compilation of the Oral Law at the end of the second century of the Common Era; the *Talmud*, the commentary on the Mishnah, compiled in the fourth century of the Common Era.
25. See Moses Maimonides, 'Introduction' to the *Mishneh Torah*, in Isadore Twersky (ed.), *A Maimonides Reader*, Behrman House, New York 1972, p35.
26. See Scholem, 'Towards an Understanding of the Messianic Idea in Judaism', pp1-36; and 'The Messianic Idea in Kabbalism', p41 in *The Messianic Idea in Judaism and Other Essays on Jewish Spirituality*, Schocken, New York 1971.
27. Scholem, 'Revelation and Tradition as Religious Categories in Judaism' (1962), in *ibid.*, pp292-303.
28. Scholem *On the Kabbalah and its Symbolism*, trans. Ralph Manheim, Schocken, New York 1969, p50 note 3. For the correspondence between Buber and Rosenzweig, see Rosenzweig, *On Jewish Learning*, (ed.), N.N. Glatzer,

Schocken, New York 1965, p118.

29. 'Über das Programm der Kommenden Philosophie', in *Walter Benjamin: Gesammelte Schriften*, Vol. II.I 167, *Walter Benjamin: Gesammelte Schnften*, (eds.), Rolf Tiedemann and Hermann Schweppenhauser, Frankfurt am Main, Vol. I-VI 1974-85); trans. 'On the Program of the Coming Philosophy', 1918, Mark Ritter, in *Benjamin: Philosophy, History, Aesthetics*, (ed.), Gary Smith, University of Chicago Press, Chicaco 1989, p8.
30. 'Über Sprache überhaupt und über die Sprache des Menschen' (1916) in *Gesammelt Schriften*, Vol. II.I 144; trans. Edmund Jephcott and Kingsley Shorter, in *One Way Street and Other Writings*, p111.
31. *Ibid.*, pp145-6, trans. p112.
32. *Ibid.*, pp146-7, trans. p113.
33. *Ibid.*, p148, trans. p115.
34. *Ibid.*, pp152-3, trans. p119.
35. *Ibid.*, p153, trans. p120.
36. *Ibid.*, p154, trans. p120.
37. *Ibid.*, p155, trans. p121.
38. *Ibid.*, p155, trans. pp121-2.
39. See Scholem,'The Crisis of Tradition in Jewish Messianism', in *The Messianic Idea in Judaism*, p69.
40. In 'Über das mimetische Vermögen' (1933), *Gesammelte Schriften*, Vol. II.I 210-13, trans. 'On the Mimetic Faculty' in *One Way Street*, pp160-3, and 'Lehre vom Ähnlichen', 1983, *ibid* 204-10, trans. Knut Tarnowski, 'Doctrine of the Similar' in *New German Critique*, 17, (Spring 1979) pp65-9 (see Anson Rabinbach's 'Introduction', 60-4), Benjamin defines the mimetic gift as being able 'to read what was never written' (213, trans. 162-3), such as, stars, entrails, runes, hieroglyphs. This circumscription represents a further derivation of language without regularity or normative force, that is, without any connotation of law.
41. Benjamin, 'Schicksal und Charakter' (1919), *Gesammelte Schriften*, Vol. II.I 173-9, 'Fate and Character', *One Way Street*, pp127-30.
42. Compare the argument in the essays on Buber, Rosenzweig and Nietzsche, in *Judaism and Modernity*, pp89-110, 127-54, 155-73.
43. 'Zur Kritik der Gewalt' (1921), *Gesammelte Schriften*, Vol. II.I pp199-200; trans. in *One Way Street*, pp50-1.
44. *Ibid.*, p200, trans. p151.
45. *Ibid.*, pp193-5, trans. pp145-7.
46. 'Theologisch-Politisches Fragment' (1921), *Gesammelte Schriften*, Vol. II.I pp203-4; trans. in *One Way Street*, p155.
47. *Ibid.*, p204, trans. p156.
48. *The Origin of German Tragic Drama*, John Osborne, New Left Books, London 1977. *Ursprung des deutschen Trauerspiels* (1928), *Gesammelte Schriften*, Vol. I.I,

p45. I retain the German *Trauerspiel* in my translation of the title, and refer to the work by this word alone in the notes.

49. *Ibid.*, pp216, 215, trans. pp36, 35.
50. *Ibid.*, p221, trans. p41.
51. *Ibid.*, p226, trans. p45.
52. *Ibid.*
53. *Ibid.*, p235, trans. p54.
54. *Ibid.*, p246, trans p66.
55. *Ibid.*, p246, trans. p65.
56. *Ibid.*, p257, trans. p78.
57. *Ibid.*, p258, trans. p79.
58. *Ibid.*, p260, trans. p81.
59. *Ibid.*, p263, trans. p84, and see Calderon, *Plays: One*, trans. Gwynne Edwards, Methuen, London 1991.
60. *Ibid.*, pp250-1, trans. pp70-1.
61. *Ibid.*, pp251-3, trans. pp72-4.
62. *Ibid.*, p274, trans. p95.
63. *Ibid.*, p276, p98.
64. *Ibid.*, p98.
65. *Ibid.*, pp276-7.
66. *Ibid.*, p294, trans. p115.
67. *Ibid.*, p298, trans. p119.
68. *Ibid.*, p330, trans. p152.
69. *Ibid.*, p334, trans. p157.
70. *Ibid.*, p317, trans. p138.
71. *Ibid.*, p318, trans. p139.
72. *Ibid.*, p160.
73. *Ibid.*, p319, trans. p140.
74. *Ibid.*, p342, trans. p165.
75. *Ibid.*, p343, trans. p 166. A note to Adorno's citation of *facies hippocratica*, Hippocratic face (taken from Francis Adams, 'Introduction' to *The Genuine Works of Hippocrates* (William Wood, New York 1886, p195), explains: 'This countenance, suffering from "the worst", is marked by "a sharp nose, hollow eyes, collapsed temples, the ears cold, contracted and their lobes turned out: the skin about the forehead being rough, distended and parched; the colour of the face being green, black, livid or lead coloured' (see Adorno, *Kierkegaard*, pp151-2, note 33).
76. *Ibid.*, pp347, 353-8, trans. pp170, 177-82.
77. *Ibid.*, p358, trans. p182, *Heilsgeschichte*, the Lutheran term for the history of the fall and salvation of man is incorrectly translated.
78. *Ibid.*, pp361-2, 362-3, trans. pp186, 187.

79. *Ibid.*, p361, trans. p185.
80. *Ibid.*, p390, trans. p216.
81. *Ibid.*, the text is cited in the translation in German and translated in a footnote, p154.
82. *Ibid.*, p404, trans. p230.
83. *Ibid.*, pp403-4.
84. *Ibid.*, p406, trans. p232.
85. *Ibid.*, p407, trans. p233.
86. *Ibid.*, p407, trans. p234.
87. *Ibid.*, p408, trans. pp234-5.
88. 'Goethe', *Gesammelte Schriften*, Vol. II.2 719, trans. 'Goethe: The Reluctant Bourgeois', Rodney Livingstone, *New Left Review*, 133 (May-June 1982), p79.
89. See 'Goethes Wahlverwandfschaften' (1921-2), *Gesammelte Schriften*, I.I 125-201; see, too, *Witte, Walter Benjamin: An Intellectual Biography*, p55.
90. 'Goethe', p737, trans. p91.
91. *Ibid.*, pp732, 717, trans. pp88, 78.
92. 'Der Erzahler: Betrachtungen zum Werk Nikolai Lesskovs' (1936), *Gesammelte Schriften*, Vol. II.2 pp438-62; trans. 'The Storyteller: Reflections on the Works of Nikolai Leskov', *Illuminations*, Harry Zohn, Fontana, London 1973, pp83-109.
93. 'Zum Bilde Proust (1929), *ibid.*, p312; trans. 'The Image of Proust', *ibid.*, p205.
94. *Ibid.*
95. *Ibid.*, p321, trans. p214.
96. Letter to Gerhard Scholem, 12.6, 1938 in *Briefe*, Vol.2 (eds.), Gershom Scholem and Theodor W. Adorno, Suhrkamp, Frankfurt am Main 1966, 763; trans. 'Max Brod's Book on Kafka: And Some of My Own Reflections', *ibid.*, p147.
97. 'Franz Kafka: Zur Zehnten Wiederkehr series Todestages', *Gesammelte Schriften*, Vol. II.2 p420; trans. 'Franz Kafka: On the Tenth Anniversary of His Death', *ibid.*, p122.
98. 'Max Brod's Book on Kafka', *ibid.*
99. *Ibid.*
100. 'Franz Kafka', *ibid.*, p424, trans. p126; 'Franz Kafka: Beim Bau der chinesischen Mauer', 1931, *Gesammelte Schriften*, Vol. 2.2 p680.
101. *Ibid.*, p678.
102. 'Franz Kafka', p437, trans. p139.
103. *Ibid.*, p432, trans. p133.
104. 'Die Aufgabe des Übersetzers'(1923) *Gesammelte Schriften*, Vol. IV.I p21; trans. *Illuminations*, p82.
105. *Ibid.*, p13, trans. p74.
106. *Ibid.*, p14, trans. pp74-5.
107. *Ibid.*, 14-15, trans. p75.

108. *Ibid.*, p21, trans. p82.
109. *Ibid.*, p21, trans. p81.
110. 'Über einige Motive bei Baudelaire' (1939), *Gesammelte Schriften*, Vol. I.2 p611; trans. 'On Some Motifs in Baudelaire', *Illuminations*, p161. A version of this with the second and third sections incorporated into the first is also included in 'Some Motifs in Baudelaire', trans. Harry Zohn, *Charles Baudelaire: A Lyric Poet in the Era of High Capitalism*, New Left Books, London 1973, pp107-54.
111. 'On Some Motifs in Baudelaire', pp162-3, trans. pp162-3.
112. 'Some Motifs in Baudelaire', p623, trans. p171.
113. *Ibid.*, p628, trans. p175.
114. *Ibid.*, pp641-2, trans. p186, amended.
115. *Ibid.*, pp646-7, trans. p190.
116. *Ibid.*, pp648-9, trans. pp191-2.
117. 'Das Kunstwerk in Zeitalter seiner technischen Reproduzierbarkeit' (1936), *Gesammelte Schriften*, Vol. 2.1 508; trans. 'The Work of Art in the Age of Mechanical Reproduction', *Illuminations*, p244.
118. *Ibid.*, p506, n 32, trans. p253 n 21.
119. *Ibid.*, p508, trans. p244.
120. *Ibid.*, p499, trans. p238.
121. *Ibid.*, pp503-5, trans. pp241-2.
122. *Ibid.*, p492, trans. p233.
123. *Ibid.*, p502, n 27, trans. p252 note 18.
124. See, too, Benjamin, 'Theorien des deutschen Faschismus: Zu der Sammelschrift 'Krieg und Krieger' (1930), *Gesammelte Schriften III, 'Theories of German Fascism: On the Collection of Essays War and Warrior*, edited by Ernst Junger', in which Benjamin argues that the theory of the German 'post-war war [*Nachkrieg*]' with its combination of Junger's 'total mobilization' and Salomon's 'landscape of the front', displays the features of baroque ethic, its idealism and its violence: 'Etching the landscape with flaming banners and trenches technology wanted to recreate the heroic features of German idealism. It went astray. What is considered heroic were the features of Hippocrates, the features of death. Deeply imbued with its own depravity, technology gave shape to the apocalyptic face of nature and reduced nature to silence – even though this technology had the power to give nature its voice. Instead of using and illuminating the secrets of nature via a technology mediated by the human scheme of things, the new nationalists' metaphysical abstraction of war signifies nothing other than a mystified and unmediated application of technology to solve the mystery of an idealistically perceived nature' pp243, 247, trans. Jerolf Wikoff, *New German Critique*, Special Walter Benjamin Issue, 17 (Spring 1979), pp124, 126-7; see, too, Ansgar Hillach, 'The Aesthetics of Politics: Walter Benjamin's "Theories of German Fascism",' *ibid.*, pp99-119).

125. 'Über den Begriff der Geschichte', *Gesammelte Schriften*, Vol. I.2 pp694-709; trans. 'Theses on the Philosophy of History', *Illuminations*, viii, amended.
126. *Ibid.*, xviii A.
127. *Ibid.*, vi.
q28. *Ibid.*, xv.
129. *Ibid.*, vii.
130. *Ibid.*, ix, vi.
131. *Ibid.*, vii, trans. amended.
132. *Ibid.*, xi, trans. amended.
133. *Ibid.*, xvii, trans. amended.
134. *Negative Dialectic*, trans. p320, E.B. Ashton, Routledge and Kegan Paul, London, p320.
135. *Ibid.*, xviii B.
136. For this argument, see Yosef Hayim Yerushalmi, *Zakhor: Jewish History and Jewish Memory*, University of Washington Press, Seattle 1982.
137. Deut, 4.32, 16.3.
138. Ex. 17.14, Deut. 25 17-19.
139. 'Critique of Violence', pp200-2, trans. p153.
140. For this idea of Halacha and ethics as a local, contextual jurisprudence, see Aharon Lichtenstein, 'Does Jewish Tradition Recognize an Ethic Independent of Halacha?' reprinted from *Modern Jewish Ethics: Theory and Practice*, (ed.), Marvin Fox, Ohio University Press, Ohio 1975, pp102-23.
141. From Lotze's *Mikrokosmos*, cited in 'N', a section of the preparatory material for the *Arcades* project, *Gesammelte Schriften*, Vol. V.I p599; trans. in Benjamin (ed.), G. Smith, p71. The words with which the second thesis on the concept of history opens are taken from the same source.
142. *Ibid.*, pp591-2, trans. p64.
143. See Scholem, 'Walter Benjamin and his Angel', *On Jews and Judaism in Crisis*, p205.
144. S.Y. Agnon, *A Guest for the Night*, 1939, trans. Misha Louvish, Schocken, New York 1968, p284. For further discussion of 'aberrated mourning', see Laurence A. Rickels, *Aberrations of Mourning: Writing on German Crypts*, Wayne State University Press, Detroit 1988.

A Communicative disclosure of the past: on the relation between anthropology and philosophy of history in Walter Benjamin

Axel Honneth

It is only in a trivial sense that Walter Benjamin seems to be still contemporaneous today. True, an ever-increasing group of scholars participates in the interpretation of his life and work, but his theory has no recognizable effect on the advancement of philosophical and sociological research. The number of theoretical camps originally confronting one another in the appropriation of his work has been augmented by new theories with every passing decade. Thus, today, not only the advocates of Critical Theory, of Marxism, and of Jewish mysticism compete for an appropriate understanding, but also the proponents of deconstruction and postmodernism as well as supporters of a conservative theory of politics. Scarcely any other author of this century has been able to trigger so many waves of reception in so short a time: hardly any other seems to possess the same stimulating potential for generating new efforts at interpretation as Benjamin. However, the importance ascribed to his writings in current research in no way corresponds to the amount of attention they attract as the object of scholarly interpretation: for the systematic questions that today play a role in philosophy, the theory of culture, or social research, the components of his work have remained virtually without significance. The disparity between interpretative effort and theoretical fruits is already anticipated in the peculiarity of Benjamin's own theory. Its scattered, frequently disparate ideas are in themselves of surprising stringency, indeed of alluring brilliance, without ever amalgamating into larger complexes which could enter philosophical discourse on a competitive basis. In accordance with their character, his writings resist every kind of theory formation so strictly that, though they continually require new interpretations like a literary text, they cannot really enter the field of scientific debate. Thus, whoever is interested in the systematic fruits of Benjamin's work has always been forced to first constructively forge a unity between the disparate ideas, a unity which they intentionally lacked. In what follows I would like to take a step in this direction by establishing a systematic connection between Benjamin's anthropologically fashioned concept of experience and his philosophy of history. I shall proceed from one of his earliest texts in order to develop the thesis that Benjamin attempts to advance the possibility of unrestricted experience against the historical process of the loss of experience only in order to solve a moral problem with which his reflections on the philosophy of history confront him.[1] The systematic fruits of his work will therefore be measured by whether he succeeds in making the moral function of an unrestricted mode of human experience sufficiently plausible.

I

Already in 'Über das Programm einer kommenden Philosophie,'[2] which Benjamin wrote while still a student, the focus of the reflections is on a critique of reductionist models of human experience. At that time Benjamin was pursuing the demanding objective of taking the Kantian critique of pure reason as the model for an epistemology according to which even religious-metaphysical knowledge could be proved to be universal and necessary. To this end, he separates in Kantian theory the epistemological procedure from the scientific material on which this procedure was originally developed in order to transfer it to the field of a superior realm of knowledge, as it were. At that time, Benjamin was not alone in his polemic against the restrictive concept of scientific experience to which Kant tied his epistemology. Like many other authors, he sees the decisive weakness of the critique of pure reason in the fact that it attempts to explore the 'certainty and truth' of knowledge on the basis of a realm of reality that is 'of a lower order, perhaps of the lowest.'[3] For Kant allows himself to be led by a concept of experience in which the *Weltanschauung* of the age of Enlightenment resonates, inasmuch as this concept takes its orientation from the model of a subject's mechanical intervention in the object realm of nature. Given this concept of simple experience, 'reduced [as it is] to a minimum of meaning,'[4] some opaque metaphysics also flows subterraneanly into Kantian epistemology, because the latter has to remain inevitably fixated on the polar contrast of an epistemological subject and a corresponding object. By contrast, Benjamin now wants to apply Kant's critical procedure to different, more demanding forms of human experience in order, as Benjamin self-confidently writes, to 'ground autonomously the sphere of knowledge beyond subject-object terminology.'[5]

If this first step is to be approximately parallel to the one Dilthey attempted to take in his epistemological justification of the historical-hermeneutical sciences,[6] then Benjamin resolutely detaches himself from this in the second step of sketching his own programme. For here he seeks the guidelines for determining a complex concept of experience not in forms of communicative knowledge, but in modes of magical world disclosure. It is not the hermeneutical experience of understanding an unfamiliar meaning context: rather it is the experience of the animated character [*Beseeltheit*] of all reality that he makes the guiding reference point for his analysis. Nor was Benjamin alone at the time in choosing this type of experience; already at the turn of the century, the attempt was made in both American pragmatism and French philosophy of life (*Lebensphilosophie*) to uncover non-instrumental forms of experience by way of an analysis of those religious and aesthetic experiences in which our relation to reality is communicatively dissipated in a peculiar manner.[7] To illustrate those borderline experiences in which reality as a whole is experienced as a field of subjective forces, Benjamin employs empirical examples, knowledge of which he largely acquired through his concern with contemporary research. Obviously following Lévy-Bruhl's highly influential investigations, he mentions 'primitive peoples' who 'identify themselves with sacred animals and plants,'[8] talks about the 'insane' and the 'sick,' in whose perception a dissolution of the borders of the self occurs, and finally even points to 'clairvoyants who at least claim to be able to receive others' perceptions as their own.'[9]

Benjamin would later return to all of these examples at different places in his writings; in different contexts he would again and again attempt to prove with these examples that to experience sometimes truly can only mean suddenly experiencing the world as a social field of analogies and correspondences. Each of the four examples vouches for the change in perception that we experience when we can no longer maintain a division between the sphere of the objectivated and that of the intersubjective. Of course, by listing these examples in the context of the early draft of a programme, Benjamin is primarily pursuing the goal of providing empirical indicators for the possibility of a form of human experience which he alternately refers to as 'religious' or 'metaphysical'. Because what is intended by this is a relation to reality that is located at the point 'of total neutrality in reference to the concepts object and subject,'[10] this relation can serve as the starting point for a grounding of true knowledge, a grounding that refers to, but transcends Kant, for it is to be located beyond subject-object terminology.

Thus, what Benjamin in his early years had in mind as the idea of a coming philosophy can, for all its metaphysical accentuation, indeed be rationally reconstructed. If, among our everyday, universally accessible experiences

[*Erfahrungen*], there are also those in which reality loses its sheer objective character and becomes the referential surface for intersubjective, lived experiences [*Erlebnisse*], then one can find in them the empirical material for a critique of knowledge concerned with the conditions of the possibility of metaphysical knowledge. Of course, what is still missing, from this point up to the critical justification of religious knowledge, is the additional step in the proof, namely, that with these magical experiences it is also a matter of universal and necessary access to knowledge about a God. Benjamin attempts to obtain an argument for this thesis by interpreting God not as the object of possible experience, but as the quintessence of everything that philosophy has to categorially imagine when it undertakes to comprehend an experience beyond the subject-object division. But such an indirect line of argumentation is probably too vague and too foolhardy for it to have played a decisive role in Benjamin's work for very long; instead, immediately after writing his early programme he turned away from the idea of establishing a metaphysics on the basis of Kantian epistemology and indeed drops the entire plan of epistemologically grounding religious knowledge. Of his original drafts, however, the core idea, that of richly meaningful, undistorted experience, survived even the sobering materialist phase of the following years. In the course of both an anthropologization and historicization, Benjamin makes an emphatic concept of experience the guide for the further development of his theory.

II

His concern with Bergson's writings on the philosophy of life, and also Ludwig Klages' theory, enabled Benjamin to give his ideas about non-mechanical, richly meaningful experience clear contours.[11] If the possibility of such a form of experience was solely dependent in the original context on the special position of archaic peoples and the physically or mentally ill, it now increasingly acquires an anthropological weight in the wake of the lessons in the philosophy of life. The path to a form of experience [*Erfahrung*] in which reality appears as a field of reference for intersubjective, lived experiences [*Erlebnisse*] should now be opened not only to particular special groups, but in principle to every human being, because access to this form of experience is tied to an ability peculiar to the human species. Like Bergson, Benjamin discloses the structure of such experience by first contrasting it to that purposive consciousness with which we lead our practical lives in the everyday world; what amounts to an experience for persons here is only that property of objects which serves to accomplish routine tasks.[12] In the normal course of everyday life we disclose the world solely in accordance with the signals through which we have learned instrumentally that they inform us of possibilities for successful action. In such cases, what is experienced is only that thin surface of things which can function as a field of instrumental reference. To that extent, however, reality must enter human experience more richly and in greater complexity whenever it is no longer disclosed under the direction of purposive action; that is the case in all those situations where instrumental attention recedes to give way to a state of lower concentration or half-wakefulness.

From many of Benjamin's writings we know what human states are said to be accompanied by such a loss of purposively directed attention: apart from the state of dreaming, it is above all the moments of awakening when the environment's perceptual stimuli cannot yet be instrumentally classified in accordance with everyday routine. Again and again he also refers to the mental state of children, whose inadequate ability to control the environment purposively allows them to experience reality as a network of animated forces. Then it is situations of reduced attention that accompany absent-minded *flânerie*, engrossment in reading or listening to music, but also intoxication. Finally, artistic creation serves for Benjamin as an example of a human state where self-forgetful engrossment in the appropriate material replaces routine concentration. What all these experiential situations demonstrate on the part of the subject is a condition that Benjamin already emphasized in his early programmatic text. Purposively directed attention disappears in such moments or states, and with it the accompanying consciousness of being distinct from the sensuous world in the sense of being the middle point of conscious acting, that is, of being the subject of action. Situations of low concentration or half-wakefulness are constituted by the circumstance that we no longer experience ourselves as being faced by a world of facts at our disposal, but tend to merge with the stream of sensuous impressions that swamps us when we no longer have the customary control of our intellects. However, it is more difficult to answer the question of how Benjamin describes the implications of such a state of consciousness for what we can perceive in reality, that is, in the object. A number of passages in his writings permit us to assume that he believed that he could defend the strong thesis that, when our purposively directed concentration is low, we tend to experience reality as a field of surprising correspondences and analogies. Thus, with regard to Proust, we read that his artificially produced remembering accompanies him back to 'a world in which the true surrealist face of existence breaks through';[13] and the *flânerie*, who finds himself in a state of half-wakeful distraction, is given the metropolis not as a field of action to master instrumentally, but as a magical place of unimagined correspondences and analogies.[14] Thus, what happens in situations when we lose our instrumental attention is not only, as we read in the essay on surrealism, a 'loosening of the self,'[15] namely, a decentring of the subject of action, but complementary to this on the side of the object, reality further acquires the properties of an animated world. With such experience, we therefore arrive at a relation to reality in which the everyday routine contrast of us as subjects facing a mere object is dissolved, because everything is drawn into a realm of the intersubjective. One may assume that Benjamin's general speculations on the human species' mimetic faculty find expression here.[16] What this first of all means for the early history of man is the faculty which human beings, in fear of natural dangers, formed in order to bring themselves into safety by developing a resemblance to the threatening object. However, Benjamin is convinced that, in the course of historical development, what has remained of this faculty is only the subjectivistic residue that enables us to establish spontaneous relations of resemblance between the objects of our sensuous world. Thus, he seems to believe that the more purposive attention is reduced in everyday existence, the more this faculty is activated, a faculty given to us for perceiving sensuous, but also non-sensuous, correspondences.

Using anthropological motifs, Benjamin also gave his theory of experience a strong historical turn; by reading sociologically oriented diagnoses of the times, as in the writings of Ferdinand Tonnies and Georg Simmel, he very soon became informed about the degree to which man's anthropologically anchored potential for experience can itself be subject to historical changes. For Benjamin, the thesis of a specific loss of experience follows from embedding his concept of experience (which was influenced by the philosophy of life) in the context of cultural and social history; as far as I can see, this thesis forms that core of his theory which is concerned with a diagnosis of the times.

III

Benjamin arrived at the assumption of an historically increasing 'loss of experience' by drawing conclusions from various studies on the social transition from traditional to modern societies, conclusions which affect the anthropologically based potential for intensifying experience by reducing attention. In the upheaval of social forms of life that the emergence of capitalist industrial production causes, the chances of legitimately lowering instrumental attention are so slight that in the end the possibility of such qualitative experiential situations threatens to disappear. It is primarily research on the historical transformations of the spheres of labour and communication that Benjamin gathers together in order to give his historical thesis fairly clear contours. If we draw together the various writings in which he investigates the process of a loss of experience, then we can distinguish three levels of change which Benjamin identifies as social preconditions for a structural transformation of experience. With regard to forms of labour – as his essay on 'the storyteller' and the studies on Baudelaire demonstrate[17] – there is a transition from craft to assembly line production, which requires 'reflex-like reactions'. If a self-forgetful engrossment in the object of labour was still possible in the former, since technical control was left to the stream of communication of those co-operatively labouring, assembly line production requires a maximum of instrumental attention, which renders every type of experience in the mode of half-wakefulness impossible. With regard to the relations of interaction, Benjamin of course expects a shift from narrative forms of exchange to the unilateral form of communication, namely 'information.' The image he employs – a somewhat nostalgic one, and obviously influenced by Tonnies[18] – assumes that, in premodern times, the integration of the social community still came about by handing down narratives in which experiences that shaped life-histories were passed on from generation to generation in a coded form; under conditions of increasing industrialization, such narrative processes of socialization are replaced by unilateral information circulated by media – that is, information about occurrences that are merely registered as 'sensations.'[19]

What is again decisive for Benjamin here is the fact that the shift in forms of communication is also accompanied by a modification of the mental conditions of reception at the expense of possibilities of reduced attention. Listening to orally transmitted narratives allows the gradual lowering of purposively directed concentration, whereas transmitting information always has to expect sharp and concentrated attention on the part of the recipient. Finally, what is most difficult to grasp is that complex of historical changes which Benjamin summarized under the heading: 'loss of aura.'[20] What is meant by this is, first of all, the shifts in the perception of the work of art; these shifts follow from the fact that the work of art is removed from the cultic distance of the sacred sphere and placed in the immediate proximity of the observer. However, this process also serves to designate a change in the form of social integration, because, along with the dissolution of ritual cults, what begins to disappear is that medium within whose horizons individual life-histories could still be collectively related to the history of a single community. To the extent that an element of the shattering of the self, that is, a moment of the disempowering of the self's purposive ability to react, is also associated with the cultic manner of perception, a site for reduced attention is lost with this mode of perception. The loss of aura means that the subject is deprived of those institutionalized situational contexts in which it was actually forced to engross itself, self-forgetfully, in something other than itself. Taking these three processes of change together, Benjamin believes he can infer a loss of experience that is said to be typical for the industrialized societies of modernity in *toto*. Experiences [*Erfahrungen*], particularly those which are possible in the mode of half-wakeful states, are increasingly replaced by the processed form of lived experiences [*Erlebnisse*],[21] a form in which occurrences and incidents are registered only in terms of their instrumental information value.

Benjamin attempts to distinguish between two forms of such a loss of experience. With relation to experiencing the past, he talks of the replacement of a qualitatively solid remembering [*Erinnerung*] (one often secured collectively) by a memory [*Gedächtnis*] in the 'service of the intellect'.[22] He owes this distinction to a historicization of the differentiation that Bergson made between '*mémoire pure*' and purposive, corporeally established habits.[23] With regard to the relation of the subject to its present, Benjamin distinguishes between, on the one hand, that mode of experience which bears features of a magical disclosure of the world and, on the other, the processed form of lived experience, which permits only the purposive side of the world to come to consciousness. Thus, all told, the structural transformation of experience, which Benjamin comprehends as the sociocultural outcome of the emergence of modern industry, comes about as a change in our perception of both the past and the present. This series of reflections, which contains the substratum of Benjamin's theory of experience, shows in more than one place points of contact with Ernst Jünger's ideas.[24] Jünger is also a rationalist, who is interested in the social transformation of modernity in terms of its negative implications for the perceptive potential of magical experiences. If, however, for Jünger such reflections lead to the consequence of an elitist re-enchantment of the world, then Benjamin, by contrast, possesses a philosophy of history that is to assign a completely different task, namely an emancipatory one, to this experiential potential.

IV

Like Benjamin, Ernst Jünger is also so strongly influenced by *Lebensphilosophie* at the beginning of the century that it provides him with the basic concepts for his critique of culture. The diary entries collected in the text *Das abenteuerliche Herz*[25] present the social world of modernity as a disenchanted realm of mechanical routine actions, one that only in rare and privileged moments provides a view of an horizon of magical appearances. In its foundation, Jünger's anthropological materialism is fixated on such extraordinary states, which, as in Benjamin, are circumscribed with the help of categories casually adopted from Bergson. In situations of danger, which originate for the child from its natural helplessness, for the warrior from the risk of death, and for the intoxicated from the maelstrom of the loss of the self – in these situations a series of self-evident values or, as he also calls them, 'standards of the heart'[26] are revealed from the magical perspective. Because man can find valuable safety here, these moments of magical rapture have a privileged status for him. Not only do they disclose the world in a synaesthetic richness of meaning – a richness not accessible to mechanical action – they also provide him with the ethical standards of orientation that dissolves, in the process of disenchantment, into a pluralism of fashionable arbitrary options. Again and again, Jünger's diary-like notes end in the description of corresponding situations of magical rapture. Intoxication, sleep, and the danger of dying are for him keys to that one experience which in a unique way establishes a correspondence between soul and world because it is not shaped by an attitude of instrumental control.[27] It is not until he describes the sociocultural developments of modern life as a particular danger for the possibility of those magical states that Jünger transforms this anthropological starting point into a critique of culture. In the metropolises, the dictates of instrumental reacting are so dominant that a 'rigid, automatic, and, as it were, narcotized attitude'[28] is spreading everywhere; through the development of military technology, the danger experienced in war is robbed of its threatening vividness, so that this danger can no longer lead into the raptured frenzy of battle as an 'inner experience.' All told, according to Jünger, the empty mechanics of routine action threatens to crush the creative richness of magical experiences, a richness that provides us with values.

From this situation of an all-dominating mechanics of time Jünger recommends an escape route: a revival of magical attitudes. It is possible to resist the draining of our world of perception only if those final bulwarks to instrumental reason are defended and expanded, namely those bulwarks found in sensitive attention to the states of intoxication, dream, and the danger of dying. But this recommendation is addressed not to everyone suffering under the dictates of purposive rationality, but only to those few who do not belong to the narcotized masses. From the outset, Jünger is too moulded by the elitist image of society entertained by the conservative critique of culture to be able to address his diagnosis of the times to more than a small minority of contemporaries. His programme is that of an elitist re-enchantment of the world that has no other goal than to provide a circle of determined, specially chosen people with the chance of magical rapture as well as the security of traditional values. But at this point, if not before, Benjamin's theory differs radically from Jünger's reflections on the times. As we can recognize today, Benjamin does indeed share with Jünger the thesis that the sociocultural upheavals of the industrial world lead to an atrophying of our abilities to perceive. With regard to the intensifying process of the loss of experience, he also agrees with Jünger that we have to find systematic ways to win back modes of such a complex perception for our present. But this idea assumes a function in Benjamin's work that is completely different from the one ascribed to it in Jünger's anthropological materialism. Winning back lost modes of experience serves not the restoration of a traditional ethics, but the attempt to settle the moral debt we have to a past in need of redemption. What represents the core of Benjamin's theory is the conviction that only magical forms of experience can provide the methodological model for an attitude within which we can disclose the past in such a way that the injustices perpetrated there can be atoned for retrospectively in the present.[29] The relation between concept of experience and moral intention hinted at here is explained by Benjamin's unique conception of history.

V

All his life Benjamin adhered to a conception of history in which there is an indissoluble connection between the injustice of the past and the emancipatory chances of the present.[30] The 'Theses on the Philosophy of History' just summarize, in metaphorical accentuation, what he saw from the outset in the tradition of Jewish Messianism as a moral debt of the historical process. 'Like every generation that preceded us,' he writes in the Theses, 'we have been endowed with a *weak* Messianic power, a power to which the past has a claim.'[31] What is meant by 'claim' here is a kind of moral right that past generations have *vis-à-vis* those living, because the latter draw advantage from the sufferings and toils which the former had to endure and which were not atoned for. Every present is enriched by the material and symbolic goods which the preceding generations created in 'anonymous toil'[32] without ever having been compensated for their sacrifices and privations. Thus, every historical process is pervaded by a chain of moral entanglements, one in which every unatoned suffering of the past further increases the objective debt of the present generation. To be freed from this growing debt is, however, for Benjamin a condition to which the success of human emancipation as a whole is attached; for without an appropriate atonement for all the wrongs that precede every present, no generation can know itself to be 'free', in a sense which includes the freedom of an unforced agreement with oneself. Thus, every attempt to continue the unconcluded struggles of the past presupposes anew in the present the endeavour to help realize the moral claim of past generations.

Yet, with this interpretation we have so far only clarified what it means to say that the past has an objective claim *vis-à-vis* each present generation. What remains open, however, is how this moral debt can ever be settled, given that the victims to be atoned belong, irretrievably, to the realm of the dead. In interpreting what Benjamin might have imagined such a rescuing of the past to be, there are two alternative paths open to us. At the end of the first one is the religious idea of the Last Judgment, the implication of which Horkheimer already pointed out critically in a letter to Benjamin. This idea is not compatible with the premises of a materialistic theory because it cannot get by without reference to a transcendent divinity.[33] The second path, on the other hand, leads to the attempt to understand the idea of a 'Messianic power' such that it remains compatible with the presuppositions of postreligious thinking. Here, the idea of the belated settlement of our debt to victims of past wrongs must assume the character of a symbolic restitution of their moral integrity.[34] Such an interpretation requires the clarification of the moral context that can persist between the suffering of past generations and history's remembering. By every wrong of the kind Benjamin imagines when he speaks of the 'barbarism'[35] of human history, a group of people is ostracized from the moral community of all human beings.

The fact that the cries for help of these victims, their silent revolt, or their loud protests, were not listened to by their contemporaries, and that they became history's anonymous losers, simply means that they could not enjoy recognition in respect of their moral rights in their own time. If a wrongdoing is not atoned for in the lifetime of the victims, they pass away as anonymous beings to whom the moral community of mankind refused admission. Because every new generation automatically becomes a part of this moral community, and thus expands the latter from epoch to epoch, it also takes over this community's past ostracizations as long as it does not, of its own accord and deliberately, subject them to correction. Every present is therefore connected anew to the unatoned victims of history through a moral band which consists in the silent demand that their personal integrity be restored retrospectively by admitting them into the moral community of mankind. If this is what Benjamin meant by the 'claim' of the past, then the act of redeeming it can of course only have symbolic character. The 'Messianic power' which continually accrues to every present means the inexhaustible ability to retrospectively make history's victims members of a continually expanding community. Now, it is my thesis that Benjamin wanted to grasp this ability as the accomplishment of a historiography that can disclose the past in such a way that the dead victims assume anew the form of animated beings. A 'Messianic power' falls to us today to the extent that we represent [*vergegenwärtigen*] the historical process in such a manner that its losers again appear as interacting partners in our present experiences and thereby become members of the moral community. Of course, such a conception of history, based on making the past present [*vergegenwärtigen*], is only possible in the first place if we adhere methodologically to the guidelines of that form of experience which is currently in danger of being destroyed.

VI

From his ceaseless study of Marcel Proust's *oeuvre*, Benjamin may have received the first inklings of the idea that the methodological perspective provided by a kind of 'involuntary remembering' (*mémoire involontaire*) is necessary in order to be able to present the past in all its presence.[36] Proust, however refracted by independent thought, was also a student of Henri Bergson. To make one's own life-history present meant for him to describe it in literature with the attitude we assume in moments of lowered attention, specifically, in moments of awakening and daydreaming. It is only in such states that the habitualized memory-sets lose so much of their power to steer action that those memory images can come to consciousness in which a trace of the original fullness of experience has been preserved.[37] It is from this use of 'involuntary remembering' in making one's childhood present that Benjamin takes his methodological orientation in order to determine the procedure of a historiography opposed to historicism. The aim he thus pursues follows from the moral function that the disclosure of history has to fulfil for him. Because it must, as with Proust, generate images of the past that can enter a communicative relation with experiences of the present, Benjamin undertakes the difficult, indeed daring, attempt to transfer Proust's narrative techniques to the depiction of history. Taking one's orientation from Proust's conception of remembering should ensure that historiography assumes the form of a world disclosure which is directed backward and by means of which former victims become the symbolically represented partners of a reopened process of reaching understanding. Thus, for Benjamin, making history present [*Vergegenwärtigung der Geschichte*] must mean projecting images of a past epoch which share with Proustian memory images the property of being so direct and so charged with experience that we can, as it were, enter into communication with them.

Benjamin was of course aware of the many difficulties that such an undertaking necessarily poses; all the methodological efforts that he made around the *Passagen-Werk* can be interpreted as attempts to circumscribe exactly the perspective that, within historiography, would correspond to Proust's narrative perspective.[38] It is of course only in a metaphorical sense that the depiction of entire historical epochs can follow from the attitude we involuntarily adopt when we recall our own childhood in states of reduced attention. In the case of historiography, the remembering subject must be replaced by an imagined group or an entire generation; and what is to be remembered is not directly accessible but must first be uncovered as historical material in a demanding study of the sources. Furthermore, within the framework of historiography, the involuntariness of the memory images – that they overwhelm the subject in the manner in which they appear – can be reproduced only artificially. Special techniques for presenting the material, for example, the associative collage of quotations, are needed in order to produce roughly the same impression that the 'magical similarities' between present and past awaken in a text by Proust. The countless attempts Benjamin made in his writings to describe the structural peculiarities of states of awakening or of cocaine have in the end only one goal: to become clear about a form of experience whose perspective on perception has to be reconstructed by historiography if it is to disclose the past as a province of communication open to the present. Here it is clear that Benjamin does not want to counteract the historical process of the loss of experience with possibilities of a re-enchantment of the world; rather, the moral impetus of his philosophy of history forces him to treat magical experiences as the methodological model for a historiography that may be able to settle our debt to the past generation.

If the systematic idea that Benjamin followed as a unity-creating motif all his life is adequately summarized in this line of reasoning, then serious doubts about its theoretical implementation are of course called for today. The programme requires a form of historiography that is capable of methodologically reproducing the pattern of magical experience to such a degree that the epochs disclosed by it open up as spheres of communication within which we can enter into interaction with forgotten victims for the purposes of moral rehabilitation. Even this brief formulation makes it unequivocally clear what kind of problems a reactivation of Benjamin's basic intentions would pose for us today. First of all, for all the seriousness of his thought, it remains unclear how a historiography is to be methodologically constituted that is to grasp its object in that attitude which we involuntarily take in states of reduced attention. It is indeed the case that recent uses of the collage technique and of multiperspectivism are suitable for retrospectively vitalizing historical events as multivoiced action occurrences, so that viewpoints of hitherto excluded groups and strata can also become visible. Even this radically conducted decentring of the narrative perspective, however, does not lead to a historiography that could enable us to experience past events as synaesthetically and imaginatively as happens in rare moments of half-wakefulness and awakening. Secondly, however, even if such a methodological reproduction of quasi-magical experience were possible, it would be still unclear to what extent it would be meaningful to speak of a communicative relationship to people or even groups of people who belong to the realm of the dead.

True, with the help of new kinds of representation techniques, a historical making-present of the past might assume such an intensive character that the voices of maltreated and oppressed victims can again be heard symbolically, as it were; but even in such cases, one can speak of a communication, however constituted, only in a metaphorical sense because the artificially revived subjects do not, for their part, have the chance to argue in language. Finally, even if this manner of speaking about 'communication' were nevertheless to be considered legitimate language usage, a third problem would still remain unresolved: whether such a communicative disclosure of the past could indeed lead to a symbolic restitution of the victims' moral integrity. However this question is answered, by posing it, Benjamin has set us a task whose fulfilment historical remembering has to force upon itself, even if we no longer share the metaphysical premises of his project.[39]

(Translated by John Farrell)

NOTES

1. I cite the following edition of Benjamin's works: Walter Benjamin, *Gesammelte Schriften*, in cooperation with T.W. Adorno and G. Scholem edited by R. Tiedemann and H. Schweppenhäuser, vols. I-VII, Suhrkamp Frankfurt am Main 1974-1989. [Translator's note: Some of the essays cited are in the following collections: *Reflections; Essays, Aphorisms, Autobiographical Writings*, ed. and intro. Peter Demetz, trans. Edmund Jephcott, Harcourt Brace Jovanovich, New York 1978; *Illuminations*, ed. and intro. Hannah Arendt, trans. Harry Zohn, Fontana, London 1973.]
2. Walter Benjamin, 'Über das Programm einer kommenden Philosophie,' in *Gesammelte Schriften*, vol.II, I, *op.cit.*, pp157-171.
3. *Ibid.*, p158.
4. *Ibid.*, p159.

5. *Ibid.*, p167.
6. See Jürgen Habermas, *Knowledge and Human Interests*, trans. Jeremy J. Shapiro, 2nd edn., Heinemann, London 1978, pp140ff.
7. On John Dewey, see, for instance, Hans Joas, *Die Kreativität des Handelns*, Suhrkamp, Frankfurt am Main 1992, tr. forthcoming (Polity); on Bergson, see Konstantin Romanos, *Heimkehr – Henri Bergsons lebensphilosophische Ansatze zur Heilung von erstarrtem Leben*, Athenäum, Frankfurt am Main 1988.
8. Benjamin, 'Über das Programm einer kommenden Philosophie,' *op.cit.*, p162.
9. *Ibid.*
10. *Ibid.*, p163.
11. Neither Benjamin's relation to Bergson's philosophy of life nor his widely documented interest in Klages has been sufficiently researched yet. An exegetical overview of his relation to Klages is provided by Werner Fuld, 'Walter Benjamins Beziebung zu Ludwig Klages,' *Akzente* 28 (1981): pp274-287; interesting references to Bergson can be found in a new, very informative, and clear work on the *Passagen-Werk* by Heiner Weidemann, *Flânerie, Sammlung, Spiel*, Fink, Munich 1992.
12. See Henri Bergson, 'Materie und Gedachtnis,' in *Materie und Gedächtnis*, Fischer, Frankfurt am Main 1964, pp43-245, esp., Chapter Two.
13. Benjamin, 'The Image of Proust,' in *Illuminations. op.cit.*, p207.
14. See, among other essays, Benjamin, 'Charles Baudelaire: Ein Lyriker im Zeitalter des Hochkapitalismus,' *Gesammelte Schriften*, vol.I, 2, *op.cit.*, pp509-690 (e.g., pp572, 627f). [Translator's note: Part 2 of this series of essays, 'Über einige Motive bei Baudelaire'(pp605-653), is translated as 'On Some Motifs in Baudelaire,' in *Illuminations, op.cit.*, pp157-202.]
15. Benjamin, 'Surrealism,' in *Reflections, op.cit.*, p179.
16. Benjamin, 'On the Mimetic Faculty,' in *Reflections, op.cit.*, pp333-336.
17. Benjamin, 'The Storyteller,' in *Illuminations, op.cit.*, pp83-109 (esp., pp91-93).; 'On Some Motifs in Baudelaire,' *op.cit.*, e.g., pp178f.
18. Ferdinand Tonnies, *Community and Association*, trans. and suppl. Charles P. Loomis, Routledge & Kegan Paul, London 1974; on the correspondences between Tonnies and Benjamin on this point, see the very informative study by Jörg Pfuhl, *Zum Erfahrungsbegriff Walter Benjamins. 'Echte historische Erfahrung' im Spätwerk*, Master's thesis, Freie Universität Berlin 1990, chap.II,1.
19. 'The Storyteller,' *op.cit.*, pp88f; 'On Some Motifs in Baudelaire,' *op.cit.*, pp160f.
20. The texts central for this complex are 'On Some Motifs in Baudelaire,' *op.cit.*, pp188ff; 'The Work of Art in the Age of Mechanical Reproduction,' in *Illuminations, op.cit.*, pp2 19-253; very helpful is the interpretation by Jürgen Habermas, 'Walter Benjamin: Conciousness-Raising or Rescuing Critique,' in *Philosophical-Political Profiles*, trans. Frederick G. Lawrence, MIT Press, Cambridge, Mass. 1983, pp129-163.

21. On tbe distinction between experience and lived experience, see 'On Some Motifs in Baudelaire,' *op.cit.*, pp162ff; as well as the interpretation by Heiner Weidemann, *Flânerie, Sammlung, Spiel*, *op.cit.*, pp67f.
22. 'On Some Motifs in Baudelaire,' *op.cit.*, p160.
23. As a whole, see *ibid.*, pp159ff.
24. Karl Heinz Bohrer drew atention to this already some time ago, see *Die Ästhetik des Schreckens*, Hanser, Munich 1978; see also Martin Meyer, *Ernst Jünger*, Hanser, Munich 1990, pp154ff.
25. I shall refer to the first version of this text, in *Sämtliche Werke, Band 9: Das abeneucrliche Herz. Essays III*, Klett-Cotta, Stuttgart 1979, pp3I ff; very informative on the context is Martin Meyer, *op.cit.*, chap.II; Hans-Peter Schwarz, *Der konservative Anarchist. Politik und Zeilkritik Ernst Jüngers*, Rombach, Freiburg 1962.
26. Jünger,*op.cit.*, p55.
27. See, for instance, *ibid.*, pp62, 72.
28. *Ibid.*, p80.
29. However, an alternative within Benjamin's works becomes visible at this point, one which is shaped by the idea of reacting to the historical process of the loss of experience not by attempting a retrieval, but by decisively abandoning all types of intact, complete, or quasi-magical experience. A model of experience, which is antiquated for social and historical reasons, is then to be replaced by the new pattern of a perception that is low in experiential content, but for that reason precise with regard to the matter and unimpassioned. At various places, Benjamin made this conception of an alternative the core of his aesthetic programme: 'The Work of Art in the Age of Mechanical Reproduction,' *op.cit.*; 'Erfahrung und Armut,' in *Gesammelte Schriften*, vol.II, I *op.cit.*, pp213-219.
30. On Benjamin's philosophy of history, see Habermas, *op.cit.*; Rolf Tiedemann, *Studien zur Philosophie Walter Benjamins*, Suhrkamp, Frankfurt am Main 1973, pp128ff. On the Jewish background of Benjamin's reflections on the philosophy of history, see Susan A. Handelman, *Fragments of Redemption. Jewish Thought and Literary Theory in Benjamin, Scholem and Levinas*, Indiana University Press, Bloomington 1991, Part One.
31. Benjamin, 'Theses on the Philosophy of History,' in *Illuminations*, *op.cit.*, p256.
32. *Ibid.*, p258.
33. See Benjamin, *Das Passagen-Werk, Gesammelte Schriften*, vol.V, 1, *op.cit.*, pp588f; on the context, see also Thomas McCarthy, 'Philosophical Foundations of Political Theology: Kant, Peukert and the Frankfurt School,' in *Civil Religion and Political Theology*, ed. L.S. Rouner, University of Notre Dame Press, Notre Dame, 1986, pp23ff.
34. Here I take my orientation from the excellent article by Lutz Wingert, 'Haben wir moralische Verpflichtungen gegendber früheren Generationen? Moralischer

Universalismus und erinnernde Solidarität,' *Babylon* 9 (1991): pp78-94.

35. Benjamin, 'Theses on the Philosophy of History,' *op.cit.*, p258.
36. On Benjamin's relation to Proust, see Weidemann, *op.cit.*, pp55ff; Peter Szondi, 'Hoffnung im Vergangenen. Über Walter Benjamin,' in *Satz und Gegensatz*, Suhrkamp, Frankfurt am Main 1964, pp79ff.
37. See Anthony E. Pilkington, *Bergson and His Influence. A Reassessment*, Cambridge University Press, Cambridge 1976, Chapter 4.
38. With regard to the methodological layout of the *Passagen-Werk*, this has been most clearly seen by Weidemann, *op.cit.*, pp55ff.
39. See, for instance, Aleida Assmann and Dietrich Harth, eds., *Mnemosyne. Formen under Funktionen der kulturellen Erinnerung*, Fischer, Frankfurt am Main 1991.

SHOAH, REMEMBRANCE AND THE ABEYANCE OF FATE: WALTER BENJAMIN'S 'FATE AND CHARACTER'

Andrew Benjamin

OPENING

Any attempt to begin will mark out an opening. Giving rise, within it, to a site, a further opening that is still to be completed. It is thus still open. It will be here that the subject in question intrudes. Here there are three beginnings. They are connected and thereby admit a complexity of subject and a complex of sites. It is the character of this occurrence, the Shoah as that which is to be determined – a determination hearing, at the same time, the fate of its register – that is at issue here. The problematic element is the extent to which it – the occurrence in question, its character – can be stated. As an approach the enduring problem of thinking this occurrence, allowing it – and in using 'it' to acknowledge, without hesitation, the poverty of any form of generality – to arise as a demand for philosophy. It is this demand that will be taken up in this instance in relation to Walter Benjamin's paper 'Fate and Character'. The twofold nature of the demand will already work to situate the present.[1] As beginnings, therefore, they will cross.

THE FIRST BEGINNING

Of that which occurred – the Shoah's occurrence – apart from factual detail and the detail, the plethora, of facts, (with their absolutely necessary, thus obligatory, accumulation) what can be known? What is being questioned here, as a beginning, is neither memory nor the project of remembrance but knowledge and with it the envisaged, given, relationship between epistemology and memory. What does memory know? The language of knowledge and with it the possibility of knowledge will always reach a limit. However the limit encountered is not located within the realm of the purely epistemological; in other words it does not pertain exclusively to what can be known. It is rather that the limit is established and thus delimited by the work of representation, since any epistemic claim is enacted within the general problematic of representation. Thus it does not just always have to appear as a representation: it is constrained to appear as one. (What is opened here, an opening that will have to be pursued elsewhere, is the complex and in the end conflictual relationship between epistemology and judgement.) The question – the question of knowing what took place – concerns therefore the representation of what is known. Representation presents the known. (Fiction's parasitism, a self-given site, is included therein.) The situation is more complex since the connection of representation and knowledge that figures in this opening question has already been and will already have been reworked by memory. The tense interplay at work here has consequences. Indeed the inability of classical epistemology to deal with memory because of the former's failure to take up, thus re-present, the ineliminable link between memory and repetition – a link opening the move from memory to remembrance – will need to be noted. The work of remembrance, initially memory, operates as the already present mediator of the present. The mediation involves memory even though it cannot be reduced to it. Here memory comprises that which, in part, gives the present itself. Furthermore it will be the work of memory in the present, working to maintain the present, that will inscribe hope. Hope, however, rather than providing an opening to the future and thus only ever being of the future, will form an integral part of the present's constitution. Hope, in marking an ineliminable spacing within the present will, as a consequence, be of the present. Given the inherently limited power of dating, temporal markers within chronology, the question that endures concerns the nature of this present.

THE SECOND BEGINNING

Benjamin's text, 'Fate and Character', was written in 1919 and first published in *Die Argonauten* in 1921. Both of these dates predate the Shoah; predate it as an historical occurrence. They take place before it. The 'before' however raises the problem of time and thus the situation of any occurrence, including their site, and of how they come to be dated. Does, however, the presence of an immediate chronological difference, the before and after, entail that a different set of questions must be asked of this text and thereby of its representation? Different, that is, from those brought to bear on any thinking of the Shoah? Maintaining difference may involve both the sundering of continuity and the possibility of another thinking. (The centrality of thinking and that within which thinking is envisaged as taking place, as having to take place – itself a happening that marks out by having to enact the constraint of tradition – must endure.). If this were the case it could only be because of the restriction imposed by its date. An important element of the task at hand therefore involves trying to determine to what extent dates, and the relationship between dates, knowledge and representation could delimit the activity of interpretation and thus of understanding. It may be the case that the time of memory, if not the temporality of the present, eschewed the temporality of dating while also maintaining the mark of chronology.

Might it not be the case moreover that despite the presence of different dates, a before and an after which in being identified and thus accepted then come to bear the mark and enact the necessity of chronology, such dates demand, nonetheless, a conception of time that would in the end be as inappropriate to Benjamin's text as it would to any thinking of the Shoah? There is more at stake here than the ontology and temporality of occurrences. In addition to the implicit problem of the relationship between any occurrence and the occurrence of the Shoah, there is also a more general problem of the relationship between time and memory. What is the time of memory? How is its location as a continual relocation in the present to be understood? Answering these questions will demand the repositioning of remembrance.

THE THIRD BEGINNING

In 1919 what could have been known? What, then, could have been predicted? Predictions always take place in the present. Moreover the act of prediction works to define and thereby to locate a specific present. A present whose specificity is identified here by 'then'. (What, *then*, could have been known?) Furthermore, a prediction opens up the future in which it will come to be realised. It should be added, of course, that this is not the future marked out within chronological time, even though it is situated within it, but the predicted future which is the prediction's future. (This distinction between natural time and the time of redemption will figure in an important way in Benjamin's own text.) Equally prediction constructs its proper past not just in terms of the time prior to prediction but as the temporality both deployed and implicated within prediction and thus in some way furnishing it. (Prediction therefore is not without its correlates amongst possible philosophies of history.)

The temporality of prediction is assumed to be fundamental to any understanding of fate and character because it constructs a totality by unifying time (albeit chronology's time). The predicted has in some sense already happened; the happening of inevitability. Within it the known has already been acknowledged as such and the future incorporated in terms of the prediction of what will be known. The future, understood in the precise sense of that which comes to be understood, will never work on the present. On the contrary, the future will only ever be the work of this present – prediction's present – on the basis of the continuity that it reinforces. It is this conception of the relationship between past, present and future that is the implicit critical point of departure for Benjamin. The assumption concerning the link between the time of prediction and fate, and character provides Benjamin's text with its opening. An opening concerned to break the link between causality on the one hand and fate and character on the other, opens Benjamin's text. In a direct sense therefore it is an opening that defies prediction. Within it, fate and character come to be re-presented in the abeyance of the hold of their traditional image. (Abeyance will mark its own inevitable demand.) The question that must be asked therefore is, to what extent does such a reformulation, or presentation, allow for an approach to the Shoah? What this question involves is the general problem of thinking it as an occurrence. Thinking its occurrence will always be a thinking in addition to that which is given by history. Furthermore this thinking should not be identified with an elementary formulation of cognition and, by extension, psychology. It is rather that what is at stake is far more significant, since it pertains to the use or deployment of the concepts and categories of thought itself. It is precisely this position that has been noted by George Steiner. While he is not alone in making such a point, the full import of his position warrants detailed attention, since it questions the possibility of retaining that which is given to determine thought.

> It may be that the Shoah has eradicated the saving grace, the life-giving mystery of meaningful metaphor in Western speech and, correlatively, in that highest organisation of speech which we call poetry and philosophical thought. There would be a just logic and a logic of justice in such an eradication.[2]

It may be that Benjamin's work – itself the reworking of fate and character – can be read as that which provides the possibility of a response to Steiner's supposition; a response after its happening. There is a problem here posed by the sense of 'after'. The problem is simply that within one possible determination nothing should have happened after it. However by allowing after's other determination what occurs after 'it' will have to have been determined by it. (The question of thinking through this latter determination endures.) Here there will be a necessity that refuses the charge of dogma. Resisting this determination – turning from necessity – will become, as a consequence, a form of active forgetting (the latter being modernity's own nihilism, the moment of forced failure and affirmed complacency within the present; the present, that is, generated by the banality of scepticism.) The response envisaged in this instance will involve a conception of singularity. As will emerge it will be the singular that obviates singularity. In other words what comes to be given – given as the demand of any thought of the Shoah – will be its insistent presence. Singularity will be defined by the absence of any pregiven relation. This apparent paradox only works beyond the work of fate. What must be resisted however is that possible aestheticisation of the Shoah in which it takes on the character of the sublime.

The difficulties that are encountered here return to the problem of the simple beginning. And yet of course all these beginnings merely begin again, though here from another site, further meditations on the occurrence of the Shoah. It should not be thought that the approach could ever be the same as any other. What this will entail is that the approach – the universality of approaching, the way of the universal in other words – is that which must be questioned; a questioning occurring here, perhaps here with these beginnings, in the approach itself.

TO BEGIN: 'FATE AND CHARACTER'

Benjamin's difficult and at times 'hermetic' text takes up the problem of the temporality of history once the dominant directional determining forces of chronology and teleology have been discarded. In being discarded what is displaced therefore is their explanatory force and thus their inclusive nature. His is a destructive text. It shakes the continuity of interpretation in order to arrive at that conclusion which is the shaking of interpretation. The shaking of continuity will allow for that occurrence or perhaps 'emergence' in which what comes to be demanded is the necessity to think the relation that is enjoined by the demise of totality – the totality of the all – and thus with it, in its path, the generation of difference outside of the pregiven and thus predetermined confines of the either/or. In *One Way Street* Benjamin expresses this break in relation to the startling of truth. 'Truth wants to be startled abruptly, at one stroke from her self-immersion, whether by uproar, music or cries of help'.[3]

In a manner prefiguring this need, Benjamin's *Fate and Character*[4] opens with a series of distancing manoeuvres that may, in the end, startle. Not only is there the attempt, to which reference has already been made, to undo the relationship, here a type of interdefinition, between fate and character, there is also the move to rework the connections – the pre-existing connections – between character and the ethical, on the one hand, and fate and religion on the other. What is essential in this instance is to trace the presuppositions at work in Benjamin's formulation and then their subsequent destruction. The already prefigured problem of relation will be seen, as a consequence, to underpin the nature of this destruction; the specificity of Benjaminian destruction. Destruction already complicates time and in so doing checks the given continuity within fate (a continuity enjoined equally by fate). The sundering of this fate, for another fate, is the redemption of time. Benjamin argues in a later text, *The Destructive Character* (1931) that, 'The destructive character . . . . because he sees ways everywhere, he always positions himself at crossroads. No moment can know (*Kein Augenblick kann wissen*) what the next will bring'.[5]

Here the centrality of the given site, the moment (*Augenblick*), falls beyond the hold of prediction. It falls moreover beyond the dominating and encompassing hold of epistemology. The emphatic moment will demand a more complex thinking. With the abeyance of prediction, and thus with the restriction of universal history, the 'moment' and with it the present will be reinvested. It will be this moment and thus another present that will become the site of hope.

Benjamin's first move in *Fate and Character* is to note the connection that pertains between both fate and character and a signifying system. Neither can be approached as though they existed in themselves, as if they were outside of such a system. Fate and character are always read through the medium of signs; moreover they generate signs to be read. This shift to reading and its inherent concomitant repositioning of the natural is of singular importance. Benjamin's interest in relation to these signs is not with their own content as signs, but with what the existence of 'such a system of signs . . . signifies'(125), in other words with what the necessity for a secondary signification reveals about fate and character. One is always 'read' through the other.[6] It will be essential to return to this question since what it opens up is the possibility of a reconsideration of both the site and the temporality of the given, that which is always predetermined and therefore is always pregiven.

The text's initial object of critique is the posited definition of fate and character where one is defined in terms of the other. In sum Benjamin's position is that the success of such definitions must be premised upon always being able to distingush between the inner person, which in some sense is character, and the outer person who is in the world and thus lives fatefully in relation to that world. Benjamin's argument is that it becomes impossible to hold these positions apart because one side of the person can always be reduced to the other. Consequently the definitions tend to collapse into each other and thereby into confusion. As Benjamin argues:

> '. . . it is impossible to determine in a single case what finally is to be considered a function of character and what a function of fate in human life . . . . the external world that the active man encounters can also in principle be reduced, to any desired degree, to his inner world, similar to his outer world, indeed regarded in principle as one and the same thing. (125-6).

The way out of this difficulty will involve a process of redefinition and therefore of considering fate and character separately. It should be added that this reconsideration will involve taking into consideration what was at work in the earlier definitions. Relation figures in the process that incorporates a reworking rather than the abandoning of the definition already given. The gift eschews any absolute giving up; the task of surrender. Once again, this then necessitates releasing the hold over them that had been established by their having been inextricably linked to either the ethical or the religious. Benjamin's methodological move is encapsulated in his claim that, 'We must banish them from both regions by revealing the error by which they were placed there.'(126) In the case of fate the error emerged not because of the relation between fate and guilt as such but because of how that relation was understood. The misconstrued position stems from the common supposition that 'fate-imposed misfortune is seen as the response of God or gods to religious offense'.(127) (It is due to the enduring force of such ideas that the present relevance of these concerns is revealed.) The argument against this position is premised on the absence of any corresponding relation of fate to innocence. Once the argument is taken a step further by the consideration of a possible connection between fate and happiness then the position of releasing fate from the hold of religion is strengthened. In sum the assumption of a link between fate and guilt presupposes one between fate and happiness. It works out that the opposite is the case. Using Benjamin's own imagery it could be said that the continuity of connection is blasted open. The fate of continuity is now fated since for Benjamin it is precisely happiness which 'releases the fortunate man from the embroilment of the Fates'(126). In cutting continuity happiness gestures towards a redemptive illumination. Guilt and misfortune are not however dismissed as elements of fate. Rather, they are relocated; moved by having been repositioned. The movement here is from religion to law. Not law in the sense of justice as though the latter were divested of fate but law in the more profound yet transformative sense of both the inevitable and inescapable laws of fate and its subsequent abstraction that takes the form of justice (this is, perhaps, an ineliminable doubling of law, necessity's complexity).

Law (*das Recht*) for Benjamin is, '. . . a residue of the demonic stage of human existence when legal statutes determined not only men's relationships but their relation to the Gods.'(127)

The confrontation with the Gods is the site of tragedy. Here it reaches beyond this restriction since Benjamin interprets Attic tragedy as the site in which fate is subdued and the web of continuity destroyed. Its having been subdued emerges as symbol. With this confrontation the tragic hero is reduced to silence. It is this silence that reinscribes the tragic hero in another fate.[7] For Benjamin no voice can be given to this overcoming. Tragedy is nonetheless the site where fate is limited and its hold delimited. 'It was not in law but in tragedy that the head of genius lifted itself for the first time from the mist of guilt, for in tragedy demonic fate is breached'.(127)

This breaching, the tear in the continuity of fate is, in the language of his work on *Trauerspiel*, the place where the 'transfigured face of nature is fleetingly revealed in the light of redemption', perhaps the startling of truth where the reign of similitude is subverted by a repetition yielding the intensity of the present. Fleeting presence is the temporality of the symbol. No longer is death the only response to fate, there is now the possibility of a release from fate by the transformation of the natural and thus the subversion of continuity. The Messianic takes the place of the historical by its emergence within it. This moment and movement of revelation is the *Jetztzeit*.

There are two important additional elements here. The first is the reworking of fate into the 'guilt context of the living' and not of the individual. The second is the introduction of 'genius' as that which provides the way out of the determinations of fate. It is essential to note that causality is being reworked in terms of human practice since guilt here is not opposed to 'purity'. Even if as has been suggested, 'fate is the guilt context of the living', this should not be understood as suggesting that fate belongs to humanity or is the possession of a single individual. It is rather that fate is in human being. It is part of the historical and temporal being of being human. Fate pertains to the 'natural condition of the living' but in terms of an illusion. It is the illusion of continuity and myth. Fate in Benjamin's argument becomes 'that part involved in the nurturing of guilt and misfortune by virtue of an illusion'.(127) Illusion here can be provisionally understood as the forgetful turning away from happiness where experience becomes no more than the re-experience of the already experienced. It is important to note that what is at stake here is a particular construal of repetition – one in which forgetting may come to play a constitutive role.

It is in relation to this description of fate that Benjamin deploys the example of the clairvoyant's activities. With them a connection is drawn with the temporality that Benjamin implicitly links to tragedy. The time where fate is wrecked. 'She discovers in signs something about natural life in man that she seeks to substitute for the head of genius.'(128)

The one who visits her gives way to fate, i.e. the guilty life within him or herself, by allowing for the substitution. Yet her activities contain something else. Benjamin concludes his treatment of fate with a complex reference to time. What he describes as 'the guilt context', (*Der Schuldzusammenhang*), has an inauthentic temporality and as such differs markedly from the 'time of redemption, or of music, or of truth'. This posited authentic temporality involves a specific relationship between the present and the future. The fortune-teller and palm-reader bring the future into the present such that while it is present the future is never co-present. (It is always mediated by a sign system yet not itself mediating the present). Time opens up another series of problems to which it will be essential to return. (As with any return, what it signals is the effective presence of the temporality of interpretation.)

Benjamin introduces his discussion of character by noting that it, as well as fate, concerns 'natural man': He starts by freeing character from its already posited relation to the ethical. The same type of argument will be used here as was deployed in the case with fate. There guilt was removed from what appears to be a simply theological context and placed in the material world of human existence. This link with materiality is fundamental to Benjamin's understanding of the Messianic and thus of redemption since for Benjamin the Messiah is the figure in which politics and time come to be thought together. (The Messiah figures in the interruption of continuity.) Here, for Benjamin, the moral terminology developed in relation to character will be retained only in its having lost its 'moral valuation'. Again he identifies another error that worked, initially, to join fate and character. He formulates this connection in terms of the weave or construction of a fabric. 'The connection is effected by the idea of a network that can be tightened by knowledge at will into a dense fabric, for this is how character appears to superficial observation.' (129)

It is in this cloth that the moral is thought to obtain, for in it a quality can be read to which moral estimation can be given. For Benjamin the mistake here is the conflation of actions and qualities. It is only the former that can have true moral significance. The metaphor of cloth must endure independently of morality. This is brought about by the process of abstraction.

> This abstraction must be such that valuation itself is preserved; only its moral accent is withdrawn, to give way to such conditional evaluations,

> in either a positive or negative sense, as are expressed by the morally indifferent descriptions of qualities of the intellect (such as "clever" or "stupid"). (129)

It is in comedy that actions appear independently of moral judgement. Within Benjamin's general argument comedy is the site where actions only 'reflect the light of character'. Character, in this sense, has no deep structure to be read. It is a surface in which a simple individuality presents itself. This is why Benjamin will argue that nothing can be learned about hypochondria and miserliness from Moliere's characters in *Le malade imaginaire* and *L'avare*. There is no hidden world to be presented. In Benjamin's own terms, 'character is unfolded in them like a sun in the brilliance of its single trait'. Character therefore is freedom; a will freed to act as pure individuality within, and against, the terms set by tragedy. Here is the link to fate. It is a subsequent and perhaps redemptive relinking. Benjamin formulates this connection in the following way: 'While fate unfolds the immense complexity of the guilty person, the complications and bonds of his guilt, character gives this mystical enslavement of the person to the guilt context the answer of genius.' (130)

Such a formulation works, as Rodolphe Gasche has argued, to identify and sustain the specificity of a given character and at the same time to provide it with whatever is necessary such that 'the knots of fate are cut apart'.[8] This means that human being is never reducible to its insertion into the work of fate. (Human being will have to work through its insertion into fate.) Furthermore it is via character that the reduction of the human to the natural is effaced. Once again there is that break with prediction such that emerging in the fissure is the generation of difference out of indifference. What is at play here is not comedy per se but the character of the comic figure as itself a figure. In Benjamin's terms the first figure is, 'not the scarecrow of the determinist; it is the beacon in whose beams the freedom of his actions becomes visible.' (127)

The second figure is the reading of character. Its figuring. It is with this final sundering of continuity – 'the blows of fate' – that another possibility will emerge.

This summation – almost an outline of an outline – presents the constitutive elements of Benjamin's complex text and with it the arguments working to reposition both fate and character. Depth does, however, need to be given to certain of these arguments. A task, however, that can only really be undertaken once there has been an attempt to clarify the description of fate as involving the 'guilt context of the living'. It should be remembered that the specific, though initial, question guiding these moves to illuminate this adumbration concerns the problem of thinking the Shoah. What will continue to be taken up, therefore, is the nature of the connection between Shoah, fate and character. The magnitude as well as the seriousness of this question necessitate that care is taken.

If fate is no longer proper to the individual or even to a universalized individual, then the guilt in question is not the consequence of original sin. Guilt appears in its being forgotten; in its being that which emerges in its transcendence by the work of character. What this means is that guilt is not part of either history or temporality as the merely given, a posited provision. It is rather, and more emphatically, that guilt is the expression of a history and a temporality. It has already been noted that the 'guilt context' is described by Benjamin as having an inauthentic temporality. One initial way of grasping the stakes of this inauthenticity, and therefore of guilt, is within the terms provided by a note to Benjamin's last work *On the Concept of History*. The note also indicates the banality, if not the potential profanity, of prediction:

> We know that the Jews were prohibited from investigating the future. The Torah and the prayers instruct them in remembrance, however. This stripped the future of its magic, to which all those succumb who turn to the soothsayers for enlightenment. This does not imply, however that for the Jews the future turned into homogeneous, empty time. For every second of time was the straight gate through which the Messiah might enter.[9]

The future is always a present possibility and as such a condition of the present. The move that takes place here therefore and which repeats the one already noted in *Fate and Character* has the effect of altering the order, while at the same time retaining the presence of past, present and future. In the earlier text the positive example concerns that which is to be learned from the fortune-teller and palmist. The first thing to note is that it is not derived from their status as those who have access to the future. It is rather, as Benjamin indicates, that they 'teach us at least that time can at every moment be made simultaneous with another (not present)'.(128) The simultaneity involves a parasitism on another life, 'a higher less natural life'. The allusion to the diminished power of nature is a reference to the possibility of Messianic time intruding into the continuity of history, the latter being the natural life of time. This other time 'has no present' (*hat keine Gegenwart*). And yet, of course, it is present as simultaneous with the present, even though one temporal domain can never be reduced to the other. (It will be precisely this present, the present that is denied, that will be of central interest for with it what must arise is the question of the site and the time of its denial and as such their present. What will figure there is the present's anoriginal complexity.10)

However there is still more than can be learnt from the fortune-teller, other considerations endure. While the time to which they gesture opens rather than precludes the possibility of the Messianic, the fortune-teller also wants to incorporate the future into the present and thereby to make the two radically distinct times not just simultaneous but co-present. (Here co-presence would be both ontological as well as temporal). Ironically fate becomes therefore a pure I present. What present means however is the present as the time which is dated and thus the continuity of its being present. This continuity – the persistence of a present yet to be breached – is that out of which the head of 'genius' comes to be lifted. It is remembrance that in opening time works in contradistinction to this reduction to the present. The approach to the future, as with the relation to the past, are both enacted as a remembrance, insofar as it is this construal of the work of memory that provides the model in terms of which the relation to any putative past and future is to be thought. (The reality of the past and the future will no longer dominate as questions, they will cede their place to the nature of the 'historical object' and the place of its presence.11) Neither the fortune-teller nor the palm-reader can be said to remember. They predict within the life of fate. Their predictions therefore form and inform the time of continuity, the pure presence of fate.

Character disrupts this continuity. It should not be thought that fate and character are absolutely distinct for to use Benjamin's own setting, comedy works within tragedy. Here Benjamin acknowledges his debt to Cohen with the reference to Cohen's argument that, in Benjamin's terms, 'tragic action. . . . casts a comic shadow'.(130-1) The casting of shadows enjoins its own play of adumbration, in sum it is that remembering, perhaps uniquely, is linked to disruption. Here the larger question will be the remembering of that whose disruption precludes any simple reiteration of continuity. It is only refusal – which will work as a type of forgetting – coupled to actual forgetting, that will allow the effect of the Shoah to be effaced. As its effect would involve thought and thus the possibility of thinking, refusal and forgetting would combine in sustaining continuity's reiteration. The disruption, the break up of that seamless present, is to be undertaken in order that it be remembered and therefore that the Shoah's consequences for thinking come to work through the demand that it be thought. As such memory and work will be part of that which constitutes the present. Part of tracking this movement demands holding together both the necessity of the task as well as that which makes it possible. The latter is the necessary yet complex interrelation between thinking and remembering.

What must be undertaken therefore – the task that will have already been demanded – necessitates building upon the other possibility for memory, namely remembrance. (A building that will involve working with Benjamin rather than being a simple reiteration of his own formulations. What is needed is work with the work, work obviates the repetition of the self-same.) Prediction will always be trapped by the conception of temporality that it demands and the conception of occurrence – an occurrence eventually opening up the event – that it envisages; the interplay of time and task that marks the epochal present. The latter is that present in which the reciprocity between time and task maintains and establishes the contemporaneity of philosophy by setting up a mutual reciprocity between the conception of the present (the 'now' that is the time of writing, writing's time) and the task demanded by that conception. The suggested way ahead here will involve taking remembrance as opening the present to both the future and the past. Remembrance in this sense will be linked to vigilance and as such it will take on a different form than that usually staked out for it. Remembrance will no longer be simple memory since with the advent of vigilance – once placed beyond the realms of loss – it takes on a political and ethical dimension. Moreover, remembrance, because of its location, means that hope will no longer be trapped by either mourning or melancholia.[12] Distance, maintaining distance and hence relation, will come to be affirmed.

The difficulty in trying to present what is at work here involves avoiding the trap of the either/or. Mourning will always be linked to a necessity. What will be necessary however is holding on to its pathos. This possibility of mourning will have to be maintained. Mourning will nonetheless only emerge as a type of remembering if incorporation and resolution are precluded and with their being precluded, almost as its announced mark, the relation of distance is allowed, its ineliminable presence maintained by being affirmed. Mourning cannot be retained simply as pathos. With the primordial presence of distance – a present spacing – and thus the given necessity to negotiate the ineliminable presence of relation (one response will of course have to be the two poles of contemporary nihilism, namely active forgetting and scepticism) it may be that mourning is no longer appropriate to delimit, perhaps, to name, *in simpliciter*, the active participation within relation. It will be, on the contrary, a participation that affirms not only the presence of relation but its necessary irreducibility; opened as marking the continual opening of the site of vigilance. Again it is this irreducibility that will have to reposition mourning in relation to vigilance. The shift in the register of mourning means that while it is not the direct consequence of vigilance – in the strict sense that it would only be possible and therefore only allowed because of the presence of vigilance – the same maintained opening must be sustained in each. Memory giving way to remembrance causes the latter to emerge as an insistent question. The necessity of remembering is never in question.

It is rather that the question pertains to what it is that remembrance is taken to be. In the context the full weight of the question must endure. Mourning will have become an affirmative remembering which in the absence of its self-enclosing finality maintains hope in the present since hope will have become linked to securing remembrance; securing in and as part of the present. Hope will be inevitably connected therefore to the maintained presence of the possibility of present remembrance. (Again the present is maintained.) If hope is to involve the future, then the future in question is not that which is there for the present. This concept of the future would eliminate the present. In other words the future in question is not that into which the present – chronology's present – is given. Not only will such a present no longer be apposite but in addition the future, in being won over from the future – again, chronology's future – will be there as a possibility within the present. However it is not present as an addition but as a constitutive part of the present itself. Hope is sustained by the affirmed sundering of continuity. The Shoah, however, in forcing the thinking of that which works beyond the confines of an inclusive and therefore predictive history, and thus eschewing continuity, is not hope. What after all would be continuous with the Shoah? Within what universal would it form a part, even diremptively? Hope exists in relation to the Shoah. What this entails is that, in its having to be thought, the consequence of that demand is the possibility of thinking hope. There is an odd and disturbing dimension of this hope – of how it comes to be thought – to which it will be necessary to return. Part of the difficulty is that what is being argued for here is hope as an ontological category. Reworking hope such that what is central is the hold of time and its interarticulated mode of being entails that its presentation no longer has an automatic and unequivocal ethical or moral dimension, one which would, by its very nature, necessitate approval.

REMEMBRANCE'S OPENING: SHOAH

What is hope for? How is remembrance to be approached? The force of these questions lies in the recognition that there are neither monuments for, nor ones marking out, what shall henceforth be called present remembrance.[13] As Benjamin's reworking of fate and character would make clear there can be no straightforward tradition for the emphatic interruption of fateful continuity (the latter being, perhaps, another name for tradition). A way of giving greater depth to what has been identified here as present remembrance will emerge from looking, albeit briefly, at the problem of connecting not simply Benjamin's thought, but thinking itself, what Steiner identifies with the terms 'poetry, philosophy, logic', to the Shoah. The problem will exist in, and for, any body of writing or philosophical thought. This is the challenge of Steiner's position to which reference was made earlier. In the case of Benjamin there could have been no explicit reference and yet the problem itself is raised within the actual formulation of another attempt to link the present and the past.

Prior to any discussion of this passage it is essential to note that what is involved here – at least initially – is an occurrence that seems to demand the description of a singularity that checks any simple formulation of the mechanisms of history, for example, the 'cunning of reason', the continuity of progress. It will be seen that it is in the work of this singularity that the further reduction to absolute singularity is rendered impossible. The trap of the absolute is exposed by the necessary presence of the relation of non-relation. Furthermore, pure singularity, because of the relation between positing and existing, will always lend itself to occlusion or absorption. The problem of absorption that threatens is more complex than it seems. Not only is there the necessity of maintaining a remembering excluding absorption – there is also the real possibility that it is the faithful who may forget. For the faithful, however, the forgetting in question would be complex since it would involve that modality of absorption in which continuity was maintained, tradition allowed to hold sway and identity to remain homogeneous. There would be a monument but not one that demanded its own thinking. Monuments will never be sufficient for remembrance. In general terms the problem, as it pertains to both philosophy and theology, of tradition and its relation to memory (accepting the initial generality of these terms) emerges at this precise point.[14]

The passage in question comes from the fifth of the sections that comprise *On the Concept of History*. Here the 'present' – the cited 'present' – is given a specific concern in relation to the past. As the passage opens, what must be noted immediately is that the connection and therefore the basis for any possible relationship between the past and the present is itself not given. The absence of such a posited connection and with it the elimination of any constitutive role for chronology means that establishing it – taking up the 'concern' – will involve the necessary sundering of any subsequent continuity of thought within the field bordered by fate and progress. 'Concerns', rather than being given, are made. The process of making therefore is central to Benjamin's project. The ineliminable presence of action and with it of inscribed presence of the actative in this formulation should not therefore pass unnoticed. '. . . every image of the past that is not recognised by the present as one of its own concerns threatens to disappear irretrievably.'[15]

These lines, the specificity of their formulation, pose three initial and here inescapable problems. The first is the nature of the recognition, the second is the meaning of 'concerns', and the third the way in which they are presented as the possession of the 'present'. (Again the insistent question is the nature of this 'present'. The question insists because of the irreducibility of this present to the time held by dates and thus chronology on the one hand and the historicism of universal history on the other.) In relation to Shoah, while the threat to it appears to take the form of its projected disappearance from memory, its being forgotten, what is actually at stake is both more significant and complicated. There has already been allusion to this founding difficulty. Indeed, it will arise from having to allow for the absence of a necessary link between the monumental and remembrance; in other words it is given by the absence of an already given foundation. The latter will always be more than memory. With regard to the Shoah there is the relation to thought that must endure since what will always have to be retained is the question of it as an occurrence for thinking. Remembrance is inscribed therefore in the very process of which its own formulation – its being in/as the reworking of memory – forms a part. It is precisely the impossibility of an outside that implicates philosophy in the practice in which it takes place.

What is involved here is twofold. In the first place there is the question of what conceptions of time and memory will allow for 'the images of the past' to be recognised at the present and as part of the present. Regardless of the answer given to this question it remains the case, as was indicated above, that it will always be more than just a memory. In the second place there is that state of affairs already noted by Adorno in which the 'effacement of memory' may be the result of what he describes as 'an all-too-wakeful consciousness'.[16] Both points indicate why the injunction, 'remember', is on its own far from sufficient.

In the different domains of the political, philosophical and theological the sense to be attributed to such a demand is neither singular in content nor generative of a single action. In relation to the Shoah and therefore to the demand that it be remembered, the injunction opens up the presence of already inscribed divisions. Each one marks out different, and at times incompatible, responses to the demands of memory. The existence of such conflicts cannot be accounted for as though the issue were simply that of differing responses to the 'same' occurrence. On the contrary they are only really explicable in terms of conflicts concerning the specificity of memory in relation to any thinking of the Shoah and thus the work of time that positions the complexity of memory. What this means is that conflicts concerning how the task of memory is best served are in fact conflicts that concern the present. The present in question is the epochal present, namely that present that is given by the reciprocity of time and task. Opening up the present will mean staying, initially, with the actual formulation of the passage.

What then is 'recognition'? At one end recognition is, in terms of function and etymology, part of the process marked by understanding and knowledge working within the ambit of representation. In general terms it pertains to representation since what is involved is the taking over of the object such that what is taken over can be presented as taken over and thus as itself; the literal move of re-presentation. It is the move that takes place within epistemology and this is the case even when taken as that which brings epistemology into play. The fulfilling of these two conditions of presentation is the operation of representation. As such it poses the general transcendental question of the conditions of possibility for any recognition. However, generality is not the issue here. Indeed, as is clear from *Das Passagen-Werk*, in strict Benjaminian terms it would be that the monadic structure of the 'historical object' would work to preclude any sustained attempt to understand 'recognition' as re-presentation. In this instance, however, it is the particular recognition of Shoah that is of concern. While it may be possible to address the conditions of possibility for knowledge and even recognition within the framework handed down as tradition and thus as providing that within which such problems are constrained to be confronted, the viability of such a response still remains an open question in regard to the Holocaust. If it were not then the Shoah would be no more than an extreme, breaking certain bounds by figuring the sublime, by being taken to be beyond any given determination or incorporation. With such a formulation the question of 'why the heavens did not darken?' would have to be taken seriously as a question rather than as a symptom. Not only is this a misconstrual of the sublime (it overlooks the role of the faculty of the supersensible) it conflates two possibilities. One is that nothing can be said because a limit is both reached and transgressed. Such a position is inherently inadequate because of its necessary parasitical relation to representation. The other is that what has arisen within thinking is a task that will, in being taken on – in the very movement of its being taken over – come to determine philosophical activity itself. It will be a determination, however, whose specificity cannot be delimited by prediction. It is this latter possibility that is captured by the procedural eventualities in the following questions. Has the possibility of 'recognition', of knowing what it is that recognition would be, been determined by the reality of the Shoah such that its actual determination remains as an open question? Is this set-up one of the factors structuring the contemporary?

If the dilemma concerns the way recognition leads inexorably to cognition and thus the incorporation, absorption and eventual forgetting of the object (the epistemological equivalent to mourning whose effective presences effaces the structure of hope), then perhaps the engagement with recognition that will retain the possibility of hope by holding open the site of remembrance and thus maintaining the demand for active participation as vigilance, would be to hold recognition apart from cognition. The distinction is not gestural. What it would mean is that while a relation would be posited, it would be a relation of distance. Distance and relation are not to be understood as though they formed no more than part of a conceptual geography. There is also a dynamic involving repetition. The repetition would involve a continuity that worked beyond the confines of mourning. The necessity for the mourning of loss and incorporation would be distanced by a vigilance working against the forgetting that would be introduced by incorporation.

The relation of distance would become a site of tension; the impossible possibility of resisting what would otherwise be inevitable, namely the formulation of recognition in terms of cognition. The move here described as a holding apart, or a relation of distance, derives its necessity from the nature of cognition as being that which demands the presentation of an absolute insofar as cognition is contingent upon such a presentation. In more general philosophical terms the absolute in question is by definition epistemological as well as ontological. It must be the latter since epistemological certitude is itself dependent upon the presentation of the object in its totality. (It would be this dependency that works to situate the opening question: Of this occurrence, apart from factual detail and the detail of facts, what can be known?) It is, of course, this absolute which provides the way into representation because the representation is the re-presentation of that which has been cognized. It comes to be presented as such. There is an inevitable logic at work here. The relation of distance will allow for presentations, and thus for knowledge, but these will work at a distance from the structure of representation and with it the logic of identity. Not only therefore does the mimetic presentation of images cede its place to a presentation within becoming; classical epistemology gives way to judgement. This double movement has a critical effect on claims to have recovered and to have represented the past. It opens up its own site of judgment.

The relation of distance is neither formal nor descriptive. It is present in Benjamin's reworking of remembrance as pertaining as much to the future as it does to the past. It also signals the reworking of historical time, ridding it of teleology and thus of the possibility for prediction. The sundering of fate in Benjamin's destructive move announces its actuality – an actuality only there *après coup* – because of that which is demanded of the present.

Remembrance needs to be situated within the relation of distance; a relation at the present and thus working to sustain present remembrance. Its continuity is provided by the tension that works within and thus provides the work of this relation. Present remembrance involves a continual recognition that is always holding open the possibility of cognition – a cognition that can neither complete nor end – another knowledge. In holding it open it reworks the present as a site of hope. (As such the possibility in question will remain an insistent and yet impossible possibility.) The absence of any closure or moment of completion demands that present remembrance become charged with vigilance. The impossibility of representation, the completion demanded by its project and thus with it the necessarily incomplete nature of cognition only betrays negativity by being its betrayal. Negativity is overcome by the projected solidarity envisaged by vigilance. It is precisely in this way that the present can make an image of the past 'one of its own concerns'.

The Shoah's occurrence, even though it is similar to all other occurrences by bearing dates and demanding knowledge, is also and at the same time radically dissimilar. It is therefore both unique and not unique. The question of its prediction; its being the work of fate; its having been known in advance reduces it to the status of a moment in historical time; a flicker in the passage of continuity. And yet it is an occurrence, one whose dates are known. The difficulty is thinking its specific impossible possibility. It goes without saying that the horror is having to think it in the first place. Nihilism is the refusal of this thinking. A thinking that once it is undertaken determines the nature of thinking and as such works to determine the specificity of modernity; the site of contemporary thought.

NOTES

1. While they cannot be addressed in detail here, running through this paper are two philosophical endeavours. The first is the attempt to identify the consequences of representation – understood as a mode of thinking – while at the same time displacing its effective presence in favour of ontology and repetition. This philosophical approach forms part of a larger project. It has been worked out, in part, in *The Plural Event* (Routledge, London 1993) and in my earlier *Art, Mimesis and the Avant-Garde* (Routledge, London 1991). The second concerns the relationship between a philosophical understanding of the present and hope. The latter is a term designating an ontological set-up rather than an ethical or utopian aspiration.
2. G. Steiner, 'The Long Life of Metaphor: An Approach to the *Shoah*'. *Encounter* Vol.68, No.2, 1987, p61. The importance of Steiner's contribution to debates on

the nature of the Shoah and the dilemmas it poses for philosophical thinking is yet to be given adequate acknowledgement.

3. W. Benjamin, *One Way Street and Other Writings*, trans. E. Jephcott and K. Shorter, New Left Books, London 1979, p95.
4. The English translation of 'Fate and Character' is included in *One Way Street*. All subsequent references to this edition are in the text.
5. W. Benjamin, *op.cit.*, p158.
6. T. Bhati makes a similar point although he pursues it in another direction. See T. Bhati, 'Theories of Knowledge: Fate and Forgetting in the Early Works of Walter Benjamin', in R. Nagele (ed) *Benjamin's Ground*, Wayne State University Press, Detroit 1988).
7. There is a similar formulation of the relationship between tragedy and silence in Franz Rosenzweig's, *The Star of Redemption* trans. W. Hallo, Routledge and Kegan Paul, London 1971, pp77-78. For a detailed treatment of the connections between them see S. Moses 'Walter Benjamin and Franz Rosenzweig', *The Philosophical Forum* Vol.XV, Nos 1-2, 1983-4.
8. R. Gasche, 'Saturnine Vision and the Question of Difference: Reflections on Walter Benjamin's Theory of Language', in R. Nagele (ed) *Benjamin's Ground*, p85.
9. W. Benjamin, *Illuminations*, trans. H. Zohn, Fontana, London 1973, p266.
10. The term anoriginal marks the presence of an origin that is divided. However the division in question is ontological in nature rather than marking the provision of a transcendental ground. For a detailed discussion of this term see *The Plural Event*, Routledge, London 1993.
11. The conception of the present in Benjamin's work has been taken up in considerable detail in 'Time and Task: Benjamin and Heidegger Showing at the Present' in A. Benjamin and P. Osborne (eds) *Walter Benjamin's Philosophy: Destruction and Experience*, Routledge, London 1993. In the same text I have provided a detailed account of the term epochal present.
12. While there are, as has been indicated, difficulties attached to the use of mourning, it is widely deployed as a way of thinking the question of remembrance. See, for example, M. Newman, 'Suffering from Reminiscences' in F. Barker (ed) *Postmodernism and the Re-reading of Modernity*, Manchester University Press, Manchester 1992. For a non-psychoanalytic thematisation of mourning see. M. Blanchot, *L'ecriture de désastre*, Gallimard, Paris 1980. The major problem with the structure of mourning is the simple implausibility of the argument for an infinite mourning. Linking mourning to the infinite rids mourning of whatever specificity it may have had.
13. I have tried to develop 'present remembrance' in the context of interpretations of Anselm Kiefer's paintings. See my *Art, Mimesis and the Avant-Garde*, Routledge, London 1991, Chapter 4, and Kiefer's *Approaches*, in (eds) A.

Benjamin and P. Osborne, *Thinking Art: Beyond Traditional Aesthetics*, ICA Publications, London 1991.

14. Within contemporary Judaism similar questions emerge. For orthodoxy, as represented by J. Sacks, 'The Holocaust has not changed the meaning of Jewish life', *Tradition in an Untraditional Age*, Vallenune, London 1990, p151. Within orthodox Judaism there is a continual preference to remember the Shoah within the festival of *Tuha B'av* (the fast day marking the destruction of the Second Temple) rather than allowing its remembrance a special day, *Yom HaShoah*. What is at issue here is the extent to which tradition already contains the resources to deal with any subsequent occurrence. In general terms the question of how to remember involves a stand, a stand defining the present, in relation to historical time.
15. W. Benjamin, *op.cit.*, p257.
16. T. Adorno, 'What Does Coming to Terms with the Past Mean?' in G. Hartman (ed) *Bitburg in Moral and Political Perspective*, Indiana University Press, Bloomington 1990, p117.

MEMOIRS AND MICROLOGIES: WALTER BENJAMIN'S ARTWORK ESSAY RECONSIDERED

Janet Wolff

This essay is not about getting Walter Benjamin 'right'. Although I do want to resist the more radical post-structuralist and hermeneutic readings of his work which are in evidence these days, in which a 'reader's' Benjamin is preferred to a 'historicized "historical" and "political" Benjamin', as the editor of one collection of essays has put it,[1] I have also come to the conclusion that there is not much profit in entering the debates – fifty years old and still going strong – about a correct interpretation of Benjamin's position. It's not that I think these debates are unimportant. I do believe it has been essential to address the question of the contradiction, resolution, or (perhaps) sequential development of Benjamin's theological and materialist modes of analysis and to consider whether, for instance, 1924 constitutes an epistemological break. In fact some of my argument will be dependent on taking a position on these issues. But having now immersed myself for some time in the contemporary versions of the Scholem/Brecht/Adorno claims on Benjamin, re-staged by (respectively) George Steiner/Terry Eagleton/Rolf Tiedemann and Susan Buck-Morss, and diplomatically mediated by Julian Roberts, Richard Wolin and Michael Jennings, I want to suggest that what is more interesting is an examination of the contemporary appropriations of Benjamin's work. Where 'getting Benjamin right' continues to be important for Benjamin-scholarship, and for the historical record, it isn't necessary or even relevant from the point of view of what is being done now, in the late 20th century, in his name and on the basis of what people *think* he said. Of course, misinterpretations, as much as interpretations, can tell us something about the political and intellectual projects in play in such appropriations, but what I want to look at here is the appropriations themselves. Specifically, I am interested in the current revival of interest in Benjamin's work in cultural criticism and cultural studies. My focus is on work in the Anglo-American tradition(s), and my particular concern is feminist cultural studies. I will make a few suggestions about the basis of the appeal of Walter

Benjamin for this work – the points of special congruence between his essays and some current concerns. And I will try to justify my own reservations about this romance. I think there are real problems, and certain risks, involved in the wholehearted enthusiasm for Benjamin (or 'Benjamin') which we are witnessing in contemporary cultural criticism, and I will address these later.

In case any justification were needed for the selective and motivated reading of the text, it is, of course, already there in Benjamin himself, as two of his major English-language commentators have pointed out. Michael Jennings concludes that 'when we use Benjamin to a particular end or in the service of a particular cause. . . . we are always proceeding in a Benjaminian way, not so much in that we use his ideas to construct our own critical constellations but in that we "mortify" Benjamin's own words, we rip them from their context and so expose Walter Benjamin's own pretensions to a higher knowledge'.[2] Susan Buck-Morss, for the same reasons, argues that 'in the service of truth, Benjamin's own text must be "ripped out of context," sometimes, indeed, with a "seemingly brutal grasp".'[3] Two of Benjamin's clearest statements about historical method and the dialectical image (a notion, as I will suggest, which is not unproblematic), both in Konvolut N of the Arcades Project, insist on this:

> It isn't that the past casts its light on the present or the present casts its light on the past: rather, an image is that in which the Then (*das Gewesene*) and the Now (*das Jetzt*) come into a constellation like a flash of lightning. In other words: image is dialectics at a standstill. (N 2a, 3)
>
> The destructive or critical impetus in materialist historiography comes into place in that blasting apart of historical continuity which allows the historical object to constitute itself . . . Materialist historiography does not choose its objects casually. It does not pluck them from the process of history, but rather blasts them out of it. (N 10a, 1)[4]

I don't read this as license for distortion, or for the free play of ungrounded readings: the insistence that objects are not chosen 'casually', I think, takes care of that. Before I address the question of Benjamin and cultural criticism, then, I want to give some thought to the basis for my resistance to certain contemporary readings of Benjamin's work, since I am also arguing against textual orthodoxy.

In the introduction to his 1981 book on Benjamin, Terry Eagleton states his intention of writing about Benjamin 'in order . . . to get at him before the opposition does'.[5] The opposition is the literary-critical establishment, the effect of whose efforts is to depoliticize Benjamin's project. More recently, Michael Jennings has suggested the national or geographical basis for disparate appropriations, according to which 'American readers have tended .... to stress Benjamin as a close reader, and to glorify, through Romantic tropes, Benjamin the brooding genius', ignoring the philosophical emphasis of his work in favour of the literary.[6] I share the critical point of view of these remarks, but am no longer certain that it is possible to argue for them in any absolute terms. For one thing, as half a century of Benjamin-criticism has made clear, the work is so notoriously elusive and, often, contradictory that it is really impossible to deny alternative readings. More importantly, though, as Benjamin himself argued and as more recent work on historiography and metahistory has demonstrated, historical accounts are always in some sense interpretations, and competing analytical or sociological models cannot, ultimately, ever be shown to be fundamentally 'right'. This is something that is at issue currently with regard to the translation of cultural studies to the United States. Commentators like Cary Nelson, John Clarke and several others have argued convincingly that the original project of cultural studies (at least in its Birmingham mode) has been transformed and depoliticized in the trans-Atlantic shift.[7] These days, cultural studies in the United States is both a growth industry and a high-profile approach, as a recent special issue of the *Village Voice Literary Supplement*, devoted to the subject, confirms.[8] But in its new, M.L.A., incarnation, cultural studies has become simply a new way of reading texts, in which any social-historical perspective itself becomes textualized (with new-historicist and post-structuralist justifications for the move), and in which the political meanings and effects of texts have little to do with the institutional and social structures of their production and reception, or with ethnography and actual readers or viewers. And yet I think we have to be wary of claiming The Truth about cultural studies, on the basis of authenticity, historical accuracy, or biographical authority ('I was at Birmingham myself'). Here I agree with Stuart Hall, who, positioned despite himself as the primary speaker at the blockbuster Cultural Studies conference in Champaign-Urbana two years ago, refused the implicit invitation to put everyone right:

> I don't want to talk about British cultural studies.... in a patriarchal way, as the keeper of the conscience of cultural studies, hoping to police you back into line with what it really was if only you knew.... I'm going to tell you about my own take on certain theoretical legacies and moments in cultural studies, not because it is the truth or the only way of telling the history.[9]

Therefore, and for similar reasons, all I want to say here about a particular, North American reading of Benjamin, which for convenience I label the 'Johns Hopkins version', is that I really have no interest in it. (This is not, of course, to say that we couldn't also examine its location, its politics, and its implications, but that it is not necessary, or, in the end, possible, to prove it 'wrong'.)

As Gershom Scholem once said, Benjamin's prose manifests an 'enormous suitability for canonization'.[10] It seems that this centenary year is already the occasion for new activities of this kind, though we will have to wait and see what residues the various conferences and conference volumes will have after 1992. With regard to cultural criticism and cultural studies the revival of interest in Benjamin's work is worth examining, because the reasons and interests behind this are no longer what they were in earlier enthusiasms. In German studies, Benjamin scholarship has proceeded uninterrupted, including in Britain and (especially) the United States, in translations, discussions in *New German Critique* and other journals, and secondary texts. But the involvements of cultural theory have been spasmodic and more than a little selective. In the early and mid-1970s there were two main versions of 'Benjamin' in circulation, identified centrally with the essays 'The author as producer' and 'The work of art in the age of mechanical reproduction'.[11] The particular sets of interest here were, first, that represented in *New Left Review* (and New Left Books) and *Screen* – an interest in questions of cultural politics, which focused on Benjamin's relationship with Brecht (and read 'The author as producer' in that context); and second, an interest in media technology and specifically the implications of reproducibility (hence, in photography, film and media studies). The second of these, particularly, is still an important debate, with the proliferation of new technologies, especially in relation to pop music (sampling, questions of copyright, and so on), but also in other media (for example, a recent copyright case involving the visual artist Jeff Koons). The 'work of art' essay continues to be reprinted in anthologies,[12] and Benjamin is often the starting point of discussion of contemporary modes of cultural reception and participation.[13] But, as Julian Roberts pointed out in the early 1980s, interest in Benjamin seemed to wane after the mid-70s. Ironically, this occurred at a time when more of his work was becoming available: notably the 'Notes and Materials' of the *Arcades Project* in 1982 (in German), and (in English) the essays in *One Way Street* and *Reflections*, 'Konvolut N', 'Central Park' and the *Moscow Diary*.[14] So the secondary books of the 1980s (Roberts, Eagleton, Smith and others) did not really engage with an active critical culture focused on his work. For a while, interest in Benjamin in cultural criticism was confined to the study of modernity.[15] Cultural studies for the most part was still preoccupied with

Gramsci and Foucault, grappling with post-structuralism and postmodern theory, and being transformed by feminism and post-colonial criticism (and with regard to these last two, despite some recent claims, Benjamin is not a great help).

I think there are two major reasons for the current revival of interest in Benjamin's work in cultural studies: memoirs and micrologies. That is, the interplay of the autobiographical and the critical in his work accords well with contemporary tendencies to integrate these two modes of writing; at the same time, the analytics of the concrete are very much in tune with the current rejection of abstract theory, and the desire for specificity. The rest of my paper will consider the appeal, and the risks, of each of these strategies. It has occurred to me, though, that there are other reasons for that 'canonization' of which Scholem speaks, which probably merit examination, but which I will simply identify and discuss briefly here. Four which come to mind are: The Photograph; The Tragedy; The Exile; and The City.

It has always seemed remarkable to me how much those *photographs* figure in Benjamin's texts. More than with any other author I can think of, it has seemed almost obligatory to include at least one image on the cover, the frontispiece, or in the body of the text. Susan Sontag's essay on Benjamin begins with a discussion of some of the best-known photographs, as if the way to read the texts is through the life, itself read through the icon: indeed, she proceeds to do just that.[16] Despite all we know about the mediation of the image (thanks, partly, to Benjamin's own work), we are constantly implicated in some fantasy of immediate knowledge of the author, compounded by the way in which most interpretations do situate the text in relation to the biography. There is a potentially interesting project here, in the analysis of the circulation and production of meaning of these images of the author.

They relate, too, to the *tragedy* of the life, and here I am thinking of what we know about other cultural heroes. There is no doubt that tragedy and, particularly, suicide 'fixes' and defines a life (and, hence, the work) in specific ways. In popular culture, the figures of Marilyn Monroe, James Dean and Jim Morrison – their myths, filmic and other biographical inventions, and canonization in the posters and T-shirts of youth culture – are only the most obvious of many examples. In the history of art, critics have demonstrated the ways in which the work of Van Gogh and of Mark Rothko has been interpreted through the suicide of those artists, which is seen to define the life (which will inevitably lead to suicide and which is, hence, tragic all along); the life, thus constructed, in turn determines the readings of the visual texts.[17] (Early or accidental death works nearly as well as suicide in this respect – for example in the cases of Jackson Pollock and Jack Kerouac.) We haven't yet had the biopic of Benjamin's life (though we have had at least one novel based on his last years),[18] but I do think there is a possible study to be made of the operation of this late twentieth-century phenomenon in relation to Benjamin's appeal.

The glorification of *exile* works in a similar, though more complex, way. (Sontag's essay is key here, too, with its themes of melancholy, solitude, the Saturnian personality.) Here I would say there are a number of different things going on. First, that romanticization of Benjamin which Jennings identifies in contemporary literary studies is greatly assisted by the notion of Benjamin as the 'outsider' – as, indeed, all romantic notions of the artist since the nineteenth century have been. His constant geographical mobility, and his final seven years of exile, are merely convenient physical expressions of that outsider status, which is also manifest, for example, in his marginality to the academy, to intellectual schools of thought, and to the family. In addition, I think there is a new romanticism of exile in play today, which has to do with the politics of post-coloniality. Nobody, of course, wants to be identified with the centre – with that oppressive, dominant, static position – and the result has partly been the proliferation of claims to alterity.[19] For those who do not claim outsider status – a politics of exile – the new ethnography provides the possibility of non-dominating, dialogic knowledge.[20] Although the more radical accounts of this project can seem somewhat disingenuous in their disavowal of power relations by simple methodological devices, the insistence on self-reflexivity as a minimal requirement is a valuable, if less ambitious, development (with a respectable pedigree in critical theory).

What is less clear, though, is the intrinsic value of the outsider status. Julian Roberts at one point suggests that being a full professor at Frankfurt University necessarily inhibited the political aspect of the work of the director of the Institute for Social Research, and that Benjamin's association with the Institute produced for him the same risks of compromise.[21] And in an essay in the most recent issue of Cultural Studies, Angela McRobbie, arguing the importance of Walter Benjamin for contemporary cultural studies, gives as one of her central reasons his status as an academic outsider.[22] In my view, though, this can only be another kind of romanticization, on a level with the Photo and the Tragedy. At the very least, it needs to be shown (sociologically and epistemologically) why marginality produces better insights. Karl Mannheim had a theory about this (the free-floating intelligentsia), but there are equally good theories of knowledge which argue the opposite case, and identify (as Foucault does) the specific intellectual or (as Gramsci does) the organic intellectual – both of these structurally and ideologically related to, even *central* to, social groups.

Lastly, I would say that the current interest in Benjamin's work has a lot to do with his *city* portraits:[23] the essays on Naples, Marseilles, Moscow and

Berlin, as well as the major work on Paris. The city is at the moment an important focus of analysis, across a range of disciplines: urban sociology, political economy, urban geography, art history. Theories of urban space are much debated, particularly with the recent translation of work by de Certeau and Lefebvre.[24] I am not entirely sure how the *city* and *exile* are related. On the one hand Peter Szondi claims that Benjamin wrote no more city portraits after 1933 because exile makes it impossible – as he puts it 'with the loss of one's homeland the notion of distance also disappears. If everything is foreign, then that tension between distance and nearness from which the city portraits draw their life cannot exist. The emigrant's ... map has no focal point'.[25] Benjamin himself, on the other hand, makes the somewhat cryptic note (in 'Central Park'): 'Emigration as a key to the metropolis'.[26] In any case, here I simply record the convergence of certain contemporary concerns with a central aspect of Benjamin's oeuvre.

Commentaries on Walter Benjamin have consistently discussed his writings in relation to his life. This is not only true of Gershom Scholem's biographical memoir, but also of the essays by Susan Sontag, Hannah Arendt and George Steiner which introduce three volumes of Benjamin's texts.[27] Even Adorno's intellectual portrait of Benjamin begins with the sentence 'The name of the philosopher who took his life while fleeing Hitler's executioners has, in the more than twenty years since then, acquired a certain nimbus, despite the esoteric character of his early writings and the fragmentary nature of his later ones'.[28] But of course Benjamin's own work operates on the borderline of subjective experience, memory and cultural analysis. There are the straightforwardly autobiographical texts (notably 'A Berlin chronicle' and *A Berlin Childhood around 1900*);[29] the personal, memoiristic essays ('Hashish in Marseilles'[30]); the individuality and subjective city portraits (of Moscow, Marseilles and Naples);[31] and the diary extracts (*Moscow Diary*, 'Conversations with Brecht'),[32] not intended for publication. Even in the philosophical and literary critical texts we are often confronted with the personal moment – as, for example, in the essay on 'Surrealism' when Benjamin recalls his hotel in Moscow in which Tibetan lamas always left their doors ajar.[33] What I want to suggest here is that this interplay between the analytic and the subjective-personal is a major factor in the current interest in returning to Benjamin. There are three areas in particular where memoir is being taken seriously at the moment in cultural criticism: feminist literary theory, cultural history, and popular culture studies.

In the past five years or so women's autobiographical writing has become highly visible. I don't just mean this in the sense that more autobiographies are being published (which is probably true), or even that there has been a proliferation of essays of autobiographical reflection by women writers (which is also the case),[34] but rather that feminist literary critics are addressing directly the question of the *nature* of women's autobiographical writing, and the ways in which women construct the 'self' through writing – what Domna Stanton calls 'autogynography'.[35] The post-structuralist critique of the existential subject has opened up the possibility – indeed the necessity – for the exploration of the discursive process through which identities are produced and maintained. Feminism has a particular investment in this, in line with the now well-known rejoinder to charges of essentialism and identity politics; as Nancy Miller has put it, 'the postmodern decision that the Author is dead, and subjective agency along with him, does not necessarily work for women and prematurely forecloses the question of identity for them .... [W]omen have not ... felt burdened by too much Self, Ego, Cogito.'[36] The emphasis here is on the political importance of identity, combined with the analytic realisation that identity is always *provisional*. In addition, feminist literary critics (including Nancy Miller) have been arguing the need to integrate the personal into academic work – what Miller refers to, in the title of her latest book, as 'Getting personal', and what Mary Ann Caws describes as 'personal criticism'.[37] This is partly about being explicit and self-reflexive about one's engagement with the subject-matter (so that one way to think about this move is as continuing the feminist project of the denial of 'objectivity' and distance, construed as 'masculine' and already challenged in philosophy by Susan Bordo and in the philosophy of science by Evelyn Fox Keller).[38] But it is also about a more clearly political choice – about the decision to identify and select certain texts and situations as worth studying, and the willingness to state the basis of one's commitment to them.

In cultural studies and cultural history, too, the transformation of method (and hence of histories themselves) by the autobiographical interruption has been radical. I am thinking here of Carolyn Steedman's 1986 book, *Landscape for a Good Woman*,[39] in which she interrogates the stories constructed by social historians, feminists and psychoanalytic critics from the vantage-point of real lives: her own and that of her mother. The inadequacies, gaps and distortions in such over-arching theories become apparent in the oblique gaze made possible by the memoir. Steedman's experiment – an experiment explicitly motivated by political as well as personal passion – has already provided the model for others who want to resist the tyranny of grand theories, the threat of excessively deconstructed identity, and the professional requirements of de-personalized academic writing. Essays in cultural studies and cultural analysis now routinely include the author in the text.

For quite different reasons, this has happened too in popular culture studies, where analysts have recently been preoccupied with their own relationship to their subjects. Janice Radway has reflected after the fact on the nature of her involvement with the readers of popular fiction whom she wrote about in her book *Reading the Romance*.[40] Constance Penley felt she needed to wonder aloud (and in print) about her relationship to the pornographic Star Trek literature and its fans, the subject of her recent research, to the extent of examining just how much she responded to the literature herself.[41] Here the issue is the ethical one of resisting any relationship of exploitation; in this, it shares with the 'new anthropology' a commitment to re-thinking ethnographic method as a dialogic process. One result of this concern has been the incorporation of fragments of memoir, diary and other modes of self-reflection in the text.

I want to make it clear that I believe that all of these are important developments in cultural theory. I think it is essential to transform ethnographic method and to deconstruct or at least acknowledge power relations in sociological research. I believe, too, that writing is a crucial arena for the production and articulation of identity. And I am also interested in breaking down the boundaries between academic and personal writing; my own work is increasingly (though tentatively) at the meeting point of cultural theory, gender studies and memoir. So my reservations about certain formulations of this project (and hence of the new enthusiasm for Benjamin's work which, I am suggesting, is related to these) have to do with how we may proceed with, and what we may expect from, such strategies. For one thing, as I indicated earlier in relation to the 'new ethnography', I contest the view that power relations (between researcher and subject) evaporate if we just manage to be dialogical enough in our research methods; it is still a matter of an encounter motivated, set up, and more or less controlled by one party, whatever the sensitivity and 'openness' to the other. Secondly, self-reflection *need* not be politically radical, ethically correct, or analytically illuminating. It *can* be simply self-indulgent, embarrassing and irrelevant. And thirdly, it can't be simply assumed that the memoiristic provides guaranteed access to knowledge, because we still have to address the question of *typicality*. So where the personal is valuable in laying bare the structures and prejudices of cultural work, it does not necessarily provide the route to 'better' cultural history, unless we can be persuaded that this particular experience is somehow *typical* or indicative of a moment.

These comments relate, too, to the last thing I want to address, namely the equivocal appeal of micrological analysis in cultural studies. Here it is not only Benjamin who is in vogue these days. Although, of course, these operate in the context of very different discourses and theoretical projects. I would link the Benjaminian concepts of the *monad*, the *dialectical image*, and the *constellation* to Barthes's notion of the *punctum*, Bakhtin's concept of the *chronotope*, Derrida's concept of the *trace*, and Adorno's discussion, influenced by Benjamin, of the *concrete particular*,[42] all of which have been taken up recently in cultural criticism. It's clear that there is a real attraction to 'micrological' approaches (as both Bloch and Adorno have described Benjamin's method).[43] I think this is partly a reaction to a growing dissatisfaction with the abstractions of Theory. To some extent, too, it is related to the desire for the connection with the personal and the subjective, which I have been discussing. Naomi Schor has made a specifically feminist case for 'the detail', as historically associated with the 'feminine' and for that reason worth studying;[44] and Norman Bryson, in his recent book on still-life painting, associates the downgrading of this genre, with its very specific attention to detail, with its identification with feminine space and women's art practice.[45] And both semiotic and psychoanalytic approaches to cultural analysis lend themselves to a focus on the concrete detail. As I said with regard to the memoir, I don't intend to question either the desire to work with the micrological, or the various factors which have prompted it. I believe that, at its best, micrological analysis can be enormously productive for a broader social and cultural history. But I am worried, too, about the risks.

Concerns about thinking in images have informed a good deal of the debate about Benjamin's legacy. Michael Jennings puts it carefully when he says that 'Benjamin's construction of constellations of images is not risk free'.[46] Susan Buck-Morss and Richard Wolin have both drawn a distinction between Benjamin's more materialist grounding of the dialectical image and his 'intuitive', quasi-mystical accounts, which verge on the irrational.[47] Behind this lies the classic debate with Adorno, according to whom Benjamin's unmediated use of the concrete is quite unacceptable. As I said earlier, I don't see that there is much to be gained from joining the discussions on just how Marxist Benjamin was (though I will say that I haven't really been persuaded by those who argue that his invocation of commodity fetishism, which seems to me to be more arbitrary than structural and systematic, rescues his project from theology and redeems it for materialism). But whether or not the dialectical image (or the monad – an earlier version of the significant concrete detail) is firmly grounded in historical materialism, I do want to maintain that it has to be grounded in *something*. In principle, I think it very likely that certain constellations capture for us the dynamic and the contradictions of a historical moment or a cultural event, and often do so by by-passing the contortions and pedantries of theory (though, of course, they are never purely 'naive' or primitive – they are never innocent of theory). What I worry about is the invisible exclusions which always come into play with the adoption of such micrologies. I therefore want to conclude my comments on Benjamin's appeal by considering this from the point of view of feminist cultural studies.

What counts as a dialectical image? Even in Benjamin's writing, this is far from clear, partly because his general discussions of the image (in Konvolut N and the Surrealism essay, for example, or the discussion of the monad in the Prologue to the *Trauerspiel* study) don't connect with the micrological thinking elsewhere. So, for instance, it seems that some of the titles of the 36 Konvoluts do identify dialectical images in relation to 19th century Paris[48] – the arcades, fashion, the interior, the *flâneur*, the prostitute – while others ('the theory of knowledge') do not. What is the basis of their selection? A few years ago, I wrote an essay on 'the invisible *flâneuse*', in which I argued (and I still think this) that the identification of the figure of the *flâneur* as a central figure of modernity, epitomizing the urban experience (an idea we find not only in Baudelaire and Benjamin but also in Simmel and later writers like Marshall Berman and Richard Sennett), totally excludes women.[49] This means that 'modernity' is defined entirely from the point of view of men, since women weren't (and, for that matter, aren't) at liberty to engage in aimless and anonymous strolling. The equation of 'modernity' with the public arena has important implications for gender studies. This isn't because the public sphere was male and the private sphere female. As many feminist historians have pointed out, women – particularly working-class women – have always had access to the public. Rather, the *ideology* of appropriate spaces operates to deny the connection public/female, and to pathologize or marginalize women who are in evidence in the street. My point here, then, is that a central dialectical image carries with it crucial gender connotations, none of which are acknowledged or thought through. Recently, certain feminist re-readings of Benjamin have been proposed. Rey Chow suggests that the aimless, non-purposive character of strolling and loitering is a 'feminine' mode, and, further, that there is good evidence of Benjamin's rejection of the mother and alliance with the prostitute.[50] Victor Burgin has argued that we should understand the arcades as a maternal space, representing the pre-Oedipal moment.[51] I'm not sure how to assess these proposals, but I still want to insist that thinking in images comes with risks, and that Benjamin's images collude with a patriarchal construction of modernity.

Is the *collector* (another Konvolut category) an example of a dialectical image? If so, it can be shown that this is similarly gendered. Naomi Schor, in her article on postcards of Paris in 1900, has argued that the collector – or rather the basis for the desire to collect- may be primarily male.[52] Clearly for Benjamin the *interior* is a central image, and one, we might think, which balances the masculine focus on the street on which the image of the *flâneur* depends. However, like Adorno in his discussion of the bourgeois interior in the study of Kierkegaard,[53] Benjamin has nothing to say about the gender dimensions of the interior space.[54] Rather, the bourgeois woman is rendered invisible in his discussion of the interior as the counterpart of the office,[55] and as the habitat of the collector, who moulds the traces of his living in the interior.[56] And where the micrological focus is on a woman, as in the case of the *prostitute*, as Susan Buck-Morss has pointed out, the whore is reduced to a sign.[57] In 'Central Park', Benjamin makes the perceptive, but cryptic, remark that 'Baudelaire never once wrote a whore-poem from the perspective of the whore'.[58] But for Benjamin too the prostitute stands for a male-defined set of possibilities and sexual (and economic) meanings.

I am not trying to take Benjamin to task for a lack of prescience of feminist scholarship of the past twenty years. What I do want to stress, though, is that, as a product of his time, his work has certain limitations, and that in the case of 'thinking in images', we have to be especially alert to how these operate (since their 'immediate' character will not necessarily direct us to their theoretical orientation). This, I think, applies to all attempts to shortcut theory with images, tropes, chronotopes or metaphors: I have recently argued this in relation to the current proliferation of metaphors of travel in cultural theory.[59] I suppose, like Adorno, I am asking for a theory of mediations, or at least for a willingness on the part of micrological thinkers to explore the origins and connotations of the images which figure in their analyses. My hope is that it will then prove possible to learn from Benjamin, and to revive and transform a deadening and depersonalized academic discourse with memoirs and micrologies.

NOTES

1. Rainer Nagele: 'Introduction: Reading Benjamin', *Benjamin's Ground, New Readings of Walter Benjamin* (Wayne State Universiy Press, Detroit: 1988), p9.
2. Michael W. Jennings: *Dialectical Images. Walter Benjamin's Theory of Literary Criticism* (Cornell U.P.: 1987), p213.
3. Susan Buck-Morss: *The Dialectics of Seeing. Walter Benjamin and the Arcardes Project* (MIT Press: 1989), p340. The quotations are from 'Konvolut N'.
4. Walter Benjamin: 'N [Re the Theory of Knowledge, Theory of Progress]', in Gary Smith ed: *Benjamin: Philosophy, History, Aesthetics* (University of Chicago Press: 1989), pp50 and 66.
5. Terry Eagleton: *Walter Benjamin, or Towards a Revolutionary Criticism* (Verve, London: 1981), pxii.
6. Jennings, *op.cit.*, p4.
7. Cary Nelson: 'Always already cultural studies: two conferences and a manifesto',

The Journal of the Midwest Modern Language Association, 24, 1, 1991; John Clarke: 'Cultural studies: a British inheritance', in *New Times and Old Enemies: Essays on Cultural Studies and America* (HarperCollins: 1991); Mike Budd, Robert M. Entman and Clay Steinman: 'The affirmative character of U.S. cultural studies', *Critical Studies in Mass Communication*, 7, June 1990; Graham Murdock: 'Cultural studies: missing links', *Critical Studies in Mass Communication*, December 1989.

8. *Voice Literary Supplement*, April 1992.
9. Stuart Hall: 'Cultural studies and its theoretical legacies', in Lawrence Grossberg, Cary Nelson and Paula Treichler, eds: *Cultural Studies* (Routledge: 1992), p277.
10. Gershom Scholem: 'Walter Benjamin and his angel', in Gary Smith ed: *On Walter Benjamin. Critical Essays and Recollections* (MIT Press: 1988), p51. Susan Buck-Morss also uses this term, referring to Benjamin's 'brilliant writing, which we are so predisposed to canonize': *The Dialectics of Seeing*.
11. Published in English in *Understanding Brecht* (New Left Books: 1973) and *Illuminations* (Harcourt, Brace & World: 1968). 'The author as producer' is also included in *Reflections* (Harcourt Brace Jovanovich: 1978), and in Andrew Arato and Eike Gebhardt, eds: *The Essential Frankfurt School Reader* (Urizen Books: 1978).
12. For example, John G. Hanhardt, ed: *Video Culture. A Critical Investigation* (Visual Studies Workshop Press, Rochester: 1986).
13. For example, John Mowitt: 'The sound of music in the era of its electronic reproducibility', in Richard Leppert and Susan McClary eds: *Music and Society: The Politics of Composition, Performance and Reception* (Cambridge University Press: 1987). Also Andrew Goodwin: 'Sample and hold: pop music in the digital age of reproduction', *Critical Quarterly* 30,3, 1988.
14. *One Way Street and Other Writings* (New Left Books: 1979); *Reflections: Essays, Aphorisms, Autobiographical Writings* (Harcourt Brace Jovanovich: 1978); 'N [Re the theory of knowledge, theory of progress]', in Gary Smith, ed: *Benjamin: Philosophy, Aesthetics, History* (University of Chicago Press: 1989) [First published in *The Philosophical Forum* 15, 1-2, 1983-4]; 'Central Park', *New German Critique* 34, 1985.
15. For example, David Frisby's study, *Fragments of Modernity: Theories of Modernity in the Work of Simmel, Kracauer and Benjamin* (Polity Press: 1985), and some essays in the journal *Theory, Culture & Society*.
16. Susan Sontag: 'Under the sign of Saturn', in *A Susan Sontag Reader* (Farrar, Straus and Giroux: 1982).
17. On Van Gogh, see Griselda Pollock: 'Artists, mythologies and media: genius, madness and art history', *Screen* 21, 3, 1980, as well as John Berger's discussion of 'Wheatfield with Crows', *Ways of Seeing* (Penguin Books: 1972), pp27-8. On

Rothko, see J.R.R. Christie and Fred Orton: 'Writing on a text of the life', *Art History* 11, 4, 1988.

18. Elaine Feinstein's *The Border* (Hutchinson & Co: 1984).
19. See, for example, Gayatri Spivak: 'Who claims alterity?' in Barbara Kruger and Phil Mariani eds: *Remaking History* (Bay Press: 1989), and Edward Said: 'The politics of knowledge', *Raritan* xi, 1, 1991.
20. James Clifford and George E. Marcus eds: *Writing Culture: The Poetics and Politics of Ethnography* (University of California Press: 1986); George E. Marcus and Michael M.J. Fischer: *Anthropology as Cultural Critique: An Experimental Moment in the Human Sciences* (University of Chicago Press: 1986).
21. Julian Roberts: *Walter Benjamin* (Macmillan: 1982), p66.
22. Angela McRobbie: 'The *Passagenwerk* and the place of Walter Benjamin in cultural studies: Benjamin, cultural studies, Marxist theories of art', *Cultural Studies* Vol.6, No.2, May 1992.
23. See Peter Szondi: 'Walter Benjamin's city portraits'(1962), in Gary Smith ed: *On Walter Benjamin. Critical Essays and Recollections* (MIT Press: 1988).
24. Michel de Certeau: 'Walking in the city', in *The Practice of Everyday Life* (University of California Press: 1984); Henri Lefebvre: *The Production of Space* (Blackwell: 1991 [1974]). See also Derek Gregory and John Urry eds: *Social Relations and Spatial Structures* (Macmillan: 1985); *Strategies* Vol.9 1990: Special Issue – 'In The City'; *New Formations* No.11, 1990: 'Subjects in Space'.
25. Szondi, *op.cit.*, p31.
26. Walter Benjamin, 'Central Park', *New German Critique* 34, Winter 1985, p42.
27. Gershom Scholem: *Walter Benjamin. The Story of a Friendship* (Schocken Books: 1981); Susan Sontag: *Op.cit.* (Introduction to *One Way Street*); Hannah Arendt: 'Walter Benjamin: 1892-1940', Introduction to *Illuminations* (Jonathan Cape: 1970) – originally published as an article in the *New Yorker*; George Steiner: Introduction to Walter Benjamin's *The Origin of German Tragic Drama* (New Left Books: 1977).
28. Theodor W. Adorno: 'A portrait of Walter Benjamin', in *Prisms* (Neville Spearman, London: 1967), p229.
29. 'A Berlin chronicle' is in *Reflections* and *One Way Street*. Part of *A Berlin Childhood around 1900* appears in English in *Art and Literature: An International Review* 4, 1965 (Lausanne).
30. In *Reflections* (Harcourt Brace Jovanovich: 1978), first published 1932.
31. All reprinted in *Reflections*; 'Moscow' originally in 1927; 'Marseilles' in 1929; and 'Naples' in 1925.
32. *Moscow Diary* (Harvard University Press: 1986). 'Conversations with Brecht' in *Understanding Brecht* (New Left Books: 1973).
33. In *Reflections*, *op.cit.*, p180.
34. For example, Carolyn Anthony ed: *Family Portraits: Remembrances by Twenty*

Distinguished Writers (Doubleday: 1989); Janet Sternburg ed: *The Writer on her Work* (W.W. Norton & Co: 1980).

35. Domna C. Stanton: 'Autogynography: is the subject different?', in Domna C. Stanton ed: *The Female Autograph: Theory and Practice of Autobiography from the Tenth to the Twentieth Century* (University of Chicago Press: 1987). See also: Estelle C. Jelinek ed: *Women's Autobiography: Essays in Criticism* (Indiana Univ. Press: 1980); Carolyn C. Heilbrun: *Writing a Woman's Life* (W.W. Norton & Co.: 1988); Shari Beinstock ed: *The Private Self: Theory and Practice of Women's Autobiographical Writings* (University of North Carolina Press: 1988); Bella Brodzki and Celeste Schenck, eds: *Life/Lines: Theorizing Women's Autobiography* (Cornell University Press: 1988); Sidonie Smith: *A Poetics of Women's Autobiography* (Indiana Univ. Press: 1987).
36. Nancy Miller: 'Changing the subject: authorship, writing, and the reader', in Teresa de Lauretis ed: *Feminist Studies/Critical Studies* (Indiana Univ. Press: 1986), p106.
37. Nancy K. Miller: *Getting Personal: Feminist Occasions and Other Autobiographical Acts* (Routledge: 1991), especially the essay 'Getting personal: autobiography as cultural criticism'; Mary Ann Caws: 'Personal criticism: a matter of choice', Chapter I of *Women of Bloosmbury* (Routledge: 1990).
38. Susan Bordo: 'The Cartesian masculinization of thought', *Signs* 11, 3, 1986; Evelyn Fox Keller: *Reflections on Gender and Science* (Yale University Press: 1985).
39. Published by Virago.
40. *Reading the Romance: Women, Patriarchy and Popular Literature* (University of North Carolina Press: 1984). See also her comments at a conference on Cultural Studies: pp78-79 of Lawrence Crossberg, Cary Nelson and Paula Treichler eds: *Cultural Studies* (Routledge: 1992), and her essay 'Reception study: ethnography and the problems of dispersed audiences and nomadic subjects', *Cultural Studies* 2, 3 1988.
41. Constance Penley: 'Feminism, psychoanalysis, and the study of popular culture', in Crossberg *et al.* eds: *Op.cit.*, p484. She asks, 'Where did I fit in to all this? – was I going to the conference as a fan, even perhaps a potential writer of K/S stories, a voyeur of a fascinating subculture, or a feminist academic and critic?' She concludes that it was all three.
42. See Susan Buck-Morss: *The Origin of Negative Dialectics* (Harvester Press: 1977) pp69-76.
43. Adorno: 'A portrait of Walter Benjamin', *Prisms* (Neville Spearman: 1967), p236. Ernst Bloch: 'Recollections of Walter Benjamin', in Gary Smith ed: *On Walter Benjamin: Critical Essays and Recollections* (MIT Press, 1988), p340.
44. Naomi Schor: *Reading in Detail: Aesthetics and the Feminine* (Methuen: 1987).
45. Norman Bryson: *Looking at the Overlooked: Four Essays on Still Life Painting*

(Harvard University Press: 1990), Chapter 4, 'Still life and "feminine" space'.
46. Jennings, *op.cit.*, p32.
47. Buck-Morss, *Dialectics of Seeing*, p220. Richard Wolin: *Walter Benjamin: An Aesthetic of Redemption* (Columbia University Press: 1982), pp179-81.
48. Here I am following scattered references in Susan Buck-Morss's book, the major study of the dialectical image to date – for example, on pages 176 (interior), 185 (prostitute), 211 (commodity), 221 (arcades, exposition, fashion).
49. 'The invisible *flâneuse*: women and the literature of modernity', *Theory, Culture & Society* 2, 3 1985: reprinted in *Feminine Sentences: Essays on Women and Culture* (Polity/University of California Press: 1990).
50. Rey Chow: 'Walter Benjamin's love affair with death', *New German Critique* 48, 1989.
51. Victor Burgin: 'The city in pieces'. See also Elizabeth Wilson's essay, 'The invisible *flâneur*', New Left Review 191, 1992, which, like her book, *The Sphinx in the City* (Virago: 1991), reclaims the city for women; for example, suggesting that the prostitute is the *flâneuse* of the 19th century city (p105).
52. Naomi Schor: '*Cartes postales*: representing Paris 1900', *Critical Inquiry*, Winter 1992, pp201-2.
53. Theodor W. Adorno: *Kierkegaard. Construction of the Aesthetic* (University of Minnesota Press: 1989), pp40-46.
54. For example, 'Louis-Philippe or the Interior', in 'Paris – the capital of the nineteenth century', *Charles Baudelaire: A Lyric Poet in the Era of High Capitalism* (New Left Books: 1973).
55. 'The private citizen who in the office took reality into account, required of the interior that it should support him in his illusions.' *Loc.cit.*, p167.
56. *Ibid*, p169.
57. Susan Buck-Morss: 'The *flâneur*, the sandwichman and the whore: the politics of loitering', *New German Critique* 39, 1986, p122.
58. 'Central Park', *op.cit.*, p42.
59. Janet Wolff: 'On the road again: metaphors of travel in cultural criticism', *Cultural Studies*, Vol.7, No.2 1993.

History, the Baroque and the Judgement of the Angels

Iain Chambers

> There is no health; Physitians say that wee,
> At best, enjoy but a neutralitie.
> And can there bee worse sicknesse, then to know
> That we are never well, nor can be so?
>
> John Donne,
> *An Anatomie Of the World – The First Anniversary* (1611)

Donne's words echo with the 'fall into secular time', with the fall into a world that 'is fractured into a series of discrete entities, dissolved from some supposed transcendent state of primal and eternal unity.'[1] An anthropomorphic universe, whose ultimate and inaccessible truth was once secured in the revelation of God, is decentred by an indifferent heliocentrism. Humankind finds itself consigned to a permanent exile, exposed to the raging sickness of the world, where time, truth and the body are ravaged by history and the error of its ways.[2]

The Baroque 'is not as an art of abstraction, but an art of imitation.'[3] It resonates with its perceived place in the universe as the art of witnessing, as the art of testimony. Lost in space (Kepler, Pascal), decentred, the uniformity of logic and nature is punctuated by the accidental: the ornamental, the decorative and the monumental. The continuum of urban space is interrupted and deviated by the ephemeral and the surprise that threatens the persistence of its order.[4] As 'mere appearance', as a *facciata*, the ornamental reveals the essential 'structure of feeling' of the baroque. Here in the aesthetics of the embellishment, in the refusal to conclude and acknowledge a natural order, in the insistence of a temporal witness and the accidental provocation of the event, we behold the senses at work as they unfold, interrupt and deviate the predestined and the ordained.

Santa Maria del Giglio in Venice was unveiled in 1683. It presents us with a *facciata* in which religious referents have been completely substituted by a sculptured paen – 'strutting statues in the common stage postures of the day' (John Ruskin) – to Antonio Barbaro and his family.[5] The façade by

Giuseppe Sardi is dominated by the statute of this Venetian admiral. Beneath his feet are scenes from six naval battles against the Turks, statues of his brothers, and maps of the six cities (Zara, Candia, Padova, Roma, Corfu, Spalato) that featured in the military and diplomatic life of this Venetian commander. The whole affair is crowned with the statue of Glory flanked by the Cardinal Virtues, and accompanied by Honour, Virtue, Fame and Wisdom. In this public display of historical triumph an apparent transcendence is knowingly undermined by a pomp and vanity built on the transient emblems of mortality.[6] We view a façade, a spectacle, a canvas, a screen, in whose glance the baroque reflects upon itself. Caught in history, guaranteed by nothing but its own death, this sensibility extracts a sense of being from a continual dialogue with its limits. Its purpose lies within itself: the erotics of the gesture, the designed frustration of form and function that supplements and subverts the closure of logos and makes of language an event whose artificial, historical, truth echoes throughout the grammar of the baroque.

Between the melancholy melody and sombre chords of John Dowland's *Semper Dowland, semper dolens* (1604) and the echoing bass ostinato and haunting arpeggios of Silvius Leopold Weiss's *Tombeau Sur La Mort De Mr De Logy* (1721), between these two lute pieces, we traverse the musical arc of the baroque. The lute itself, delicate and intricate in its construction, tuning and the execution of its music, is an allegory of that fragile bridge of melancholia spanning the extremes of the rational and the unrepresentable that so characterises the age. Already by 1750, the year in which both Weiss and Bach died, it was destined for the antiquarian, its place taken by the altogether more robust, rational simplicity of the guitar.

The lute masters of England, France and Germany cast their sonorities in the shapes and tempos provided by existing dance patterns subsequently collected into suites: the galliard, the alman, the gigge, later the courante, the minuet, the gavotte, the bourée and the sarabande. But alongside the exploration of these ready-made structures, of equal importance were the musical freedoms of style and execution that were cultivated from Dowland to Weiss, from René Mesangeau to Denis Gaultier and Robert De Visée, in the fancies, preludes, fantasies, and their sombre culmination in the funeral oration of the *tombeau*. What pulls me to the lute, and to the latter group of compositions, is the insistent inscription of the melancholic in these scores. Dowland's titles are, as always, emblematic reminders of this sensibility: *Lachrimae antiquae, Forelorne Hope, Fancy, Farewell*; but it is with the seventeenth-century *tombeau* of the French and German lutenists that this tendency reaches its apotheosis. These compositions mark and name past time – Monsieur Bianrocher (Dufaut), Monsieur de Lenclos (Gaultier), Baron d'Hartig

(Weiss) – in a perpetual dialogue with the dead. To interpret the past is also, as Michel de Certeau points out, to inter it: to honour and exorcise it by inscribing it in the possibilities of language.[7] To name and mark past time and recover it for the present is to produce a *tombeau*, a funeral commemoration that simultaneously celebrates life.[8] For it 'is to make a place for the dead, but also to redistribute the space of possibility, to determine negatively what must be done, and consequently to use the narrativity that buries the dead as a way of establishing a place for the living.'[9] It is, perhaps, from this encounter, along the borders of different worlds, of life and death, where certainties are transmuted into circumscribed limits, and the ego mocked, destabilised, and temporarily held in melancholy before being irreversibly undone by a mean mortality, that the poetics of the baroque draws its greatest resources.

In the ornamental the baroque reveals the corner-stone of its structure: 'Artefice, as sublime meaning for and on behalf of the underlying, implicit nonbeing, replaces the ephemeral.'[10] A sustained *appoggiatura* in the melody, rhythmic variations in the bass, a lingering dissonance hovering between notes (*acciaccatura*), a rapid trill or accidental note, the tremolo, the mordent or the bite, are all ornaments that register tonal uncertainties; shades of potential dissonance that conduct us into the folds in sound. Although seemingly auxiliary they reveal themselves to be obligatory.[11] As if a jewel, the ornament or 'grace note' is not an afterthought, a subsequent embellishment added to the finished work, but is rather the essential point towards which the work strives.[12] Like the small windows high up in the baroque *cupola* the ornamental notes cast light down into the interiors. They direct us into the creases in the body of sound. We traverse the melody and descend into the *basso continuo* of the world.[13] A sombre dissonance, hovering over the formless abyss that lies at the bottom of being, pulls us down through the sound to release a tragic vision of the world and a musical redemption of truth.[14] Over our heads the 'centre' continues to oscillate in the arabesque of an elaboration that is never an 'extra', but is essential to the execution, to the unfolding that disseminates the tonality.[15] As an opening in the sound, usually improvised, it surprises the form with the individual responsibility and freedom of the performance. It forcefully reminds us that the language of the baroque is elliptical. It neither pretends to be transparent nor presumes to be eternal. Sense is unfolded into a sensibility where language becomes the art of the interruption.

The Platonic idea of a perfect form, the circle which functions as the transcendental guarantee of a harmony to which the heavens were expected to correspond, is displaced by Kepler's discovery of the ellipse traversed by the planets. The circle is breached. The centre is duplicated and dispersed within the ellipse. The archetype fractures, the orbit vacillates, the mind migrates. The closed order of cosmology gives way to the infinity of astronomy.[16] Suspended between anterior and posterior certainties – the precedence of Renaissance humanism and the subsequent convictions of scientific logic and rationalism – the baroque involves a self-conscious act of throwing a construction over nothing. Alone, and responsible for our actions and the place of our making, we acknowledge Giordano Bruno's 'heresy' in Zarathrustra's joy.[17]

In the parable of the Nolan heresy lie the seeds of a dilemma that will cast its shadows over the century that opens with his public execution in Rome, February 1600. Alongside the popular mythology of the persecuted man of reason and science speaking out against Papal obscurantism, is the more significant claim to be made on his behalf against the Inquisition for a freedom that permits a highly erudite magician to speak his mind without being reduced to ashes at the stake. This, of course, is the argument so brilliantly sustained by Frances Yates in her book *Giordano Bruno and the Hermetic Tradition*.[18] But where she sees in Bruno (and Campanella), for example, the public termination of an esoteric Renaissance discourse before its disappearance underground into more obscure settings (the Rosicrucians, the masons), and its inevitable replacement by the scientific, post-Copernican formation of the modern epoch, I prefer to think that Bruno's thought constitutes a perennial disturbance. The provocation of Bruno thinking the infinite draws our attention both into the ambiguous languages of the baroque and into the usually repressed shadows of rationalism. Giordano Bruno, after all, was condemned as a 'man of letters'. His 'errors' stemmed from textual hermeneutics, from his interpretation of certain gnostic texts, particularly those carrying the collective name of Hermes Trismegistus. He was a sixteenth century semiotician who proposed an erudite, however mystical, reading of a decentred infinity that happened to formally coincide with the emerging, scientific geometry of space.

Yet that form of reading the logic of the universe does not simply disappear, it haunts and shadows subsequent enquiry. Before his death, and well into another century, Isaac Newton consigned his manuscripts to a trunk. The trunk was discovered by Keynes in 1936. The writings in it are concerned with Biblical exegesis, and with works on alchemy and magic. They starkly illustrate how 'the primary physicist was also the ultimate magician'.[19] We are here dealing, as Loup Verlet points out in his recent book on the contents of that trunk, with the occlusion of an initial discontinuity, with the hiding of the fractured foundation of a discourse. We are presented with a version that excludes breaks and fissions, with a version in which the contents of the trunk are ignored and denied. Newton's years of study of 'mystical language' are invariably separated and subsequently cancelled from his scientific production. But, as Verlet points out, the mathematisation of reality with which Newton's model established the basis of modern science, perhaps finds its genetic moment within a religious problematic that is inspired by and continues to seek responses in other, 'non-scientific', forms of knowledge. Here, suspended between the co-ordinates of mathematics and magic, we are back with Bruno.

The sense of loss, the rude displacement, the fall from grace into the immense landscape of an incomprehensible and infinite (dis)order, in which humankind 'rolls away from the centre towards X' (Friedrich Nietzsche), surely inaugurates the geography of baroque melancholia, the installation of irony, and the modern sensibility of historical secularism. Trapped in the fragility of a desire for transcendence, for completion, for the homecoming of truth, the baroque acknowledges in the very fabric of its language, in its voluptuous accommodation of loss, a destiny of interminable peregrinations that reveal in every instance, in 'all the mornings of the world', the folly of such a presumption.[20] Every statement, gesture or expression is immediately doubled by doubt, every resolution by the uncertain shadows of an imminent dissolution. It is this realisation 'of a truly temporal predicament' that so profoundly animates the baroque dissemination of allegory and irony.[21]

> In this doubling, where the subject refuses to stand unequivocally by his own statement, irony shows both the refusal to give up expository discourse and the impossibility of assuming it totally. The interplay between statements about objects and reflection about these statements as objects is ambiguous. The subject is placed in a transcendent position with respect to discourse, but only to deny the possibility of being the guarantor of transcendence.[22]

The empty sockets of a skull, fresh flowers between its teeth, gaze blankly upon the everyday street.[23] The world, words, women ... truth, have become fickle, unstable tokens of a destitute cosmology: falling stars, children begot with mandrake root, the sound of mermaids' singing – signs destined to reveal their falsehood 'ere I come, to two or three.[24] The temporary abeyance of transcendental guarantees, prior to an imperious rationalism once again claiming the universe of humankind, permits the recognition of the full autonomy of representations whose only reason lies within themselves. Fallen to earth, language, images and signs 'stunningly joined to nothing', can only respond to their passage and presence in this world.[25] The acknowledgement of the image in and for itself, of the temporal construct of the artifice, of the simulacrum, 'implies the closure of metaphysics and the complete acceptance of the historical world.'[26] Yet this is compounded, rather than contradicted, in a contemporary intolerance to loss. For the fierce consolation of Protestantism and the aggression of the Inquisition are only seemingly opposed symptoms of a deep reluctance to forgo: both institutionalise an intolerance to loss. In refusing to give up the lost object, the primal thing, the terrestrial signatures of signs and sounds continue to gesture across the abyss of time in a perpetual mourning that contributes directly to the baroque affect:

> Like a tense link between Thing and Meaning, the unnameable and the proliferation of signs, the silent affect and the ideality that designates and goes beyond it, the *imaginary* is neither the objective description that will reach its highest point in science nor theological idealism that will be satisfied with reaching the symbolic uniqueness of a beyond. The experience of nameable melancholia opens up the space of a necessarily heterogeneous subjectivity, torn between the two co-necessary and co-present centers of opacity and ideal. The opacity of things, like that of the body untenanted by meaning – a depressed body, bent on suicide – is conveyed to the work's meaning, which asserts itself at the same time absolute and corrupt, untenable, impossible, to be done all over again. A subtle alchemy of signs then compels recognition – musicalization of signifiers, polyphony of lexemes, dislocation of lexical, syntactic, and narrative units – this is *immediately* experienced as a psychic transformation of the speaking being between the two limits of nonmeaning and meaning, Satan and God, Fall and Resurrection.[27]

So, the world is not only decentred but also doubled by the coeval insistence on dogma and doubt in every discourse. Open to construction and determinism, the world is also susceptible to a poetics of ambiguity, to a cleft in reason where rational design can slip into the alliterative contours of a dream.[28] The straight lines employed in astronomy and architecture for the geometrical rationalisation of time and space are shadowed, mimicked and mocked by alchemy and necromancy, by magical equations, emblematic insignia and the terrestrial trappings of life, before it all evaporates in the deceptive order of music: the note hangs in the air, and then falls away. In the fall . . . in that transient, dropping away, in that excess of representation, the functional and the rational are exposed as fragile faiths: logics, despite their declared neutrality, that are always circumscribed by human desire. Nowhere is this more starkly displayed than in the insistent application of 'science' to music found in the writings of Pierre Gassendi, Marin Mersenne and René Descartes. Seeking a universal harmony in the geometry of sound and an arithmetic of the passions, they employed mytho-mathematics of Greek and Byzantine provenance that invariably betrayed the alchemical, astrological and magical drives that continually shadowed baroque reason.[29]

If the shortest distance between two bodies is a straight line, it is the shock of the allegoric that provides the most rapid transport from the obvious into the hieroglyphic and the other, obscured centre of the ellipse.[30] Nicholas Dyer, architect, responsible for the building of seven new churches in the cities of London and Westminster in 1711, here reveals a logic that accords with an unsuspected design:

> And thus will I compleet the Figure: Spittle-Fields, Wapping and Limehouse have made the triangle; Bloomsbury and St Mary Woolnoth have next created the major Pentacle-starre; and, with Greenwich, all these will form the Sextuple abode of Baal-Berith or the Lord of the Covenant. Then, with the church of Little St Hugh, the Septilateral Figure will rise above about Black Step Lane and, in this Pattern, every straight line is enrich'd with a point at Infinity and every Plane with a line at Infinity. Let him that has Understanding count the Number: the seven Churches are built in conjunction with the seven Planets in the lower Orbs of Heaven, the seven Circles of the Heavens, the seven Starres in Ursa Minor and the seven Starres in the Pleiades. Little St Hugh was flung into the Pitte with the seven Marks upon his Hands, Feet, Sides and Breast which thus exhibit the seven Demons – Beydelus, Metucgayn, Adulec, Demeymes, Gadix, Uqizuz and Sol. I have built an everlasting Order, which I may run through laughing: no one can catch me now.[31]

In his classic account of the English intellectual thought of the period, *The Seventeenth Century Background* (1934), Basil Willey returns again and again to the deep seated ambiguity in its voice. He carefully tempers talk of the dawning of the age of reason and the triumph of science by insisting on the Janus-like quality of the epoch, with its ability to live 'in divided and distinguished worlds' (Sir Thomas Browne). For what was new did not necessarily imply an irreversible cut in time, but rather a novel configuration of elements that simultaneously encouraged and deviated the possibility of an indivisible truth to be located in a mechanical rationalism 'which supposes that which is fluctuating to be fixed' (Bacon). Writing in an epoch in which uncertainty had become a principle within the paradigm of the natural sciences (Heisenberg), Willey justly queries a rationalist vision of the earlier period. He notes:

> The distinctions were only beginning to be made which for later ages shut off poetry from science, metaphor from fact, fancy from judgement. The point about these different worlds was not that they were divided, but that they were simultaneously available.[32]

This framing of thought, and life, was suspended in a fluctuating and ambiguous balance between light and shadows, between the flat, tabular frame of reason and the infinite spread and inter-layered folds of explanation. Fernand Hallyn writes:

> ... we can consider the seventeenth and eighteenth centuries as the period of transition from the predominance of the vertical axis, linking several levels of reality, to the predominance of the horizontal axis, reducing everything to a single level.[33]

Between a *spiegare* (to explain, expound, unfold) and a *piegare* (to fold, wrap, crease), emerges the *spiegamento* (the explication, the spread, the unfolding). Contrary to the fixed point of the rationalist a priori sought by Descartes lies the mutable point of view found in the body, where to explain is to unfold a complexity and to trace the in-finite in the folds, creases and envelopment of the world; in the finitude of our physical frame, time and place, in the world of our possibilities.[34]

> To explain does not simply imply to extend, expand and lay out an argument, but is rather to be involved and evolve with it. Although the organism defines itself through its capacity to endlessly bend and fold its parts, it explains them not by referring to infinity but with reference to the limits available to the species.[35]

Sometimes the construction, in architecture, the theatre, and thought, leaned more towards the light, sometimes more towards the shadows; invariably it recognised its hybrid provenance in both. The constraints of mortality were inscribed as much in its rational flights as in the vivid movement of bodies and light that are obliquely pictured in Caravaggio: temporarily caught but not centred, falling away, out of the frame.[36] Like the dying note on the lute or viol de gamba, the texture and tonality is decentred, transient, melancholic. This passionate view of things emerges from the events of suffering history – 'bound upon a wheel of fire'- and not from the secluded security of logic. In its violent affirmation this temper also announces the precarious space of the emergence of the modern urban world, and anticipates what in later centuries will be referred to as 'mass culture'.[37]

Along with the systematic installation of centralised government and court life (Madrid, Versailles, London), and the public rationalisation of financial, juridicial, educational and military control, renewed imposition of seigniorial rights on the land induced, sometimes physically enforced, the rural migrations of peasants, sharecroppers and small landowners from the countryside towards the cities. It led to the growth of a landless and propertyless street dweller: the anonymous faces of the future urban 'mob', 'crowd' and 'masses', as well as the urban criminal underworld. To these violent dislocations are to be added interminable religious wars and persecution resulting in rural regions being scoured by bandits and roving armies of disbanded soldiers and ex-mercenaries. Added to this were regular outbreaks of witch hunts and the plague. In an 'age drunk with acts of cruelty both lived and imagined', these were all immediate exemplars of the 'baroque pedagogy of violence', terrifying reminders of a fragile world and a precarious mortality.[38]

In the first half of the seventeenth century London was ravaged by plague – 1603: 33,500 deaths; 1625: 35,500 deaths; 1636: 10,500 deaths; 1665-6: the Great Plague; 69,000 deaths, followed by the Fire.[39] Similarly, baroque Naples is studded with allegorical *guglie* or obelisks built to exorcise plagues, earthquakes and volcanic eruptions: the eruption of Vesuvius in 1631, the plagues of 1656 and 1657, the earthquakes of 1688 and 1694.[40] What was once held at a distance through the promise of another world, life and salvation, is dramatically brought close; it is re-presented (*vor-stellen*) and re-membered, in-corporated and rendered flesh. It becomes some 'thing' (*res*) that concerns and disturbs us.[41] So the last things – death and judgement – become immediate things.[42] The Italian philosopher Mario Perniola associates this baroque acknowledgement of the historical and ontological import of death in life, as opposed to something separate and extraneous to terrestrial existence, with Loyola and the Jesuits. It is not a head full of reason, but a body inscribed with terrestrial constraints, dwelling in the perishable shelter of the Earth and destined for the worms of time, that provides the constant and tragic corpus of baroque drama, of the epoch's aesthetics and ascetic sensibility.

Yet in this powerful proximity, in the marked inscription of mortality into truth, there existed a remarkable amnesia.[43] As though in compensation for a lost centrality the century of the baroque is also witness to the violent and extensive elaboration of a eurocentrism that seeks to model and mould the rest of the world in its image and imaginary. In the moment that European thought considers itself to be a prisoner of time and is cast into the unprotected vicissitudes of history it discovers a terrible freedom. For elsewhere, in the wide avenues, the giant plaza and imposing church façades that the baroque realised in urban Mexico and South America, there is mounted an architecture in which non-European bodies and histories were included only to be ruthlessly negated. Silence, the intractable and the untranslatable was forced to bear testimony to a European narcissism which sought 'to represent even those experiences that resist it with a stubborn opacity.'[44] This invisible presence was traced in the labour, slavery, blood, torture and death of those beings that colonial government, military repression and the Inquisition administered and occluded. Maintained on the colonial periphery by force, fear and terror, the limits of a European possession, and position, were simultaneously installed and repressed as the west brutally insisted on becoming synonymous with the world.

* * *

> The Talmudic legend assigns to each instance of time a specific angel, that is to say its specific quality, or, in other words, its irreplaceable messianic virtuality . . . this figure of paradoxical thought, according to which the end can be realised immediately 'in the very heart of history', subverts the very foundations of historical Reason. It implies that time is no longer to be considered as a directive axis, where one thing inevitably follows another, or as a river that flows from its source towards its mouth, but rather as a juxtaposition of instances, each of them unique and irreducible to a totality, and which therefore do not follow one another as if they were stages in an irreversible process. Here the past, the present and the future no longer succeed each other along a direct line as though viewed externally, but coexist as three states of permanent consciousness . . .
>
> Stéphane Mosès[45]

> . . . all manifest discourse is the repression of what is not said which, in turn, undermines all that is said.
>
> Noreen O'Connor[46]

The complex play of the lights and shadows of the baroque, its limits and interrogation, opens up a critical space that returns to inhabit our present. It raises a question, creates an opening in the construction of our understandings, a rent in the fabric of our knowledge. It draws us into the shadows of illumination, into the repressed zones that our sense of being seeks to avoid. For it forces us to confront and converse with what we most avidly seek to ignore: our limits and our mortality. The baroque critique of permanency and essentialism, complemented by the re-centring of sixteenth-century

Europe in colonial directives, this simultaneous decentring and recentring, returns as a ghost – 'Remember me'- to haunt the dusk of western modernism. It erupts in the heterotopic challenge to the rational, utopic design of the latter. It calls out for an ethical reply to the needs of another scene, another story, another possibility, reminding us that historical reason is itself to be judged. For behind the 'perverse absolutism' (Lévinas) of western knowledge, and its universal desire for an unfractured, unitary logic, a rational teleology of time and causality, there lies the evasion of that judgement. To refuse to register the enigmatic, the discontinuous, the regressive and the hungry shadows of oblivion, and to eradicate them in the violent insistence on coherence, is to flee from life and the anguish of death, and is to repudiate responsibility for that condition.[47]

When the earth is refused and violently reduced to an ethereal pact between thought and trancendental logic, when the world is abrogated and distilled into the pure spirit and transparency of the rational word, all those unresolved, mutant, incomplete, uncanny, cracked, silent and undone languages that contribute to the insistent 'worlding of the world' are denied.[48] As we draw back from that blinkered perspective, turn away from that narrow path, and reinvest ourselves with the responsibility for our lives and what sustains them, other lives, we catch the echoes of our baroque antecedents in the duplicity, disturbance, excess, folds and opacity of knowledge, while at the same time listening to the counter-point of cultural amnesia and European narcissism. We re-member in that mortal mess-age and its history of shadows, the questions that permit us to continue to question, that permit us to live.

It is why, for some of us, the ragged, unwoven and incomplete *chiaroscuro* patterns of the baroque are far closer to our present sensibilities and modalities of being than the subsequent faith in instrumental reason and confident subjectivity. To recall that earlier interruption is to remind ourselves of the complex, sometimes indifferent, contingency of the world before positivism stepped in to reassure us with the secular god of 'science'. The proximity of the allegorical landscapes of the baroque to the radical and disruptive experiences of modernity has been well caught by Christine Buci-Glucksmann:

> Here one can see, well before modern art, allegory as the testimony of the domination of the fragment over everything, of the destructive principle over the constructive one, of passion, as the excavation of an absence, over the mastery of reason. Only the fragment is able to demonstrate that the logics of the body, of feeling, of life and death do not coincide with those of Power or the Idea. In the fragment there

> appears precisely that which is mute (hence music), that which is new (even if it is death), that which is unmastered and profoundly ungovernable: catastrophes that embody the very act of representation.
>
> Reality is here consigned to a perennial antinomy, to the deceptive game of reality as an illusion, in which the world is simultaneously evaluated and devaluated. 'The profane world, considered from the point of allegory, is simultaneously evaluated and devaluated.' In it there lies the specific seduction of the baroque, in which the pre-eminence of the aesthetic – of play, of appearance – is united with metaphysical loss against a background of affliction and melancholy. The metaphor of the theatre – of the world as theatre and the theatre as world – portrays the particular temporality of the baroque . . . Over this eternal displacement of appearances there lies the presence of an omniscient, but now distant, spectator: God. The abyss between reality and illusion, however, is insuperable: the theatre now knows itself to be theatre.[49]

This exposes and advances the contemporary baroquisation of the world in which the rationalist drive, and a facile faith in the linear accumulation of 'progress', is now perhaps to be considered as an interruption, an interval. In an altogether wider constellation the seventeenth century baroque, with its fragile allegories of excess and mortality, with its melancholy acknowledgement of the limits of reason and life, is affinitively linked to the reappearance of neo-baroque styles in the late twentieth century, where 'style', like the earlier baroque ornament, is not a trivial extra but rather exemplifies the self-conscious pathos of the languages we inhabit.

It is in the insistence of our being captured in time, subjected to history and mortality, rendering sense from the crisis and fragility of human existence, that the baroque sensibility flares up into an image that projects light into our world. Like the illumination from dead stars, the baroque arrives to become part of our lives, as something that is simultaneously present and absent.[50] The palpable instability of what we are accustomed to refer to as 'knowledge' and 'truth' provides a telescopic link between two historical constellations. It leads us to the suggestion that historical specificity does not lie in the factual annotation of the passage of time, but in our receiving and acknowledging a discontinued moment by interpreting it and ourselves in its present light. That moment is both unique and repetitive, 'irreversible and recurrent'.[51] For its truth does not lie in a 'foreclosure through facts . . .' but in the event and resonance of language.[52] Truth is not our personal property, restricted to the range and intention of our will.[53] It is something that both invests us and escapes us: it is discontinuous.[54] So the transient past, apparently lost forever, can and does return to activate another, even novel, sense of the present, and, with it, an opening towards the future.

This is to suggest an ethical and involved, rather than a positivist and distanced, paradigm of knowledge.[55] In this mode, the past is never recaptured 'as it was', as though, in a reversal of time, we could simply retrace our steps back along the path of homogeneous evolution to an earlier moment. The past does not come down to us smoothly across the passage of time. It erupts and resonates in our time as a disconcerting and discrete event: as the voice and body of the other that challenges our own. The past becomes the scene of traces. As signs, silences and resonance, we are directed towards what is irredeemably lost to us yet which continues to haunt our language and thoughts, and thereby interrogate our sense of the present. To translate (and transform) the past in this manner may well be to betray how things 'actually were', but it is also to refuse to discard the body of the past. If we were to reduce the baroque to the uniform tread, and ultimate oblivion, of 'progress', we would be cancelling the possibility of its return: the possibility of past generations continuing to interrogate, disturb and challenge our time and our custody for their times.

To temper and test time in this manner is to punctuate it in order to hear the respiration of other ways of being in time. It is to acknowledge our own precariousness in which the past is not given and the future is not predictable: all is to be undone, inter-preted, contested, again and again and . . .

To open up the body of history, and expose it to the vindications of the world, involves the adoption of a figure of time, of knowledge, that is also a figure of speech, of writing, able to hold in suspension the ambiguous 'truth' that language sustains in our continual rewriting of the past as we research the historical potential of the present. For style is the body, the physicality of language. So, we acknowledge in the gesture of a style – of thought, of writing, of speech – the co-presence and responsibility for past, present and future. There the intractable, rebus-like quality of baroque allegory, as the speech and writing of a sensibility, as epochal expression, suggests to us something more than merely a literary technique or archaic poetics. Walter Benjamin writes:

> . . . in allegory the observer is confronted with the *facies hippocratica* of history as a petrified, primordial landscape. Everything about history that, from the very beginning, had been untimely, sorrowful, unsuccessful, is expressed in a face – or rather in a death's head. And although such a thing lacks all 'symbolic' freedom, all classical proportion, all humanity – nevertheless, this is the form in which man's subjection to

> nature is most obvious and it significantly gives rise not only to the enigmatic question of the nature of human existence as such, but also of the biographical historicity of the individual. This is the heart of the allegorical way of seeing, of the baroque, secular explanation of history as the Passion of the world; its importance resides solely in the stations of its decline.[56]

In the interregnum between religious faith secured in the divine stability of the pre-Copernican universe and later consolation in the idolatry of science, the baroque exposed a naked, unprotected being, in which any 'person, any object, any relationship can mean absolutely anything else. With this possibility a destructive, but just verdict is passed on the profane world . . .'[57] Stripped of an obvious symbolic function, caught in the fall of the world, in the profanity of decay and ruin, the baroque points elsewhere by tunnelling into the body, the physicality, of language. As Benjamin points out, the typographic extremes and charged metaphors of the baroque are only the most obvious examples of a language that tends towards the visual, towards the illumination that emanates from an independent and autonomous image. But it is a marked, a wounded autonomy, for:

> In the field of allegorical intuition the image is a fragment, a rune.[58]

The image is both a fragment, a ruin, but also a rune, a hieroglyph.

> The false appearance of totality is extinguished. For the *eidos* disappears, the simile ceases to exist, and the cosmos it contained shrivels up. The dry rebuses which remain contain an insight, which is still available to the confused investigator.[59]

Beneath its flourish of pomp, the baroque insists on the imperfection and incompleteness of the world, it insists on our physical and terrestrial enclosure, on the inevitability of decay and ruin, and so wins for itself, out of the depths of its language, an insight destined to endure: 'Where man is drawn towards the symbol, allegory emerges from the depths of being to intercept the intention, and to triumph over it.'[60] José Maravall also insists on the centrality of the interruption and the incomplete to the baroque, suggesting that it offers, for example, a key to the reading of Shakespeare's later 'unfinished' plays.[61]

The idea that historical time might be multiple and discontinuous, that history is an allegorical construction exposing the ruins of time, is not only what links Benjamin to the excessive and poetic underside of modernism

(Baudelaire, Kafka), but it is also what links the German Jewish thinker to the baroque and his own marvellous and deeply allegorical reading of modernity. The key texts here are the volume on the mourning theatre (*Trauerspiel*) of the German baroque published in 1928, the only book that Benjamin actually completed, the massive and incomplete project on the Parisian arcades that he worked on in the last years of his life in exile, and the 'Theses on the philosophy of history' (1940).

To subvert and discard the links in the temporal chain of irreversible causality, in order to turn time back against itself and release another story, and another way of telling, is what animates Benjamin's continual engagement with the languages of time and being, with the writing of history. It is to give a name to the defeated and deceased, to return again to the overlooked and the shadows, and there to reveal in a diverse scansion of time the detailed instances that make up the eternal pathos of terrestrial existence in the repetitive discontinuities of mortality. In the ambiguous gesture of the collector – simultaneously salvaging and reifying the past – Benjamin seeks to actively re-member, rather than merely recall, such traces and fragments.[62] Like the baroque *tombeau*, he seeks to open up a space in language and time in which another history can appear and, with it, an alternative future in which each historical moment can be sundered to reveal an opening towards paths and possibilities not yet taken. Hence historical time, as opposed to the linear tyranny of physical time, becomes reversible. It permits a re-membering, a return, that produces the 'open' time of writing, of politics, of aesthetics and ethics, ready for judgement in every instance (Emmanuel Lévinas).[63] For it is the history of the 'untimely, sorrowful, unsuccessful', that is, in the discontinued, discarded and dispersed histories of the vanquished, that Benjamin continually sought to snatch from the hands of the victors, from the oppression of the continuity of *their* time and 'progress'. For this 'progress' is founded upon the continuity of catastrophe, on the defeat of the denied bodies and stories of those excluded: the ruins of history.

This is to establish a new type of historical intelligibility that binds us to the time of the other, that binds us to a response and a response-ability (Shoshana Felman) for the excluded, for oblivion. In the transient act of writing under the eternal sign of ethical redemption, Benjamin, like Franz Rosenzweig, but the Heideggerian echoes here should also not be overlooked, sought an intelligibility that was not closed, 'scientific', or metaphysical, but was rather consigned to the custody of language; to the vital unfolding of my being in language and my language in being in which the breath of the living fans the ashes of the past that flare up to cast light on our future.

* * *

A passing note. In the centrality of music to the black Atlantic experiences of modernity we encounter not simply a historical and cultural archive, a vital storehouse of memories, but also a constellation of perpetual redemption.[64] Here past, present and future fuse in an abrupt interruption – the blue note on the bent guitar string, the shout, the saxophone growl, the bass story, the rap – that challenges immediate circumstance to reveal the presence of other histories. For rap invokes an interruption of language, a cut which folds language in upon itself, and then unfolds it across the fields of English rock music and urban style. It constitutes the act of testimony, of bearing witness, that reveals a diverse scansion of historical time, a different cultural inscription and musical signature. Unchaining such languages from their presumed referents, the supplement of rap proposes another centre. Usually considered to be an addition, an ornament, to the centrality of rock music, viewed from elsewhere rap registers an essential relocation and reciting of the musical (and cultural) score.[65] In this separation of sound from the earlier signified, we enter the) 'topos of Unsayability'.[66] Like the baroque insistence on the ornament that permits us to glance into the interior and bear witness to the 'underground of language', rap's decoration and decentring of readily available languages and styles suggests that music reflects more than is accessible to the categories of reflection, and invokes the 'effort to say that of which one cannot speak.'[67] On this point Andrew Bowie concludes:

> The importance of music in the history of modernity seems to me in part at least explained by its role as part of the counter discourse of modernity, that discourse that in the face of the determination to ground the subject in rules, codes and systems always reveals the extent to which these systems cannot be self-grounding.[68]

* * *

> Art is not about communication, it is a form of resistance against communication, against the deceit of communication.
>
> Jean-Marie Straub

To return to the lost harmony of the circle. In the circle of investigation we set out confident that we will return to our point of departure complete with our survey and solutions. In the ellipse we discover our decentring, and never return to our point of departure. Like a baroque column spiralling upwards in a twisting formation, we find ourselves caught in a movement in which beginning and end do not correspond. We encounter other centres, other perspectives, disseminated along the spiralled ellipse of our trajectory.

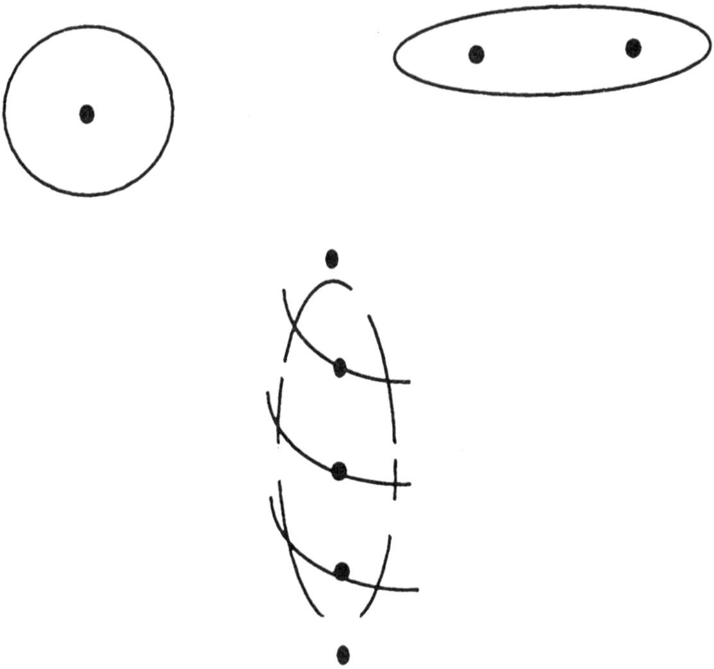

* * *

> Reason is entitled to a home in the world, but the world is just that: a home; it is not totality.
>
> Franz Rosenzweig[69]

In this exposure I encounter the judgement of the angels, the disturbing judgement of the other that resists my language, refuses my view and repudiates my history. For angels are creatures of an ambiguous provenance that move between worlds refusing allegiance. Amongst them is the allegorical angel whose wings brushed Walter Benjamin's writings: the famous figure contemplating the growing debris of the past as it is blown backwards into the future. Then there are the black and white angels that inhabit the fragmentary, dream-like cinema of Isaac Julien's extraordinary *Looking for*

Langston (1989). There is also the angel that sings through the trees in the final sequence of Sally Potter's film *Orlando* (1992). These angels condense past. present and future. Under their gaze I find myself caught between two centres: between the apparent ineluctability of time and the obscure centre of its continual crisis.[70] For the angels announce history as a perpetual becoming, an inexhaustible emerging, an eternal provocation, a desire that defies and transgresses the linearity of abstract logic with the insistent now, the body, the *Jetz*, of the permanent presence of the possible.[71]

Apparently caught in the scissors of time, a space opens up between past and future that reveals the ever-present body of language: 'The being of language – the language of being.'[72] I 'live here, forever taking leave', called upon to lend my ear and body to the miracle of the terrestrial call:

> Wasn't all this a miracle? Be astonished, Angel, for we
> *are* this, O Great One; proclaim that we could achieve this, my breath
> is too short for such praise. So, after all, we have not
> failed to make use of these generous spaces, these
> spaces of ours. (How frighteningly great they must be,
> since thousands of years have not made them overflow with our feelings.)[73]

NOTES

1. Thomas Docherty, *John Donne, Undone*, Methuen, London & New York 1986, pp37-8.
2. On the baroque as a period of 'general crisis' which monarchical absolutism sought to control and direct, see José Antonio Maravall, *Culture of the Baroque*, Manchester University Press, Manchester 1986.
3. Suzanne Clercx, *Le Baroque et le Musique: Essai d'estethétique musicale*, Éditions de la Librairie Encyclopédique, Bruxelles 1948, p18.
4. Severo Sarduy, *Barroco*, Editions du Seuil, Paris 1975; I am using the Italian translation: *Barroco*, Il Saggiatore, Milano 1980, pp50-3.
5. John Ruskin, *The Stones of Venice*, quoted in Mary Laura Gibbs, *The Church of Santa Maria del Giglio*, Venice Committee, Venice & New York n.d. Ruskin considered the church 'so grossly debased that even the Italian critics . . . exhaust their terms of reproach . . .', *ibid.*
6. See Mario Perniola, 'L'essere-per-la-morte e il simulacro della morte', in Mario Perniola, *La Società dei Simulacri*, Bologna, Capelli 1983.
7. Michel de Certeau, *The Writing of History*, trans. Tom Conley, Columbia University Press, New York 1988, p101.

8. For the resonance of the idea of the *tombeau* in historical reasoning see Iain Chambers, *Migrancy, Culture, Identity*, Routledge, London & New York 1994.
9. Michel de Certeau, *op.cit.*, p100.
10. Julia Kristeva, *Black Sun: Depression and Melancholia*, trans, Leon S. Roudiez, Columbia University Press, New York 1989, p99.
11. Robert Donington, *A Performers Guide to Baroque Music*, Faber & Faber, London 1978.
12. For a discussion of the origin of the term 'baroque' in the context of jewellery, and Portuguese (*barrucco* – an irregular shaped pearl), see Severo Sarduy, *op.cit.*
13. See the description of Leibniz's multi-storeyed 'house of resonance' in the opening pages of Gilles Deleuze, *Le Pli: Leibniz et la Baroque*, Editions de Minuit, Paris 1988; I am using the Italian translation, *La Piega, Lebaiz e il Barocco*, Einaudi, Torino 1990, p17. The English edition is *The Fold: Leibniz and the Baroque*, trans. Tom Conley, University of Minnesota Press, Minneapolis, 1993. The ever-present, and ever evolving, *basso continuo* can be compared to the modern day 'rhythm section' of guitar, bass, keyboards and drums in both jazz and rock music, see Thurston Dart, *The Interpretation of Music*, Harper & Row, New York 1963, p78.
14. Christine Buci-Glucksmann, *Tragique de l'ombre*, Éditions Galilee, Paris 1990, pp229-30. 'De la musique, comme art de l'emotion sans concept, comme Affect de tout affect.', *ibid*, p230.
15. *Ibid.*, p202.
16. For the detailed nuances of this 'cosmological break' in the making of the baroque sensibility, see in particular Severo Sarduy, *op.cit.*
17. See Thomas Docherty, *op.cit.*, pp17-29.
18. Frances Yates, *Giordano Bruno and the Hermetic Tradition*, Routledge & Kegan Paul, London 1964.
19. Loup Verlet, *La malle de Newton*, Gallimard, Paris 1993.
20. The reference is to Pascal Quignard's *Touts les matins du monde*, and its subsequent realisation as a film, with Quignard's screenplay, by Alain Courneau in 1992. On 'sad voluptuousness', see Julia Kristeva, *Black Sun: Depression and Melancholia*, trans. Leon S. Roudiez, Columbia University Press, New York 1989.
21. Paul de Man, 'The Rhetoric of Temporality' in Paul de Man, *Blindness and Insight*, Methuen, London 1983, p222.
22. Fernand Hallyn, *The Poetic Structure of the World: Copernicus and Kepler*, Zone Books, New York 1993, p22; translation modified.
23. The church of Santa Maria delle Anime del Purgatoria (1604), Via Tribunali, Naples. The flowers are changed daily.
24. John Donne, *Song*.
25. Hélène Cixous referring to Shakespeare, in Hélène Cixous and Catherine

Clement, *The Newly Born Woman*, Manchester, Manchester University Press 1987, p98.
26. Mario Perniola, 'Icone, visioni, simulacri', in Mario Perniola, *op.cit.*, p122.
27. Julia Kristeva, *Black Sun: Depression and Melancholia*, trans. Leon S. Roudiez, Columbia University Press, New York 1989, pp100-1.
28. Kepler's *Dream*, published posthumously by his son in 1634, describes celestial phenomena as they would have appeared from the moon. Earlier versions had circulated in manuscript form and Kepler thought it was known to John Donne; see Fernand Hallyn, *op.cit.* 'A Dream' is also the title of a fine fantasy for the lute by John Dowland.
29. See Marin Mersenne, *Questions Inouyes*, Fayard, Paris 1985, and Pierre Gassendi, *Initiation à la théorie de la musique*, Aix-en-Provence, Edisud 1992. Descartes wrote a *Compendium Musicae* that was published posthumously in Utrecht in 1650. It is available in a French translation as *Abrégé de musique*, Press Universitaires de France, Paris 1987.
30. To Heidegger's proposal that we dwell in language is to be added Vico's on the metaphorical character of reality: Ernesto Grassi, 'Il dramma della metafora', in *Informazione Filosofica*, n.6, marzo 1992.
31. Peter Ackroyd, *Hawksmoor*, Abacus, London 1985, p186.
32. Basil Willey, *The Seventeenth Century Background*, Doubleday, New York 1953, p50.
33. Fernand Hallyn, *op.cit.*, p20.
34. 'The point of view is found in the body': Leibniz, letter to Lady Masham, June 1704, cited in Delenze *op.cit.*, p17.
35. Deleuze, *op.cit.*, p13.
36. Sardoy, *op.cit.*, p50.
37. See Maravall, *op.cit.*
38. The first phrase is Benjamin's: Walter Benjamin, *The Origin of German Tragic Drama*, Verso, London 1990, p185; the second is from Maravall, *op.cit.*, p163.
39. Figures from Christopher Hill, *The Century of Revolution*, 1603-1714, Sphere Books, London 1969, p278.
40. Gaetano Cantone, *Napoli barocca*, Laterza, Bari 1992.
41. Martin Heidegger, 'La cosa', in Martin Heidegger, *Saggi e discorsi*, Mursia, Milano 1976.
42. Martin Heidegger, 'The Origin of the Work of Art', in Martin Heidegger, *Basic Writings*, Harper & Row, New York 1977, p152.
43. I am extremely grateful to Kathy Biddick for directing me to this amnesia.
44. Rey Chow, *Writing Diaspora*, Indiana University Press, Bloomington 1993, p38.
45. Stéphane Mosès, *L'Ange De L'Histoire: Rosenzweig, Benjamin*, Scholem, Editions du Seuil, Paris 1992, pp19-20.
46. Noreen O'Connor 'The Personal is Political', in R. Bernasconi & D. Wood, *The*

Provocation of Lévinas, Routledge, London & New York 1988, p59.

47. E. Robberechts, 'Savoir et mort chez F. Rosenzweig' in *Revue Philosophique de Louvain*, volume 90, Mai 1992.
48. Martin Heidegger, 'La cosa', in Martin Heidegger, *op.cit.*, p119.
49. Christine Buci-Glucksmann, *La Raison Baroque: De Baudelaire a Benjamin*, Éditions Galilee, Paris 1984, pp71-2; *Baroque Reason: The Aesthetics of Modernity*, Sage, London 1994. She is quoting Benjamin.
50. Walter Benjamin, *Charles Baudelaire: A Lyric Poet in the Era of High Capitalism*, New Left Books, London 1973.
51. Stéphane Mosès, *op.cit.*, p139.
52. Dori Laub, in Shoshana Felman & Dori Laub, *Testimony: Crises of Witnessing in Literature, Psychoanalysis, and History*, Routledge, London 1992, p73.
53. Emmanuel Lévinas, *Totality and Infinity*, Duquesne University Press, Pittsburgh 1969.
54. Stéphane Mosès, *op.cit.*, p132.
55. *Ibid*, p127.
56. Walter Benjamin, *The Origin of German Tragic Drama*, Verso, London 1990, p166.
57. *Ibid*, p175.
58. *Ibid*, p176.
59. *Ibid.*, p176.
60. *Ibid.*, p183.
61. Maravall, *op.cit.*
62. On the political ambiguities of collecting, and its place in the articulation and disarticulation of modernity, see Chow, *op.cit.*, pp43-4.
63. I have borrowed the concept of 'open time' from Stéphane Mosès, *op.cit.*, p177.
64. For the concept of a counter-history of modernity articulated around the black Atlantic see Paul Gilroy, *The Black Atlantic*, Verso, London 1993.
65. Ted Swedenburg, 'Homies in the Hood: Rap's Commodification of Insubordination', *New Formations*, 18, Winter 1992.
66. Carl Dalhaus, *Die Idee der absoluten Musik*, quoted in Andrew Bowie, 'Music, Language and Modernity', in Andrew Benjamin (ed), *The Problems of Modernity, Adorno and Benjamin*, Routledge, London & New York 1989, p70.
67. The 'underground of language' comes from Shoshana Felman, in Shoshana Felman & Dori Laub, *op.cit.*, p15; while the second voice is that of Theodor Adorno, quoted in Bowie, *op.cit.*, p80.
68. Bowie, *op.cit.*, p83.
69. Franz Rosenzweig, *The Star of Redemption*, trans. William W. Hallo, Holt, Rinehart and Winston, New York 1971, p13.
70. See Mosès, *op.cit.*
71. This paragraph is a modified reprise of the coda to Chambers, *op.cit.*

72. Martin Heidegger, 'The Nature of Language', in Martin Heidegger, *On The Way To Language*, Harper & Row, New York 1982, p76.
73. Rainer Maria Rilke, from the Seventh Elegy of the Duino Elegies, in *The Selected Poetry of Rainer Maria Rilke*, Picador, London 1987, translated by Stephen Mitchell, p191. The phrase 'we live here, forever taking leave' comes from the concluding line of the Eighth Elegy, *ibid*, p197.

EXPERIENCE WITHOUT A SUBJECT: WALTER BENJAMIN AND THE NOVEL

Martin Jay

'However paradoxical it may seem,' Hans-Georg Gadamer writes in *Truth and Method*, 'the concept of experience seems to me one of the most obscure that we have.'[1] 'Of all the words in the philosophical vocabulary,' Michael Oakeshott agrees in *Experience and its Modes*, 'it is the most difficult to manage.'[2] Derived from the Latin *experientia*, which meant trial, proof and experiment (an acceptation still current in French), it has come to mean a welter of different things. Accordingly, the term has generated enormous controversy. Literary critics like Philip Rahv have denounced the 'cult of experience' in American literature, while historians like Joan Scott have bemoaned its privileged role as evidentiary foundation in the work of figures as diverse as R.G. Collingwood and E.P. Thompson.[3] And for all those who resist so-called 'identity politics,' in which legitimation comes from who you are – your 'subject position,' in the current jargon – and not from the force of what you say, the appeal to something called experience has also become a prime target.

And yet, obscurity and unmanageability not withstanding, 'experience' remains a key term in both everyday language and the lexicons of esoteric philosophies. Indeed, Gadamer, Oakeshott and a host of other twentieth-century thinkers, from Buber to Bataille, from Husserl to Dewey, from Jünger to Lyotard, have felt compelled to mull over its multiple meanings and contradictory implications. But perhaps no one has had as profound an effect on our appreciation of its varieties as Walter Benjamin; nor has anyone else made us as sensitive to the crisis of at least one of those varieties. Indeed, experience has rightly been called 'Benjamin's great theme . . . the true focal point of his analysis of modernity, philosophy of history, and theory of the artwork.'[4]

As a result, a formidable exegetical literature has developed around Benjamin's discussion of the concept, a literature whose central contributors would include Richard Wolin, Marleen Stoessel, Thorsten Meiffert, Michael

Jennings, Miriam Hansen, Michael Makropolous, and many of the contributors to this collection.[5] It is not my goal in this paper to rehearse their complicated arguments, or provide a way to adjudicate their differences. Instead, I want to suggest that we might find an important confirmation of Benjamin's theory of experience in a place where he himself never thought to find it: in that modern literary genre towards which he felt so ambivalent, the novel. I want to argue that this confirmation can be found in a vital linguistic resource of the novel which Benjamin, for all his fascination with language, failed to explore.

Before making this case, however, it will be necessary to present in very general terms Benjamin's theory of experience. Most of the attention paid to it has been to his mature reflections, in particular the crucial distinction between *Erlebnis* and *Erfahrung* he developed in such works as *One Way Street*, 'Experience and Poverty,' 'The Storyteller', and 'On Some Motifs in Baudelaire.'[6] Benjamin's juxtaposition of these terms was not, to be sure, his own invention. Following the lead of Rousseau and Goethe, Wilhelm Dilthey had contrasted *Erlebnis* (or sometimes *das Erleben*), which he identified with 'inner lived experience,' to *aüssere Erfahrung*, by which he meant 'outer sensory experience.'[7] Whereas the latter was grounded in the discrete stimuli of mere sensation, the former involved the internal integration of sensations into a meaningful whole available to hermeneutic interpretation. Edmund Husserl had likewise disdained the scientific and neo-Kantian notion of *Erfahrung*, based on conceptual reflection, as inferior to the richer, intuitively meaningful *Erlebnis* of the pre-reflexive *Lebenswelt*.[8] And Ernst Jünger had celebrated war as the arena of an authentic *Erlebnis* absent from the desiccated *Erfahrung* of bourgeois, civilian existence.[9] In all these cases, *Erlebnis* was an honorific term for subjective, concrete, intuitive responses to the world that were prior to the constructed abstractions of science or the intellect.

What set Benjamin apart from his predecessors was his disdain for both the alleged immediacy and meaningfulness of *Erlebnis* and the overly rational, disinterested version of *Erfahrung* defended by the positivists and neo-Kantians. Instead, he favoured an alternative closer to what Gadamer has called a dialectical concept of experience, a learning process over time, combining negations through unpleasant episodes as well as affirmations through positive ones to produce something akin to a wisdom that can be passed down via tradition through the generations.[10] Unlike Dilthey, he did not give the name *Erlebnis* to such a dialectical process. The immediate, passive, fragmented, isolated and unintegrated inner experience of *Erlebnis* was, Benjamin argued, very different from the cumulative, totalizing accretion of transmittable wisdom, of epic truth, that was *Erfahrung*. Here the echoes of the German word for taking a journey (*fahren*), a narrativizable exploration of parts hitherto unknown, could be heard.

Such an historically grounded notion of experience, moreover, was necessarily more than individual, for cumulative wisdom could occur only within a community, which could transmit the tales of the tribe through oral traditions such as story-telling. Thus, it was the Haggadic quality of truth, its ability to be handed down from generation to generation, like the Passover story, through collective memory rather than official historical records, that marked genuine experience. The contrast between the Jewish notion of *Zakhor*, group memory, and historical science, to which Yosef Yerushalmi has recently drawn attention, was thus implicitly active in Benjamin's antithetical concepts of experience.[11]

Benjamin, as we know, was deeply sceptical about the possibility of restoring genuine *Erfahrung* in the modern, capitalist world.[12] Although he resisted claiming it had been completely extirpated, he spoke movingly about its 'atrophy' (*Verhummerung*),[13] in particular after the First World War. The continuum of *Erfahrung* had already been broken by the unassimilable shocks of urban life and the replacement of artisanal production by the dull, non-cumulative repetition of the assembly line. Meaningful narrative had been supplanted by haphazard information and raw sensation in the mass media. Only the Revolution, he contended in his more Marxist moods, might create a new community in which the lost 'integrity of the contents'[14] of transmitted dialectical truth would be regained.

But even when his theory of experience can be called most materialist,[15] his doubts about the restoration of the fabric of genuine *Erfahrung* remained strong. A primary reason for those doubts was the stubbornly theological dimension of Benjamin's work, which was never fully disentangled from its Marxist counterpart. For it was here that a powerful component of his theory of experience can also be found, a component Gershom Scholem called his quest for 'absolute experience.'[16] In one of his first considerations of this theme, his 1917-1918 essay 'On the Programme of the Coming Philosophy,' Benjamin explicitly faulted the neo-Kantian concept of experience, exemplified in Hermann Cohen's *Kants Theorie der Erfahrung*, for being too narrowly empirical and scientific, and thus excluding metaphysical and religious experiences.[17] Although unwilling to make the latter the only source of genuine experience, which he pluralistically called 'the uniform and continuous multiplicity of knowledge,'[18] Benjamin clearly thought that without a religious component, experience would remain woefully impoverished. For 'there is a unity of experience that can by no means be understood as a sum of experiences, to which the concept of knowledge as theory is immediately related in its continuous development. The object and the content of this theory, this concrete totality of experience, is religion.'[19]

Religious experience is particularly important, Benjamin suggested, because it transcends the problematic dichotomy of subject and object, which underlay both the scientific notion of empirical *Erfahrung* and the non-rationalist notion of *Erlebnis*. It is a 'true experience, in which neither god nor man is object or subject of experience but in which this experience is based on pure knowledge .... The task of future epistemology is to find for knowledge the sphere of total neutrality in regard to the concepts of both subject and object, in other words, it is to discover the autonomous, innate sphere of knowledge in which this concept in no way continues to designate the relation between two metaphysical entities.'[20] Later, in his more Marxist phase, Benjamin contrasted a collective subjective experience, that of the community to be created after the Revolution, to the isolated individual *Erlebnis* of modern, capitalist life, but here he was arguing for an experience that paradoxically went beyond that of any subject, collective or individual, an experience that might justly be called noumenal or ontological. As such, it was far less a synonym for active human making than his later concept of *Erfahrung* has seemed to Benjamin's commentators.[21]

Rather than musing on the 'varieties of religious experience,' in the manner of William James, Benjamin focused on only one. The locus of that experience, he argued in 'On the Programme of the Coming Philosophy,' was to be found not in sensation or perception, but rather in language, that region of human endeavour Johann Georg Hamann had been the first to challenge Kant in stressing. 'A concept of knowledge gained from reflection on the linguistic nature of knowledge will create a corresponding concept of experience,' Benjamin insisted, 'which will also encompass regions that Kant failed to integrate into his system. The realm of religion should be mentioned as the foremost of these.'[22] Here language reveals itself as more than a mere tool of communication in which the feelings, observations or thoughts of a subjective inferiority reveal themselves to another subject. Here the divine word manifests itself ontologically, prior to the subjective conventionalism of human name-giving.

A religiously inflected notion of language in which the dichotomy of subject and object is transcended and ontological truth revealed – the early Benjamin is clearly invoking a concept of experience unlike any we have previously mentioned. Kantian *Erfahrung* is the empirical experience of the transcendental, scientific, cognitive subject; Diltheyan *Erlebnis* is the inner experience of the contingent subject prior to rational reflection or scientific cognition; even the Haggadic epic truth transmitted through narrative continuity can be understood as that of a collective subject, a communal meta-subject beyond the isolated, damaged subjects of modern life. But religious (or 'absolute') experience, as Benjamin describes it, implies a point of indifference between subject and object, an equiprimordiality prior to their differentiation. As Winfried Menninghaus has put it, 'his emphatic concept of experience' is 'an ultimately Messianic category of unrestricted synthesis,' which is linked to forms of meaning that might even be called mythical.[23] It was for this reason that even his close friend Adorno could grow uneasy:

> His target is not an allegedly over-inflated subjectivism but rather the notion of a subjective dimension itself. Between myth and reconciliation, the poles of his philosophy, the subject evaporates. Before his Medusan glance, man turns into the stage on which an objective process unfolds. For this reason Benjamin's philosophy is no less a source of terror than a promise of happiness.[24]

As a consequence, suggestive comparisons might be drawn to a similar notion of ontological experience in the work of Martin Heidegger, who was also sceptical of the overly subjective bias of individual *Erlebnis* and scientific *Erfahrung*, and had no use for collective meta-subjects either.[25] Or perhaps the poetry of Hölderlin, important for both Benjamin and Heidegger, might be adduced to demonstrate what they were after.[26] It might also be fruitful to situate Benjamin's search for an experience that transcends the subject/object opposition in the context of many other such attempts by twentieth-century artists. The Surrealists, whose writings Benjamin himself claimed were concerned primarily with experiences, come immediately to mind.[27] And we might focus on the heterodox means, such as hashish, Benjamin explored to provide non-religious glimpses of absolute experience, those profane illuminations that broke down the barrier between subject and object.

But, rather than follow these well-trodden paths, I want to go down instead the one that Benjamin himself suggested was the locus of non-subjective experience, that of language. And I want to suggest that even if we jettison the religious and magical underpinnings of Benjamin's own complicated theory of language, with its hope for the recovery of divinely inspired names and nonsensuous, mimetic similarities, we can still discover in the highly secular language of the modern novel unexpected warrant for his argument. We can, I want to claim, identify an intriguing example of experience without a subject that is independent of a redemptive, quasi-mythical notion of metaphysical or religious truth, or a magical notion of analogical correspondences, which are bound to make many of us uncomfortable in this age of cynical reason.

Benjamin's own mixed feelings about the novel are, to be sure, widely appreciated. Following Georg Lukács's lead in *The Theory of the Novel*, he saw it as the genre for an age of 'transcendental homelessness' in which the community underpinning the oral transmission of tales was shattered.[28] The invention of the printed book undermined the need for collective group memory through public narration; epic meaning survived only in the endangered form of the tale. 'The birthplace of the novel,' Benjamin charged, 'is the solitary individual, who is no longer able to express himself by giving examples of his most important concerns, is himself uncounseled, and cannot counsel others. To write a novel means to carry the incommensurable to extremes in the representation of human life.'[29]

Although novels centre on 'the meaning of life,' they never get beyond demonstrating that life in the age of information is inherently meaningless; the experience they depict is thus that of *Erlebnis* at its emptiest. The fate of its characters, indeed their very deaths, can only provide a simulacrum of meaning for readers, whose lives are deprived of it. Novels rely on psychological explanations instead of depicting the inherent meaning of the world of the epic, a meaning which is self-evident and in need of no external explanatory scaffolding. Even when novels like Proust's *À La Recherche du Temps Perdu* attempt to restore coherent retrospective meaning, they can only do so through the subjective gloss of memory rather than through a presentation of objectively intelligible experience.[30] Although 'involuntary memory,' the technique Proust appropriated from Bergson, was closer than its voluntary counterpart to the anamnestic moment in true *Erfahrung*, it was only artificially generated through the novelist's fiat.

How then, we might ask, can the novel provide any confirmation of Benjamin's belief in the possibility of experience without a subject? How can it serve as the placeholder of an 'absolute experience' beyond mere *Erlebnis* or even the lost *Erfahrung* of the storyteller? The answer resides in an aspect of the novel, which Benjamin, to my knowledge, never acknowledged: its frequent adoption of a stylistic mode that was absent from virtually all previous genres, a mode which is known in French as the '*style indirect libre*,' in German as '*erlebte Rede*,' and in English as 'represented speech'. It is further connected to the grammatical variant known as 'the middle voice,' which differs from active and passive voices and has been identified by critics like Roland Barthes as characteristic of 'the intransitive' writing of modernism.[31] Although the presence of these linguistic phenomena does not suggest that the novel taken as a coherent, generic whole represents a prefiguration of 'absolute experience,' they allow us to believe that within certain novels, there exist moments that do. Such moments, to be sure, may not prefigure the full redemptive version of that experience hoped for by Benjamin at his most utopian, but perhaps they are instances of what he liked to call the 'weak Messianic power'[32] permitted to us even in the darkest of times.

The *style indirect libre* was first singled out for serious analysis by the Swiss linguist and student of Saussure, Charles Bally, in 1912,[33] and then given special significance by Proust in his celebrated essay of 1920 on Flaubert's style.[34] A year later, Etienne Lorck coined the term *erlebte Rede* for its German counterpart, and in 1924, the Danish linguist Otto Jespersen introduced the less widely adopted 'represented speech' for the English variant.[35] In the years since, a host of linguists and literary critics, among them V.N. Volosinov, Stephen Ullmann, Dorrit Cohn, Roy Pascal, Hans Robert Jauss and Ann Banfield, have explored every aspect of its usage.[36] Even intellectual historians like Dominick LaCapra have evoked it to argue that Flaubert's prose style, rather than his apparently salacious content, led to the trial of Madame Bovary in 1857.[37]

Its significance for the issue of experience is suggested, if in somewhat misleading ways, by the fact that the German variant was called *erlebte Rede* by Lorck, who was a student of Karl Vossler, the Romantic linguist of individualist subjectivism. Vossler, an opponent of Saussure, stressed the psychological content of linguistic performance, psychology understood not in positivist/empiricist terms, but in those of *Lebensphilosophie*.[38] That is, language expressed the internal, subjective state of mind of the speaker, rather than an impersonal sign system, and the linguist studied stylistics and *Spracheseele* (the soul expressed through style) rather than grammar. Accordingly, as one commentator has noted, 'the chief reason Lorck invented the term *erlebte Rede* was to stress the irrational and rapturous in contrast to the informational function of language. It was thus related to philosophies of "life" and immediate "experience".'[39]

How then can we claim that the indirect free style instantiates Benjamin's notion of 'absolute experience' prior to the split between subject and object, if it seems to be an example of *Erlebnis* at its most objectionable? Let us examine more closely its implications for the answer. Lorck contrasted *erlebte Rede* to the direct discourse he called *gesprochene Rede* (repeated speech) and the indirect discourse he dubbed *berichtete Rede* (communicated speech). Direct discourse or repeated speech is uttered by a speaker, say a hero in a play, as his own thoughts, for example, Faust saying 'Habe nun, ach! Philosophie, Juristerei . . .' Indirect discourse or communicated speech occurs when a second person cites the speech of a first to a third. e.g. 'Faust hat gesagt: "Habe nun, ach! Philosophie, Juristerei . . ." ' But *erlebte Rede* takes place when a second person wants to create in his own mind Faust's thoughts, e.g. 'Faust hat nun, ach! Philosophie, Juristerei,' or insofar as they are past thoughts, 'Faust haste nun, ach!'

Another, much discussed example comes from *Madame Bovary*. Emma, looking in a mirror after her first act of adultery, is described in the following way:

> Elle se répétait: J'ai un amant! un amant! se délectant à cette idée comme à celle d'une autre puberté qui lui serait survenue. Elle allait done enfin posséder ces plaisirs de l'amour, cette fièvre de bonheur donc elle avait désespér. Elle entrait dans quelque chose de merveilleux, où tout serait passion, extase, délire. . . .
>
> She repeated: 'I have a lover! a lover!' delighting at the idea as if a second puberty had come to her. So at last she was to know those joys of love, that fever of happiness of which she had despaired! She was entering upon a marvellous world where all would be passion, ecstacy, delirium . . .[40]

What made this passage so scandalous and confusing to Flaubert's critics was their inability to attribute with certainty the shocking sentiments in the last sentence to either the character or the author. Was Flaubert identifying with Emma's fantasy or merely reporting it? His style did not seem to permit a firm answer.[41]

For Lorck, indirect free style was a means of one person re-experiencing the experiences of another (what Dilthey had called *nacherleben*),[42] but not of communicating it to a third. Thus, it is not something actually said in normal conversation, but only exists as a literary convention, only, that is, in written prose. If spoken aloud, it would sound more like a hallucination than a communicative speech act. Lorck thus emphasized its function as an incitement to fantasy, an example of language's ability to transcend the intellect and create anew, as evidence of its status as living energeia, to use Humboldt's terms, rather than dead *ergon*.

Subsequent students of free indirect style have agreed with Lorck's claim that intersubjective, public communication is not the goal of language used in this peculiar way. They have further endorsed his belief that it is inherently a written rather than spoken form, showing that language development does not always come from innovations in verbal performance. And they have shared his sense that it provides evidence of a creative capacity in language that calls into question seemingly watertight distinctions like direct and indirect discourse.

But they have vigorously challenged Lorck's Vosslerite assumption that *erlebte Rede* is the re-experiencing of an irrational *Erlebnis*. Instead, as Pascal has argued, the subjective function of the style is combined with a narratorial one, which is 'communicated through the vocabulary and idiom, through the composition of the sentences and the larger passages, and through the context.'[43] That is, there is a subtle distinction preserved in the style between character and narrator, even if the inferiorities of the two seem to be perfectly conflated. Similarly, Volosinov claims that we hear a conflict between the evaluative orientation of the character whose speech is reported, and the narrator whose smooth narration is disrupted by its representation. 'We perceive the author's accents and intonations being interrupted by these value judgments of another person,' he writes. 'And that is the way, as we know, in which quasi-direct discourse differs from substituted discourse, where no new accents vis-à-vis the surrounding authorial context appear.'[44] The result of all this, as Banfield makes clear, is that the self whose thoughts are reported in the indirect free style, is not equivalent to a single, coherent, egocentric subject at all, a subject whose *Erlebnis* could be *nacherlebt*. 'Represented thought,' she thus argues, 'is an attempt to render thought as nonspeech through the medium of language. Language makes this attempt feasible because it is not synonymous with speech or communication, because speaker and self are distinct concepts, both required by linguistic theory and, hence, both posited as part of the speaker's internalized linguistic knowledge.'[45]

In addition to the stylistic expression of this non-personalized notion of experience, there is a grammatical correlate that was most clearly identified by Emile Benveniste in his 1950 essay 'Active and Middle Voice in the Verb.'[46] Not evident in all languages or equally prominent throughout the history of those where it can be found, the so-called 'middle voice' challenges the alternative between active and passive voices, just as the *style indirect libre* calls into question the opposition between direct and indirect discourse. Voice, or to use the technical term, diathesis, indicates the way the subject of a verb is affected by its action. According to Benveniste, whereas verbs in the active voice signify a process in which the subject is outside the action that it achieves, the middle voice signifies a subject *within* that process, even if it entails an object as well. The passive voice was only a late off-shoot of the middle voice, produced only when the distinction between agent (subject) and patient (object) came to be regarded as strict. But the middle voice did not entirely die. Familiar examples in French would be *Je suis né*, I was born, and *il est mort*, he died. Another from Sanskrit grammar concerns the ritual self-sacrifice of a person, who takes the knife in his own hands and plays the roles of executioner and victim (*yajate* rather than *yajati*, when the priest does the killing).

Benveniste's stress on the importance of the middle voice has had a powerful impact on recent French theory. In his influential 1968 essay on 'Différence,' Jacques Derrida invoked it to explain the meaning of that crucial deconstructionist neologism. Claiming that *différance* is an operation that also cannot be conceived either as a passion or an action of a subject, he argued that 'the middle voice, a certain nontransitivity, may be what philosophy, at its outset, distributed into an active and a passive voice, thereby constituting itself by means of this repression.'[47] Undoing – or at least deconstructing – this repression, he implied, would be an emancipatory gesture, allowing some more primordial operation to re-emerge.

Also extrapolating from Benveniste, Roland Barthes contended, in an essay originally written two years before Derrida's, that the middle voice had recovered its central place in modernist writing, writing in which the authorial function was incorporated into the text, which seemed to write itself. Such writing could thus be called intransitive rather than transitive in the sense of not having an object exterior to it. Whereas Romantic writing involved a subject *an*terior to the actions about which it wrote, modernist writing's subject was *in*terior to and simultaneous with the writing itself. According to Barthes, 'in the modern verb of middle voice *to write*, the subject is constituted as immediately contemporary with the writing, being effected and affected by it: this is the exemplary case of the Proustian narrator, who exists only by writing, despite the reference to a pseudo-memory.'[48]

Rather than accepting Benjamin's critique of Proust for providing a retrospective and subjective simulacrum of *Erfahrung* through involuntary memory, Barthes insisted that the writing itself contained what Benjamin was seeking. For here we have example of a linguistic version of experience without the subject, of *écriture* without an *écrivain*.[49] Although Barthes identified intransitive writing with modernism, where techniques like interior monologue are often employed, it would be possible to see its antecedents in the realistic novel in which the *style indirect libre* also appeared, for example in Flaubert. Thus, both on the level of style and of grammatical voice, there is evidence in the novel of those attributes Benjamin denied to it.

One might also note parenthetically that Benjamin's own vaunted style (or rather several styles, because he did not always write in the same manner) can usefully be described as a form of intransitive writing. Even in his most seemingly autobiographical texts, his own expressive subjectivity was ruthlessly suppressed. Nowhere was Benjamin's yearning to efface his authorial presence more evident than in his celebrated desire to write a work composed entirely of quotations.

Whether or not one reads Benjamin's own writing as an example of how experience without a subject can appear outside of the novel, it is significant that several recent theorists have found it in non-literary phenomena as well. Ann Banfield, for example, has claimed that in certain modern recording instruments, such as the camera, the thermometer and the tape recorder, non-sensed sensibilia can manifest themselves without an actual subject present when the event occurs.[50] These phenomena she compares to the *style indirect libre* in the novels of Virginia Woolf and the narrative of Maurice Blanchot, and employs them to criticize the claim that sensibilia always need a subject to do the sensing. 'The novel,' she writes, 'contains sentences with deictics which can be said to represent the perspective of no one; not objective, centreless statements, but subjective yet subjectless, they render the appearances of things to no one, akin in this to the light-sensitive plate.'[51] Although she does not draw on Benjamin's famous discussion of photography's revelation of an 'optical unconscious,' her remarks suggest a similar concern for realities that escape subjective apprehension.[52]

In another context, the philosopher Berel Lang and the intellectual historian Hayden White have suggested that intransitive writing in the middle voice may be a helpful way to present the historical narrative of events such as the Holocaust that defy traditional attempts to write about them as an objective story.[53] For White, following Roland Barthes, modernism is 'nothing less than an order of experience beyond (or prior to) that expressible in the kind of *oppositions* we are forced to draw (between agency and patiency, subjectivity and objectivity, literalness and figurativeness, fact and fiction, history and myth and so forth) in any version of realism.'[54] This modernist experience, White suggests, is somehow appropriate to that of the Holocaust, 'a new form of historical reality, a reality that included, among its supposedly unimaginable, unthinkable and unspeakable aspects, the phenomena of Hitlerism, the Final Solution, total war . . .'[55]

The claims of Lang and White that the unspeakable acts of twentieth-century totalitarianism are best represented in the unsayable sentences we have been calling instances of subjectless experience are, to be sure, controversial; indeed, I have myself vigorously challenged them elsewhere.[56] But they suggest how powerful the appeal of that notion of experience now is. Benjamin's early hope for an 'absolute experience,' an ontological experience expressed in non-communicative language prior to the privileging of subjectivity in irrational *Erlebnis* or scientific *Erfahrung*, has found an echo in unexpected quarters, where no explicit residue remains of his theological concerns. Although few commentators have noticed the continuities – Banfield is an exception, as she uses the celebrated lines from 'The Task of the Translator' 'No poem is intended for the reader, no picture for the beholder, no symphony for the listener' as an epigraph for one of her articles[57] – it is clear that, shorn of its religious aura, Benjamin's early theory of experience has shown itself to be remarkably durable.

Can it also be said in conclusion to be persuasive as well? In a recent essay addressing many of the themes we have just been discussing, the literary critic Vincent Pecora has expressed alarm at the way in which Benveniste's work on the middle voice has functioned to short-circuit serious discussions of political agency.[58] Betraying a kind of ethnological nostalgia for an allegedly prior state of undifferentiated unity, its celebrants, he claims, fail to ask the hard questions about how we are to find our way back to such a utopian state. 'Like the jargon of phenomenology,' Pecora protests, 'middle voice only superficially 'dissolves' older logical and ethical dilemmas of subject/object relations.'[59] As a result, it may even prove an unwitting handmaiden of an authoritarian politics, as Heidegger's philosophy, itself based on a search for experience without a subject, unfortunately did.

A somewhat less sinister scenario is suggested, however, by a reading of the *style indirect libre* that emphasizes its still contestatory impulses as a 'dual style.' Volosinov, Pascal and LaCapra all argue for a dialogical rather than empathetic interpretation of it. That is, they stress the ways in which character and narrator remain in tension rather than smoothly absorbed one into the other, as the Vosslerite theories of *nacherleben* suggest. Volosinov was a member of Mikhail Bakhtin's circle in the Soviet Union – in fact, some critics have claimed they were actually the same person[60] – so it is not surprising to find the now familiar idea of carnival associated with that of the *style indirect libre*. According to LaCapra, writing about *Madame Bovary* in particular, 'the effect here is a carnivalization of narrative voice and a dissemination of the narrator – at times the author – in the text.'[61]

It would not be the first time, moreover, that Bahktin's notion of carnival has been introduced to flesh out Benjamin's arcane ideas. Terry Eagleton already did so in the early 1980s, even suggesting certain similarities between the theological premises of each position.[62] The implication of this reading of the style indirect fibre is perhaps not quite as nostalgic and affirmative as the one Pecora attributes to those who have used the middle voice as a way to overcome subject/object dichotomies. For it suggests a less settled notion of a unity prior to the split into direct and indirect discourse, active and passive voice. Here experience without the subject turns out to be experience with more than one subject inhabiting the same space.

Although Benjamin's early notion of absolute experience might not at first glance appear congenial to this version, it does fit well with one of his most intriguing contentions: that the aura involves an unsublatable interaction of gazes. As Habermas notes, 'The experience released from the ruptured shell of the aura was, however, already contained in the experience of the aura itself: the metamorphosis of the object into a counterpart. Thereby a whole field of surprising correspondences between animate and inanimate nature is opened up, wherein even things encounter us in the structures of frail intersubjectivity.'[63] Habermas' version of that intersubjectivity is, to be sure, more harmonious and reciprocal than the dialogic heteroglossia of Bakhtin, but he insightfully recognizes the importance of multiple subjectivities (indeed, of objects metamorphosed into subjectivities) in Benjamin's concept of *Erfahrung*. If such a reading of absolute experience is allowed, and admittedly it is highly speculative, it might help rebut the charge of recent critics like Leo Bersani that Benjamin was hopelessly nostalgic for a putative lost wholeness, which came dangerously close to the Fascist aestheticization of politics he decried.[64]

However one interprets the political implications of absolute experience, the *style indirect libre* or the middle voice, Benjamin's contention that experience is a multi-faceted and internally contested concept has thus been confirmed by the linguistic evidence of novels that Benjamin himself failed to appreciate. Whether or not we then conclude that absolute experience has virtually vanished from the world or that its utopian spark remains hidden in the pages of those novels, waiting somehow to be actualized by their readers in ways that are impossible to foretell, is a question that no one can confidently answer.

NOTES

1. Hans-Georg Gadamer, *Truth and Method,* New York 1986, p310.
2. Michael Oakeshott, *Experience and its Modes*, Cambridge, 1933, p9.
3. Philip Rahv, 'The Cult of Experience in American Writing,' *Literature and the Sixth Sense*, New York, 1969 and Joan W. Scott, 'The Evidence of Experience,' *Critical Inquiry*, 17,4 (Summer, 1991).
4. Gary Smith, 'Thinking Through Benjamin: An Introductory Essay,' in Smith, ed., *Benjamin: Philosophy, Aesthetics, History*, Chicago, 1989, pxii.
5. Richard Wolin, *Walter Benjamin: An Aesthetic of Redemption*, New York, 1982; Marleen Stoessel, *Aura: Das vergessene Menschliche*, Munich, 1983; Torsten Meiffert, *Die enteignete Erfahrung: Zu Walter Benjamins Konzept einer 'Dialetik im Shilsand'*, Bielefeld, 1986; Michael Jennings, *Dialectical Images: Walter Benjamin's Theory of Literary Criticism*, Ithaca, 1987; Miriam Hansen, 'Benjamin, Cinema and Experience: "The Blue Flower in the Land of Technology",' *New German Critique*, 40 (Winter, 1987); Michael Makropolous, *Modernittät als ontologischer Ausnahmezustand? Walter Benjamins Theorie der Moderne*, Munich, 1989.
6. Benjamin, *One Way Street and Other Writings*, trans. Edmund Jephcott and Kingsley Shorter, London, 1979; 'Erfahrung und Armut,' *Gesammelte Schriften*, II.I; 'The Storyteller' and 'On Some Motifs in Baudelaire,' in *Illuminations*, ed.

Hannah Arendt, trans. Harry Zohn, New York, 1968.

7. See Dilthey, *Das Erlebnis und die Dichtung: Lessing, Goethe, Novalis, Hölderin*, 13th ed., Gottingen, 1957. For a discussion of Dilthey's usage, see Michael Ermarth, *Wilhelm Dilthey: The Critique of Historical Reason*, Chicago, 1978, p97ff.
8. Edmund Husserl, *Experience and Judgment*, ed. Ludwig Landgrebe, trans. J.S. Churchill and K. Ameriko, Evanston, 1973.
9. Ernst Jünger, *Der Kampf als innere Erlebnis, Werke*, vol.5 (Stuttgart, n.d.).
10. Gadamer, *Truth and Method*, *op.cit.*, p317, where he credits Hegel for a dialectical concept of experience as 'scepticism in action.'
11. Yusef Hayim Yerushalmi, *Zakhor: Jewish History and Jewish Memory*, New York, 1989. Curiously, Benjamin is never mentioned in this remarkable book. For a discussion of the relevance of Yerushalmi to Benjamin, see Susan A. Handelman, *Fragments of Redemption: Jewish Thought and Literary Theory in Benjamin, Scholem, and Levinas*, Bloomington, Ind. 1991, p164. It would be fruitful to compare Benjamin's distinction between two types of memory, *Gedächtnis* (the memory of the many) and *Erinnerung* (the interiorization of the past) or *Eingedenken* (the memory of the one) with Yerushalmi's distinction between memory and history. For a helpful account of Benjamin's ideas on this issue, see Irving Wohlfarth, 'On the Messianic Structure of Walter Benjamin's Last Reflections,' *Glyph*, 3 (1978).
12. A similar argument is suggested by Reinhart Koselleck in ' "Space of Experience" and "Horizon of Expectation": Two Historical Categories,' in *Futures Past: On the Semantics of Historical Time*, trans. Keith Tribe, Cambridge, Mass. 1985). Koselleck argues that modernity is defined by the growing gap between experience, which he defines as 'present past, whose events have been incorporated and can be remembered' (p272), and an expectational horizon which distances itself radically from the status quo. He links this transformation with the notions of 'history in general' and 'progress,' both of which were anathema to Benjamin.
13. For a discussion of the implications of this word, see Makropolous, *Modernität als ontologischer Ausnahmezustand*, *op.cit.*, chapter 3.
14. Benjamin, 'On Some Motifs in Baudelaire,' *Illuminations*, *op.cit.*, p165. Benjamin's ambivalence about the ability of the masses to recover *Erfahrung* is discussed in Hansen, 'Benjamin, Cinema and Experience.' She stresses the links between his concept of aura and experience, and argues that 'with the denigration of the auratic image in favor of reproduction, Benjamin implicitly denies the masses the possibility of aesthetic experience.' *op.cit.*, p186.
15. For an analysis of it in these terms, see Wolin, chapter 7; and 'Experience and Materialism in Benjamin's *Passagenwerk*,' in Smith, ed., *Benjamin: Philosophy, Aesthetics, History.*
16. Gershom Scholem, *Walter Benjamin: Thc Story of a Friendship*, trans. Harry

Zohn, New York, 1981, p60. Here Scholem describes the lengthy discussions he had with Benjamin in Muri, Switzerland in 1918 over the issue of experience in the work of Hermann Cohen.

17. Benjamin, 'On the Programme of the Coming Philosophy,' in Smith, ed., *Benjamin: Philosophy, Aesthetics, History*. For discussions of the importance of this essay, see Smith's introduction and Jennings, *Dialectical Images*, chapter 3. Prior to this piece, when he was in the Youth Movement, Benjamin published a short essay in 1912 entitled '*Erfahrung*' in which he attacked the concept as an excuse for adults to lord it over the young. See Benjamin, *Gesammelte Schriften*, vol.II.I, ed. the Cartesianism it purports to transcend in *Grundfragen der Philosophic: Ausgewählte 'Probleme' der 'Logik', Gesamtausgabe*, vol.45, ed. Friedrich-Wilhelm von Herrmann, Frankfurt, 1984, p149.
18. Benjamin, 'On the Programme of the Coming Philosophy,' p10.
19. *Ibid.*, p11.
20. *Ibid.*, p5.
21. For an example, see Peter Bürger, 'Art and Rationality: On the Dialectic of Symbolic and Allegorical Form,' in Axel Honneth et al. eds, *Philosophical Interventions in the Unfinished Project of Enlightenment*, trans. William Rehg, Cambridge, Mass., 1992, where an *Erfahrung* 'deserving of the name' is defined as something that 'does not happen to us but rather is *made* by us.' (p234).
22. *Ibid.*, p9.
23. Winfried Menninghaus, 'Walter Benjamin's Theory of Myth,' in Gary Smith, ed., *On Walter Benjamin: Critical Essays and Reflections*, Cambridge, Mass. 1988, p321-322. Benjamin, to be sure, was sceptical of certain types of mythic thinking, even attacking *Lebensphilosophie* as proto-fascist for its interest in myth. (See, 'On Some Motifs in Baudelaire,' p158). But Menninghaus shows the extent to which he distrusted the simple myth/enlightenment dichotomy.
24. Theodor W. Adorno, *Prisms*, trans. Samuel and Shierry Weber, London 1967, p235.
25. See, for example, his critique of *Erlebnis*.
26. For an attempt to do so, see Rainer Nägele, 'Benjamin's Ground,' in Nägele, ed., *Benjamin's Ground: New Readings of Walter Benjamin*, Detroit, 1988.
27. Benjamin, 'Surrealism: The Last Snapshot of the European Intelligentsia,' *Reflections: Essays, Aphorisms, Autobiographical Writings*, ed. Peter Demetz, trans. Edmond Jephcott, New York 1978, p179.
28. Georg Lukács, *The Theory of the Novel*, trans. Anna Bostock (Cambridge, Mass., 1971), p41, cited by Benjamin, 'The Storyteller,' p99. Rolf Tiedemann and Hermann Schweppenhäuser, Frankfurt 1977.
29. Benjamin, 'The Storyteller: Reflections on the Work of Nikola Leskov,' *Illuminations*, p87.
30. According to Benjamin, 'the important thing for the remembering author is not

what he experienced, but the weaving of his memory, the Penelope work of recollection.' 'The Image of Proust,' *Illuminations*, *op.cit.*, p205.

31. Roland Barthes, 'To Write: An Intransitive Verb?,' in *The Rustle of Language*, trans. Richard Howard, Berkeley, 1989.
32. Benjamin, 'Theses on the Philosophy of History,' *Illuminations*, *op.cit.*, 257. In a letter to the author of 23 August 1992, Richard Wolin contends that Benjamin would not have accepted the formalist distrust of plenitudinous meaning evident in critics like Barthes; for him, the stylistic moments of absolute experience demanded the experiential fulfillment that such critics thought impossible.
33. Charles Bally, 'Le style indirect libre en français moderne I et II, *Germanisch-Romanische Monatsschrift*, Heidelberg 1912. There were some prior discussions in the work of the linguists A. Tobler and Th. Kaplevsky, but it was not until Bally, who was one of the two students of Saussure who published the notes of the *Cours de linguistique générale* in 1916, that a sustained analysis was made. 'Libre' means syntactically independent.
34. Marcel Proust, 'About Flaubert's Style,' in *Marcel Proust: A Selection from his Miscellaneous Writings*, trans. Gerard Hopkins, London 1948.
35. Étienne Lorck, *Die 'Erlebte Rede': Ein sprachlische Untersuchung* (Heidelberg, 1921); Otto Jespersen, *The Philosophy of Grammar*, London 1924.
36. V.S. Volosinov, *Marxism and the Philosophy of Language* [1930] trans. Ladislav Metejka and I.R. Titunik, New York 1973; Stephen Ullmann, *Style in the French Novel*, New York 1964; Dorrit Cohn, *Transparent Minds: Narrative Modes for Presenting Consciousness in Fiction* (Princeton, 1978); Roy Pascal, *The Dual Voice: Free Indirect Speech and its Functioning in the Nineteenth-Century European Novel*, Manchester 1977; Hans Robert Jauss, 'Literary History as a Challenge to Literary Theory,' *Toward an Aesthetic of Reception*, trans. Timothy Bahti, Minneapolis 1982; and Ann Banfield, *Unspeakable Sentences*, Boston 1982.
37. Dominick LaCapra, *'Madame Bovary' on Trial*, Ithaca 1982.
38. For an account of Vossler and the Vosslerites, see Volosinov, *op.cit.*, p32.
39. LaCapra, *op.cit.*, p138.
40. *Ibid.*, pp57-58.
41. It also might be conjectured that anxiety about another confusion was also reinforced by the *style indirect libre*, that between character and reader. In the eighteenth century, the moral implications of the novel were contested precisely because of the dangerously fluid boundaries between amoral characters and sympathetic (often female) readers. *Madame Bovary* itself, of course, draws on the fear that impressionable readers will confuse their lives with those of romantic heroines.
42. Interestingly, one of the other Vosslerites who worked on *erlebte Rede*, Gertraud Lerch, used the Diltheyan notion of *Einfühlung* (empathy) as the key to the style. See the discussion in Volosinov, p150.

43. Pascal, *op.cit.*, p25.
44. Volosinov, *op.cit.*, p155.
45. Ann Banfield, 'Where Epistemology, Style, and Grammar Meet Literary History: The Development of Represented Speech and Thought,' *New Literary History*, IX, 3 (1978), p449.
46. Emile Benveniste, *Problems in General Linguistics*, trans. Mary Elizabeth Meek, Coral Gables, Fla.1971, chap. 14.
47. Jacques Derrida, 'Différence,' *Margins of Philosophy*, trans. Alan Bass (Chicago, 1982), p9.
48. Barthes, 'To Write – An Intransitive Verb?', *op.cit.*, p19.
49. For an analysis of *écriture* in terms of intransitive writing, the middle voice, and the *style indirect libre*, see Ann Banfield, 'Écriture, Narration and the Grammar of French,' in Jeremy Hawthorn, ed., *Narrative: From Malory to Motion Pictures* (London, 1985). She makes the point that the impersonal grammatical function of writing was lost in America when the pragmatists substituted 'The Experience Curriculum' in the 1930s (p17-18). In the Benjaminian terms we have been using, the 'absolute experience' of *écriture* was replaced by mere *Erlebnis*.
50. Ann Banfield, 'Describing the Unobserved: Events Grouped Around an Empty Center,' in Nigel Fabb et al., eds. *The Linguistics of Writing: Arguments Between Language and Literature*, Manchester 1987: 'Le miroir qui ne reflète personne,' in *Transparence et Opacité: Litterature det Sciences Cognitives, Hommage à Mitou Ronat*, Paris 1988; and 'L'Imparfait de l'Objectif: The Imperfect of the Object Glass,' *Camera Obscura*, 24 (Fall, 1991).
51. Banfield, 'L'Imparfait de l'Objectif,' p77.
52. Benjamin, 'A Short History of Photography,' *Screen*, 13,1 (Spring, 1972). For a discussion of the links between Benjamin's visual concerns and the issue of experience, see Hansen, 'Benjamin, Cinema and Experience.'
53. Berel Lang, *Act and Idea in the Nazi Genocide*, Chicago 1990 and Hayden White, 'Historical Emplotment and the Problem of Truth,' in Saul Friedlander, ed., *Probing the Limits of Representation: Nazism and the 'Final Solution'*, Cambridge, Mass. 1992. White has explored these issues in an unpublished paper entitled 'Writing in the Middle Voice,' which he has kindly allowed me to read.
54. White, 'Historical Emplotment and the Problem of Truth,' *op.cit.*, p49.
55. *Ibid.*, p52.
56. Martin Jay, 'Of Plots, Witnesses and Judgments,' in Friedlander, *Probing the Limits of Representation.* The distinction between active agent and passive victim seems to be nowhere as important to maintain as in accounts of the Holocaust; otherwise, we risk the travesty of even-handed remembrance evident at Bitburg and in the work of certain historians during the *Historikerstreit.*
57. Banfield, 'Where Epistemology, Style, and Grammar Meet Literary History: The Development of Represented Speech and Thought,' p415.

58. Vincent Pecora, 'Ethics, Politics and the Middle Voice,' *Yale French Studies*, 79 (1991).
59. *Ibid.*, p212.
60. See the discussion in Katerina Clark and Michael Holquist, *Mikhail Bakhtin*, Cambridge, Mass. 1984, chapter 6; and the translators' introduction to Volosinov, *Marxism and the Philosophy of Language, op.cit.*
61. LaCapra, *'Madame Bovary' on Trial, op.cit.*, p149.
62. Terry Eagleton, *Walter Benjamin: Or Towards a Revolutionary Criticism*, London 1981, where he claimed that in Bakhtin exists a 'Judeo-Christian mysticism in some ways akin to Benjamin's – that *Marxism and the Philosophy of Language*[which he takes to be written by Bakhtin] contains as its secret code a theological devotion to the incarnational unity of word and being similar to that which marks Benjamin's own meditations.'(p153-154).
63. Jürgen Habermas, 'Consciousness-Raising or Redemptive Criticism: The Contemporaneity of Walter Benjamin,' *New German Critique*, 17 (Spring, 1979), p45-46.
64. Leo Bersani, *The Culture of Redemption*, Cambridge, Mass. 1990, p60. Bersani's own anti-redemptive concept of experience derives in large measure from Bataille's *Inner Experience*, trans. Leslie Anne Boldt, Albany, N.Y. 1988.

THE AESTHETICS OF CONFLICT

Julian Roberts

I AESTHETICS AND MORALITY

Aesthetics – saying what makes things beautiful – moves uneasily between two competing models. On the one side, there is the pull towards description; aesthetics should conform to the norms of the natural sciences, and dispassionately describe the phenomena presented to it. That may result in formal inventories of beautiful properties: beauty is about, say, proportions, harmonies, and other features amenable to quantification. Or it may engender concern with the psychology of responses to beauty. That is, for its exponents, a more satisfyingly rigorous approach, assimilable as it is to the current philosophical fashion for cognitive psychology.

On the other side, practical aesthetic work – 'criticism' – tends strongly towards moralistic thematization. In this, of course, it has tradition on its side. Horace, for example, thought that literature was, in the end, merely a sweet coating for the pill of moral precept. The moralistic approach has gained in strength in recent years. It adopts a slightly different manner, admittedly, preferring apocalyptic lamentation about the evils of the age ('postmodernity') to Horatian instruction about the right conduct of individuals. But its impetus remains the same; and, whatever else, it is resolutely antipathetic to the scientism of descriptive aesthetics.

The lamentational mode is much in evidence among those who use the work of Walter Benjamin. Benjamin was caught by the catastrophes of the century more even than most of his contemporaries: his work was unappreciated and largely unpublished during his life, he was an exile, and he eventually perished fleeing from the Nazis. Moreover, Benjamin was a failure as an academic. This latter aspect gives the brew particular spice, since Benjamin is now at the centre of a world-wide scholarly industry: scarcely a monograph where the author omits to don sackcloth and ashes, in order, by that gesture at least, to join the general chorus against iniquity.

In this paper, however, I wish to argue that Benjamin's work in aesthetics is not moralistic. It is practical, indeed, in the sense that it locates any human enterprise, including the scientific one, in a pragmatic context. But it is also, indeed fundamentally so, *descriptive*, in its attempt to provide a general categorical framework for aesthetics. In particular, moreover, Benjamin's work *refutes* moralism in disallowing any suggestion that involvement, emotion and 'subjectivity' have a proper role in criticism.

I shall not here present Benjamin's comments on the illusory radicalism of subjective lamentation (they appear most obviously in his comments on Karl Kraus, also on Kafka).[1] Rather, I shall display the elements of his categorical structure. There are two basic elements to this. First, it is necessary to understand the role of *history* as a component of aesthetics. This is presupposed rather than argued by Benjamin; but it is important to trace the argument of his predecessors in order to disentangle him from the rhetoric of millennarianism. Second, I shall present the descriptive categories that inform Benjamin's own aesthetics.

II HISTORY AND AESTHETICS

Why should aesthetics be concerned with history?

In its eighteenth-century origins, aesthetics was not directed towards history.[2] For Baumgarten, judgements of pleasure were to be assimilated to a version of cognitive psychology; specifically, they were to be regarded as emerging from a 'lower' faculty of knowledge. This was an attempt to confront the question why judgements of pleasure are irredeemably subjective and difficult to explain in distinct terms. For example: '*I like* this painting' is acceptable as an aesthetic explanation, while '*I think* seven plus five equals twelve' would not be acceptable as an explanation in arithmetic. For Baumgarten, the lower cognitive faculty produces judgements which, by virtue of being associated with that faculty, are not suceptible of further distinctness.

This does not, of course, get us terribly far. Are these 'lower' forms of judgement to be regarded as general even though not distinct? If so, does their generality rest on some anthropological or psychological state of affairs (i.e., are they empirically accessible), or are they in some more profound way ineliminably constitutive of those parts of our cognition relating to pleasure?

Kant appropriated Baumgarten's initiative to what became the framework for the subsequent discipline of aesthetics. In Kant, the framework is still fragmentary, its elements only partially connected. The point, however, is this. First, *all* cognition is conditioned by sense (this is what in the *Critique of Pure Reason* is identified as the 'transcendental aesthetic'). In that respect, the qualitative distinction Baumgarten drew between 'distinct' cognition (the upper faculties) and 'confused' cognition (judgements of pleasure) becomes redundant. All judgements are, in the Kantian scheme of things, restricted by the elements of sensuality – space and time. Space and time (as Kant explains the point) are subjective: they are not absolute, they are my space, my time. All cognition, even of the most abstracted theoretical variety, takes place within a subjective spatio-temporal environment. Because of this, a limit has to be set to the apparent universality of 'distinct' reasoning. Kant discusses this in the 'transcendental dialectic' of his first *Critique*. His most famous examples, probably, are the 'antinomies of reason': we cannot legitimately answer questions about the beginning of the world in time, or the first cause of all other causes, because these exceed our spatio-temporal environment. Science concerns itself with those phenomena that happen, at least potentially, within the horizons of our experience. Things outside those horizons (including, say, the ultimate substance of the world) are simply beyond our insight; and questions about them merely lead to bad metaphysics.

In the twentieth century this vision has been systematically applied to the philosophy of arithmetic. Its guiding metaphor is that arithmetical truths (such as Kant's famous '7+5=12') are not 'found', but *constructed* in our practice of computation. That means that all absolute, ontologically independent 'truths' ('thoughts of God', so to speak, rather than constructions by men and women) are ruled out. A problem without an answer (Goldbach's conjecture, for example) is no more than that, neither true nor false, and not an indication that there is an answer somewhere, even though we have not yet found it. Hence the rejection, by proponents of this view (who are called constructivists, or intuitionists) of the 'law of excluded middle', whereby all assertions are either true or false.[3]

If all reasoning is limited, the apparent limits of aesthetic judgements (their 'indistinctness') becomes less of a problem. One feature of them, however, leads to a not previously envisaged radicalization of the Kantian scheme. The difficulty is: even though all truths, including the majestic abstractions of arithmetic are ultimately limited to *our* experienced environment, this environment seems at least in the case of the 'sciences' to be indisputably general and persistent. We have no basis to *dispute* the findings of arithmetic, even though there may be occasional (very broad) restrictions on our 'metaphysical' use of them. But the whole point about aesthetic judgements is that they are eminently disputable, and conspicuously variable from person to person. So on what basis can taste claim, as it does, to be 'good' and in some sense binding on others?

It is here that Kant makes a move decisive not only for the subsequent impact of his theories, but for the development of philosophy generally. The point is this. Implicitly, Kant's earlier thinking had assumed that 'non-distinct' judgement fell somewhere on a continuous scale of *universal* cognitive activity. Following Baumgarten, he assumed that what was needed was a tidying-up of our cognitive psychology. Confronted with the *intrinsic* variability of judgements of taste, however, he realized that this variability would have to be related to something; and, perforce, he saw that it must be related to the *material individuality of the person making the judgement.* In other words, while in the case of mathematics one could prudently abstract from who in particular it was judging '7+5=12', this abstraction could no longer be made in the case of judgements like 'Gothic cathedrals are beautiful'.

Accordingly, the framework of a *particular individual sensibility* comes to determine the environment of aesthetic judgements. (In principle, it already sets the environment of arithmetical and other 'distinct' judgements; but, as a matter of experience, these are not variable, or, at least, not in a way obvious to Kant.)

And the particular individual sensibility, then, comes for Kant to be situated collectively and historically. Taste, in the *Critique of Judgement*, is related to what he calls *Gemeinsinn* – the 'sense' (*Sinn*) that is shared by, or common to (*gemein*) a particular group of people. This, so to speak, is the spatial 'limit' of judgements of taste; the full historical structure appears with the temporal limit, and what Kant calls 'culture'. Culture is the taste of a *particular* group of people acquired through *time*. Subject to that restriction, it enjoys the same binding universality as judgements of science.

The significance of this move is hard to overestimate. Emphatically, it must not be understood as acquiescence in the notion that artistic criticism is no more than a review of dogmas and prejudices. The point is: truth – all truth – is historical, and the historicity of judgements of taste, far from being anomalous and 'confused', becomes paradigmatic for cognitive activity in general.

The problem of how to use this paradigm has dominated post-Kantian philosophy. (It is also increasingly concerning 'analytical' philosophy, though much of this tradition, as Habermas has remarked, should if anything be regarded as *pre*-Kantian.) What does it mean that strict rationality should be in some respect contingent upon sense and particularity? Does it, for example, mean that we *do* have to abandon the certainties of science and arithmetic?

Extremer versions of phenomenology, most notably that of Heidegger, would answer the last question with 'yes'; for such thinkers, the experiential environment (Husserl's 'life-world') is delineated by the absolute relativities of fate, *Geworfenheit* and so on. Another approach, since Hegel, has followed a different line. For him, the historicity of the experienced environment does have a logic. Or, to put it the other way round, logic (the computational understanding) is not simply imposed upon or imported into the life-world; it emerges from the practices that articulate the life-world in the first place. This is the essence of the 'constructivist' interpretation of Kant. Arithmetic, as the central example, is generally valid because, or to the extent that, it expresses universal structural practices. The primitive structural practice, in this account, is interaction with others (or 'intersubjectivity'). All the instruments of the understanding are, ultimately, derivable from this. (This is Paul Lorenzen's well-known 'dialogical' elimination of the logical constants.)[4]

III INTERSUBJECTIVITY AND CONFLICT

Much still turns, however, on how 'intersubjectivity' is to be interpreted. In the twentieth century, it has generally been understood (most famously, by Habermas) as a vindication of our need for others. Rationality, from such a perspective, happens only once the level egalitarian playing field (the 'ideal speech situation') allows it to. So we have a 'quasi-transcendental' commitment to harmony, equality and justice.

This, however, is a view different from that taken by Hegel. Hegel interprets intersubjectivity not as a primitive disposition to cooperation, but, with Hobbes, as primitive *desire* – for survival and hence for conflict.[5] Cooperation, along with the rationality it grounds, is itself derived from the primary struggle of each individual. The first relation between consciousness and its other is negation, both practically (as destruction and consumption) and logically. Only after a complex, and, indeed, dangerous process of struggle (the famous Master-Slave episode in Hegel's *Phenomenology*) do we attain self-consciousness, and with it practical and logical identity.[6]

Now, the consequences of this view do not appear in Hegel's own work on aesthetics. They do, however, appear in his view of history, which is presented as a sequence of struggles for identity. His conflictual ontology carries through to a conflictual teleology. History ends with the victory of the fittest.

In essence, this is what is taken over by Marx, complete with the notion that history can indeed end at some point (with the victory of the proletariat and the transition to socialism). And with the Marxist view of history we arrive, finally, at the basic structure for Benjamin's aesthetics. These work, in summary, as follows.

First, the questions of aesthetics (what is beauty? is this beautiful?) can only be resolved on the basis of an ontology (what is this, such that it is beautiful?). A purely naturalistic ontology of objects and psychological responses will not work (we will assume, starting 'after' Kant). A historicist ontology, on the other hand, presupposes some sort of account of whet 'history' is – of what 'practices' are to be taken as constitutive, or at least characteristic, of the world of objects.

Such an account is given by the Marxist theory. In it, practice ('labour') is taken to be constitutive of the semantically accessible universe. Labour is, however, an implementation of each individual desire. This means that the 'substance' of 'things' is, ultimately, derived from the practice, the desire, the struggle that put them there. Furthermore, labour is not an abstract category (as 'practice' is); it is a historical category describable in the vocabulary of political economy. Labour is the production of the means of existence within a given historical organization of society.

The ontology of things, from this perspective, is inextricably bound to the social and political aspects of 'labour'. The Marxist scheme runs: 'things' are produced by 'labour', and in that respect, labour is a general condition of ontology. At that level of abstraction, however, the argument obscures labour's character as practice by concrete individuals in particular circumstances. Those circumstances are, that labour is a saleable commodity that arises only by virtue of the existence of a labour market. And a labour market 'always already' expresses relations of power – that is, relations brought about as a result of conflict and struggle. (Crudely: the worker, on confronting the issues of personal survival, finds herself facing a market. This means two things: first, goods are defined as objects of exchange – commodities – and second, the only way of acquiring those goods is to enter the exchange process. For those not already in control of the process – control which consists of being able to manipulate the process of exchange, e.g. by possession of scarce resources – the only means of entry is *to become a commodity oneself*.)

So, understanding labour demands its recovery not as a term of cooperation and harmony, but as one delineating the primitive conflictual dimension of existence. Life is, to be sure, a struggle against recalcitrant nature; but before that, it is a struggle against human enemies. And that struggle, at least to the extent that we can envisage it, is a struggle between competing interest groups. In Marx's terms: all previous history is the history of class struggle

IV HISTORY AND AESTHETICS

The implications of all this for aesthetics are not as direct as they have seemed, to some thinkers at least. Two conclusions need to be resisted. One is the classical 'Marxism' of the base-superstructure model, where 'aesthetics' is taken to account for the way in which ontologically prior states of affairs (economic relations and so on) are represented in ontologically secondary ones ('ideology', which includes art). Such a conclusion represents a reversion to a simplistic naturalism. Marxism's pragmatist claim that substance derives from labour supplies no grounds for distinguishing certain sorts of (superstructural) activity as being epiphenomena of the others. In other words, art is not to be regarded as a mere 'reflection'; it is a practice like any other.

The second conclusion to be resisted is the moralistic one we have already noted. The perspective of 'class struggle' lends itself to a sympathy for the underdog and for history's losers. More generally, it leads to the apocalyptic lamentation that it is always the evil characters who win. But Marxism's claim, at least, was that it described and did not value. We should give this claim a chance.

The overall point is this: the historical ontology we have described means that a 'scientific' understanding of human affairs can, and should, derive them directly from a locus in social conflict. This is independent of any particular conflict: the straightforward legacy of Hobbes, that life is struggle, means that we do not have to resort directly to higher-level explanations in terms of developed political economy. The initial question is much simpler: does the practice under investigation engage in struggle? Or: what struggles might it engage in, and to what extent does it successfully do so?

This fundamental level of questioning is a persistent theme throughout Benjamin's writings. It represents the historical ground against which the rest of his thinking is set. And it is independent of doctrinaire attachments. Although Benjamin usually formulates his notions of social struggle in Marxist terms, these are very broad. In many respects his analysis accords equally well with another 'conflictual' theory he was familiar with, namely that of Carl Schmitt. (Although, of course, Schmitt's own Hobbesianism eventually issues in nationalism and Fascism.)

To illustrate this point: the conflictual theme guides the first of Benjamin's essays on Baudelaire, 'Paris of the Second Empire in Baudelaire'. The perspective taken is that Baudelaire was, like all writers of the time, faced with a collapse of traditional social environments. Capitalism was destroying the old systems of status with, in the case of intellectuals, their mechanisms of patronage, and was replacing them with a simple labour-market arrangement. For the writer, that meant: contract on the terms of the market, or starve.

Benjamin understood the available choices in stark terms. Either the writers resisted, or they went under. 'Going under', here, included simple prostitution to the demands of the market. The Dumas family, who employed literary hacks to produce their wares in a kind of writer's factory, had, for all their affluence, destroyed their position as writers just as surely as those who simply starved.

The market, as Benjamin understood it (in directly Marxist terms, it must be said), was an arrangement run in the interests of those who, as beneficiaries of past struggles, now controlled the relations of production. The only answer to this was to take a leaf from their book, and to re-institute the struggle in an attempt to reverse present conditions. The lesson from the past was: the collective solidarity of those who are at present the winners must be matched by the collective solidarity of those who would overthrow them which, though oriented by different indicators, was precisely what Schmitt too would have said).

So the terms which structure the discussion of the first Baudelaire essay – *flâneur*, hero, putschist, conspirator and so on – are a mapping of the failure to achieve this solidarity. The essay is a narrative of the weakness of intellectuals – especially in nineteenth-century Paris, but just as forcefully in the terrifying world of 1930s Europe.

This aspect of Benjamin's writing tends to be resisted by his academic readers, perhaps because (as Benjamin believed, at any rate) academics are precisely that part of the intellectual world defined by their having been *officially* coopted by the other side. (The first Baudelaire essay was rejected by Adorno on the grounds that it consisted only of 'astonished presentation of simple facts'.[7] This objection is silly: the essay is a carefully structured argument. The real problem was Benjamin's conflictual position, which Adorno could never understand as any more than naive Brechtian activism.) It is, however, fundamental to the structure of his thinking. In particular, it underpins his formal analysis of art – in a word, of his theory of beauty.

V BEAUTY AND DECLINE

Giving art an ontological location is different from explaining its modes of articulation. Kant had attributed art to the *Gemeinsinn*, and then declared that its modes were beauty and the sublime. The systematic unity of his position works adequately for the sublime (the sublime is what cultured people are able to feel), but rather leaves out an account of beauty, which emerges as a drily conceptual kind of response. Benjamin's system, I would venture to say, is more successful.

At its heart is the notion of *decline* (or passing-away – *Vergehen*). Beauty, in this account, emerges in the fading of the idea. Dürer's representation of his aged mother, one might say, evokes beauty in a way that the boisterous flesh of a Boucher nymph does not. There is a *memento mori* at the heart of beauty which distinguishes it from mere sensuality. Spring is sensual; autumn is beautiful.

How does this notion combine with the principle of conflict to produce an account of aesthetics?

In general terms, we might say, conflictualism is anti-idealist. This means, most importantly, that norms and truths cannot precede their combative generation in struggle. It rejects, for example, the idealism which believes that 'natural law' provides universal values for humankind. Norms bind because they *have been fought for*, not because they exist absolutely. This means two things. First, no law, however desirable, exceeds the commitment to it of those who benefit from it. Enlightened political order, for example, is not self-justifying; it has the force only of a provisional tally, of the current state of play. It is constantly on the edge of collapse as those who would fight for it lose interest or pass away.

Second, aspirations to liberty may direct themselves to some vision of perfect enlightenment, but this vision is never more than a dream. Utopias are unreal concatenations of past fragments; they are not true, really existing goals (there are, so to speak, no 'future facts'). The paradox of hope is that its object is always an illusion.

Within this scheme the struggling parties express their hopes and fears, along a spectrum of dream, illusion and passing wakefulness. The dream is that the ideal exists, and that we either have it, or have lost it. Wakefulness is the point where we realise that the ideal can never exist, but also that its substance is nonetheless available to us in the struggle itself. Within this pattern of naive optimism, foolish disillusion and defiant realism, hope weaves its figures of beauty, poised always on the brink of loss and transience.

Benjamin's theory of passing beauty envisages three fundamental moments. They are *symbol*, *melancholy*, and *construction*. They work as follows.[8]

In Benjamin's own work, symbol is associated principally with mythic world-views. It is, we shall say, the notion that the intelligible world is continuous with the sensory one. Our patterns of thought mirror, or partake in, the structures of reality. So, for example, language is 'mimetic' (in Benjamin's essay on the topic) of reality; it imitates it in the intimacy of some profound nominative grounding. Or: the structures of reality *are* the very same as those formulated, for example, in mathematics and scientific thought (this is the Platonism re-invigorated, at the beginning of this century, by Frege). Most generally: each thing invokes, microcosmically, the universe of which it is a part. Everything that is near is at the same time far; each object, however humble, recalls the ideal order that endows it with intelligibility. This is what Benjamin (with Klages) calls the 'aura'; and it is the root of such diverse phenomena as the love of the collector for her pieces and the absorption of the pre-industrial craftsman in his works. (We use the term 'symbol' because it is more general than 'aura', can readily be explained in terms of its theological background and is the subject of systematic exposition by Benjamin himself in the *Wahlverwandtschaften* essay and in *Origin of German Tragic Drama*. Other equivalent terms might be Platonism or mimesis.)

This belief in a pure and accessible universe produces its own kind of beauty. In the first part of this century they were perhaps typically visible in the 'platonic solids' of Corbusian architecture – for example. the Villa Savoie.

The belief that we are in possession of the truth is, at least politically and ethically, difficult to sustain in an era of universal cruelty; Corbusian optimism takes on elements of the inhumanity it so briskly disregards. The clean-limbed vigour of egalitarian utopias becomes the voyeuristic body-fetishism of the fascists; the denizens of the garden cities emerge with the coiffured pubes of a Ziegler, or as the monumental Aryans of an Arno Breker.

Far more characteristic of art in a world of horrors is what Benjamin calls melancholy. Melancholy recoils from a symbol now seen to be vacuous or tainted. What was once real presence is now an empty shell. From being each one a vehicle of truth and clarity, worldly things have now become the inscrutable death masks of departed spirit. At best, they perform the allusive role of allegory, which subverts denotation with the deliberate employment of ambiguity, fragmentation and self-reference. In theological terms (as Benjamin expounds it in *Origin of German Tragic Drama*), the naive symbolist idolatries of Catholicism are followed by the dour piety of Protestantism, with its passionate grieving for the *deus absconditus*. In general philosophical terms, perhaps, Platonism and scientism are followed by scepticism.

The classic representation of this is Durer's etching *Melencolia I*; in it, an angel sits despondent, surrounded by mathematical figures and geometrical devices, the accoutrements of a now futile science. In more recent terms, the impulse of melancholy is captured by much 'post-modernist' art and architecture, with its embrace of dislocated citation, its self-referential thematization of ruin, and, above all, its rejection of classical notions of form and proportion (which, for a Platonist, are the insignia impressed by reason on matter). Architecture, for example, revels to a now clichéd degree in the sublime, eliciting Burke's 'delightful horror' by the immensity (Kant's 'unmeasurable size') of colossal towers faced with sheer drops of mirror glass and polished granite. Art, in the work of Francis Bacon, turns angrily on the integral human body and represents it as no more than twisted meat bereft even of the minimal structure of a skeleton. (For a Platonist such as Winckelmann, by contrast, the body's bone and sinews related to its flesh as the soul did to the body as a whole: they guaranteed the imposition of form and identity on amorphous matter.)

In melancholy, the moment of the *memento mori* comes to the fore; and in that sense, it may be regarded as an advance on the potentially tiresome sensuality of symbolism. Its own subjectivism, however, is equally unstable. According to Benjamin, the melancholic retreats from a now meaningless world into an 'interior'; from here, or so he believes, he can safely observe the senseless doings outside. But this belief that there is any privileged vantage-point is an illusion. A consistent sceptic is sceptical also about himself; and that leads not further into despair, but into the realization that all reality is pragmatic, provisional and variable. It is not that the world is deceptive, and the subject is sovereign; world and subject are together involved in a continuous process of change whose engine (as we saw) is *struggle*, and whose truth lies not in contemplations of eternity but in the grasping of the moment.

Such an 'awakening', of course, is itself only momentary, or, at least, transitional. The default position, so to speak, is always the dream of eternal verity, expressed either optimistically as symbol or pessimistically as melancholy. Emergence from this dream is a matter of hard and continuing work. And in that respect, the art of the third moment is itself an activity and not confinable to the static condition of the 'art-work'. In grasping the moment, the work of art is itself absorbed into ephemerality and transition; it resists incorporation into a canon of fixed objects.

Nonetheless, it is possible to give examples of this third moment of art; Benjamin's tend to be associated with Soviet constructivism, but also with essentially kinetic forms such as the cinema. In Eisenstein's movies, for example, form rests on the aggressively de-naturalizing effect of montage; and substance is related typically to the ephemerality of the newsreel, where (in Benjamin's example) the crowd as audience becomes conscious of itself as the crowd on the screen.

This principle of *construction* can be generalised as that form of art which thematizes its own instability.[9] This is not, however, to be understood simply as the melancholic *memento mori*; it may be better compared, perhaps, to those 'fly-by-wire' aircraft which only remain stable by virtue of constant intervention and re-direction by a computer. A striking example is Tatlin's 'Monument to the Second International' (the 'Tatlin Tower'), whose defiant instability proclaims a truculent faith in the capacity of engineering to hold it up. Constructivist art of this kind is expressly technical, though without the scientism of the modern, and, indeed, without being confined to the twentieth century. The mature work of Balthasar Neumann, for example, is characterized by an eminently 'constructivist' combination of breathtaking engineering with intense sculptural fluidity and playfulness (preeminently, of course, at Vierzehnheiligen). It may be even that the literary genre of tragedy could be characterized as 'constructive' in this sense, to the extent at least that it combines sorrow at death with triumph at human achievement, however hubristic and short-lived.

VI CONCLUSION

Benjamin's work is often read as a collection of fragments informed only by the pathos of his own life and by a sense of doom and decline – as part of the genre of prophetic lamentation, in other words.

In this paper I have argued that Benjamin's sense of history is in fact secular and systematic, being rooted in a conflictual social ontology that derives from Marx, Hegel and, ultimately, Hobbes. The aesthetic theory he builds on this basis contains, to be sure, a celebration of 'melancholy'; but this is only one moment in a spectrum of attitudes to beauty.

Aesthetics is a relatively modern enterprise. I would argue that Benjamin is the most penetrating and, at least programmatically (given that the work as it stands is incomplete), the most comprehensive aesthetic theorist so far.

NOTES

1. For details see Julian Roberts, *Walter Benjamin*, Macmillan, Basingstoke 1982.
2. For detailed exposition, see Julian Roberts, 'German Cultural Criticism 1755-70 and its Theoretical Assumptions'; Cambridge, Ph.D. diss., 1979 and *German Philosophy. An Introduction*, Polity, Cambridge 1988.
3. For detailed discussion see Julian Roberts, *The Logic of Reflection*, Yale, London and New Haven 1992.
4. *Ibid*, chapter 5.
5. For a recent discussion of Hegel's appropriation of Hobbes, see A. Honneth, *Kampf um Anerkennung. Zur moralischen Grammatik sozialer Konflikte*, Suhrkampf, Frankfurt 1992.
6. For more on this part of the *Phenomenology*, see Roberts, *German Philosophy*, chap. 2.

7. For more on this, see S. Buck-Morss *The Dialectics of Seeing*, MIT Press, Cambridge, Mass. 1989: 205ff.
8. For a more detailed exposition, see Roberts 'Melancholy Meanings', in N. Wheale (ed.) *Postmodernism*, Routledge, London.
9. The notion of construction is also usefully developed in Adorno's aesthetics – though his overall stance is probably 'melancholic' (see Roberts, *German Philosophy*, chap. 10.)